ARISTOTLE'S

POLITICS AND POETICS

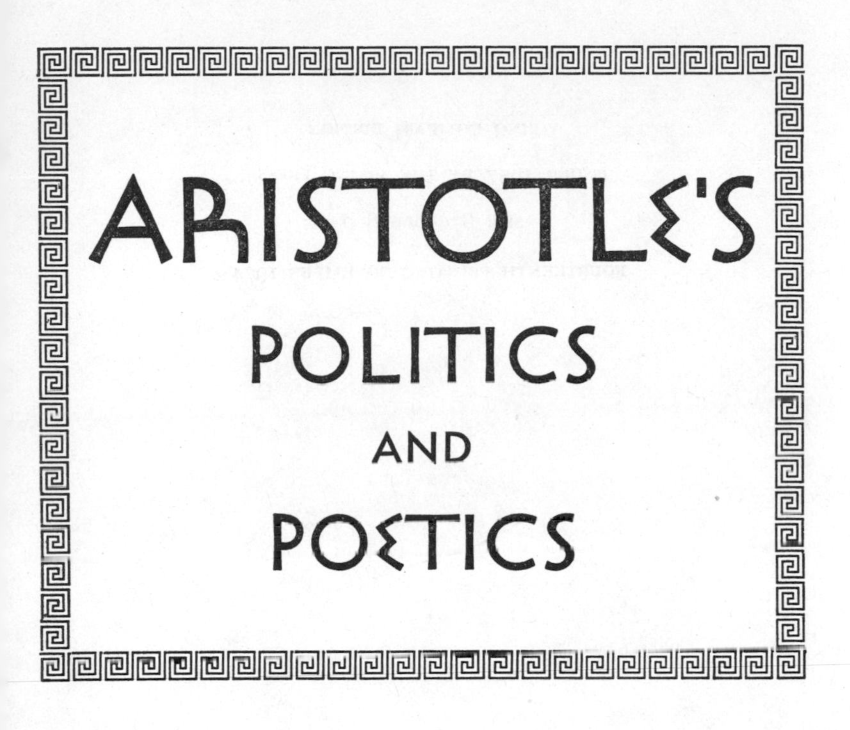

ARISTOTLE'S POLITICS AND POETICS

Translated by

BENJAMIN JOWETT & THOMAS TWINING

with an Introduction by

LINCOLN DIAMANT

New York: The Viking Press

VIKING COMPASS EDITION

ISSUED 1957 BY THE VIKING PRESS

SBN 670-00028-0

FOURTEENTH PRINTING NOVEMBER 1974

DISTRIBUTED IN CANADA BY
THE MACMILLAN COMPANY OF CANADA LIMITED

PRINTED IN U.S.A. BY THE COLONIAL PRESS INC.

CONTENTS

INTRODUCTION

Aristotle, the greatest thinker of antiquity, was born at Stagira in northern Greece in 384 B.C., the son of a wealthy physician, and died at Chalcis sixty-two years later. He filled his lifetime with such profound speculation on the nature of man and the universe that he effectively laid the groundwork for all of contemporary scientific philosophy. The most brilliant of Plato's students, Aristotle studied under that great master in Athens from the age of eighteen until he was thirty-seven. His own growing fame as a scholar spread throughout the Eastern Mediterranean area, and at forty-one he was called to Macedonia to tutor Alexander the Great, then a boy of thirteen. He remained at the Macedonian court for eight years, returning to Athens in 335 B.C., after a prolonged series of arguments with his pupil over Alexander's lack of restraint and his assumption of personal divinity.

Back in Athens, Aristotle founded his own school (Plato had died a decade earlier) called the *Lyceum*, where he lectured regularly for twelve fruitful years. Then, in 323 B.C., a mounting wave of anti-Macedon "nationalism" swept Greece. Aristotle, suspect because of his past association with Alexander, was forced to flee to Euboea, a large island in the Aegean Sea not far from Athens, where he died the following year, 322 B.C.

The most famous of Aristotle's extant works are *Organum, Metaphysics, Physics, On the Heavens, History of Animals, On the Parts of Animals, De Anima, Nicomachean Ethics, Rhetoric, Politics,* and *Poetics*. In the narrow sense, none of these are books written by Aristotle; they are actually collections of his lecture notes edited and filled in after his death by former students. Their scholarly style is so compact and pithy that they are not easy to digest; of the eleven works mentioned above, the *Politics* and *Poetics* are perhaps best suited for modern reading. Nevertheless, every one of these books has exerted a tremendous influence on the history of thought, a fact obvious to anyone who considers the very vocabulary of dialectic, of natural science, or of metaphysics.

All men, Aristotle taught, are actuated with the desire for a knowledge of First Principles—a quest that did not start with the Greeks but which can be traced back to man's speculative beginnings, glorified in the oldest legends. Our own modern efforts to explain and rationalize our existence, facing the more imposing difficulties presented by the complexities of technology and contemporary social relations, continue the same quest. Today, the call for this very kind of Aristotelian identification is well-nigh universal.

Aristotle's contribution to the search for the meaning of human existence was his development of the *teleological* point of view—the belief of a purpose in the world. With his system of primary categories, reached through and constituted by the unpredictable process of temporal change, he became the first in a long and honored chain of rational materialists. His studies make brilliant deductive guesses about the nature of things, and his writings are a kind of "scientific poetry." However, although Aristotle was the founder of logic—the system that concerns itself with the validity of thought—his works are not really founded on scientific method. The world had to wait until the end of the sixteenth century for the growth of genuine scientific, materialist thinking, arising from very practical needs of the Bourgeois Revolution.

This revolt, however, with its primary emphasis on the intensive development of special sciences, lost for centuries Aristotle's view of the world as a single interconnected whole in endless motion. Only in the most recent times—our own tremendously exciting era—have Einstein and other great contemporary explorers of the physical and social scene brought us back once again to Aristotle's materialist view—a view, we should hasten to add, now enriched by the whole thought content of almost two and a half thousand years of the historical development of philosophy, natural science, and the social structure. With this perspective of twenty-three centuries, let us examine the great Greek thinker's ideas on the social structure.

POLITICS

Aristotle's discussion of government in the *Politics* is so packed with ideas that the book has been argued over ever since it was written. It is an empiric description of the nature of man under various historical circumstances, filled with information on what had happened to former states and what was happening in Aristotle's own time, coupled with a profound analysis of the structure of human society. The debt which our own American political system owes this book is deep and well-acknowledged. Aristotelian thinking underlay the ideas of Harrington and Locke and the seventeenth-century English school of political economy, shaped the conclusions of Madison and Hamilton and John Adams, and ran in an undercurrent through all the long and arduous sessions of the Constitutional Convention in Philadelphia.

Of course, Aristotle himself was indebted to Plato as a springboard for many of his ideas (and Plato in turn to Socrates), but in truth, the *Politics* is a reaction against the platonic ideal of what a state *ought to be*, for it presents the state *as it is*.

"Man," says Aristotle, "is a political animal," the only animal endowed with speech and therefore able to associate himself with other men to build communities and erect the state—the highest form of community, "the community of free men." It is this use of the term "free men," coupled with Aristotle's normal acceptance of the "expediency and rightness" of slave and master classes as a necessary foundation for any social structure, that unsettles most modern critics who profess the proper contemporary abhorrence of the institution of bodily servitude. More words have probably been written and spoken about this one Aristotelian concept than about any other in the *Politics*.

The modern reader properly resolves the dilemma by recalling that only slavery made possible the flowering of Hellenism in the ancient world. Without slavery there would have been no Greek state; no Greek art or science (Aristotle himself owned two hundred slaves); no Roman Empire. And without Hellenism and the Roman Empire, there could have been no modern civilization. Without the slavery of antiquity, as necessary as it was universally recognized, you could not sit here comfortably today, reading this page. Slavery in that period actually represented a great social step forward—a barbaric and almost bestial means whereby man extricated himself from among the beasts. A reader who finds himself troubled by Aristotle's statement that all human society must be founded on the principle of slavery might just as well reproach the Greeks for their lack of antibiotics or atomic power.

Nevertheless, despite the ideological limits imposed by the slave society in which he lived, it is to Aristotle's lasting credit that he recognized the transcending characteristic of all social and political systems; that they must involve a prior consideration of some principle or standard of good, and that politics, therefore, presupposes a system of ethics. This concept, as we shall see again in the *Poetics,* runs throughout all of Aristotle's thought. He makes it plain that not only ordinarily recognized moral questions but every problem of politics is, in a very real sense, a moral problem—a view to which modern scientific philosophy, after centuries of preoccupation with the traditional concept of virtue, is once again slowly but inevitably returning.

Aristotle's discussion of states has influenced all of modern political thinking through its concept of what constitutes a good and bad state. Good government, he says, is liberty under law. "Governments which have regard for the common interest are constituted under strict principles of justice, and those which regard only the interest of the rulers are despotic." Although he believes man will never achieve a *perfect* form of government, Aristotle postulates three forms of good, or tolerable, government: *Kingship,* which he defines as a state in which one person rules in the common interest; *Aristocracy,* the rule by the best in the common interest; and *Commonwealth,* "the most tolerable form of government," represented by today's constitutional democracy, in which the citizens at large administer the state in the common interest.

All bad governments, Aristotle continues, are merely perversions of these three basic forms. Kingships degenerate into tyranny when the monarchy turns to serve only the interest of the King and his satellites; Aristocracies degenerate into oligarchy when the wealthy turn to rule in their own interest; and even Commonwealths can degenerate into the tyranny of mob rule—"a tyranny no less dreadful than the tyranny of the few," which *The Federalist* (deriving most of its ideas directly from the *Politics*) mortally feared.

To avoid these forms of governmental degeneration, Aristotle proposes moderation, restraint, and temperance on every level. A man who acts virtuously and honorably and performs the noblest deeds for the common welfare can find as great a satisfaction for himself as "people who assign to themselves the greater share of wealth, honors and bodily pleasures." A thoroughgoing anti-imperialist after his disappointment with Alexander, Aristotle preaches that even nations tend to lose their national virtue and all characteristics of their culture when they overreach themselves politically.

The Aristotle of the *Politics* is primarily a man of reason, anxious to observe and ponder, believing virtue consists not necessarily in absolute morality, but in reasonable thought; and that reasonable thought occurs not only to someone sitting somewhere in solitude, but also derives from the continuous cross-fertilization of ideas and endless observation.

Aristotle realized that man contains within himself the seeds of both good and evil. He concerned himself most with suggesting conditions that would exalt the good and suppress the evil. That is perhaps the most important word the *Politics* brings to us today—*to face things as they are and to do our best to correct abuses.* This is realism—not in the narrow platonic sense—but as we ordinarily use the word. Aristotle's concept of government is that process which brings together people with different outlooks on life, people who represent different things. Government therefore must deal not with *unity* but with *diversity;* having accepted diversity as a virtue, the state can then encourage people to *be themselves*—which is a good, simple statement of the ultimate aims of democracy.

Aristotle believed a common interest existed between all men everywhere—a community of necessity which through reason, realism, and humanism could eventually overcome all difficulties and bind mankind together. His greatest wish was to see the individual integrated with society. Our goal, which he set for us two thousand years ago, is still that identical interplay between individual contribution and public organization—a symphony of voices in which each singer carries his individual tune and each tune merges into the total melody, moving the entire world towards its "singing tomorrows."

POETICS

"Criticism in our times," Malcolm Cowley once remarked, "has advanced scarcely further than in those of Aristotle." Certainly in the case of the *Poetics,* the sparkling, diamond-like prose of this brilliant little book, short and fragmentary as it is, has truly had more influence on criticism than anything written since.

As the *Politics* is a book mainly on how to organize a government, this is a book mainly on how to write plays. In common with all Greeks of his class, Aristotle had a great love for the theatre. His tremendous knowledge of drama and deep awareness of poetic beauty spurred the preparation of this scientific and aesthetic analysis that would actually help playwrights write plays.

The Greeks were wildly excited at their plays, laughing their heads off at comedies and being thrilled to the point of tears and hysteria at the tragedies. Plato, who dogmatically insisted that emotions were wrong, announced that the drama was wrong.

The *Poetics* is therefore another of Aristotle's humanized "reactions" to his mentor, whom he answers most platonically by affirming that poetry (which includes drama) is really a much higher form of writing than history, since it deals with the general, whereas history deals only with the particular. He explores that splendid generality of emotional excitement induced in audiences of dramatic poetry, elucidating the concept of tragic pleasure and "purgation of emotions"—that famous Aristotelian phrase which lays bare the social function of catharsis produced by mimed pity and terror, awakening in its spectators a collective ecstasy, elevation, loss of self, and gained awareness of the meaning of human greatness in the world through terms of physical suffering.

Aristotle is more interested in the created thing, e.g., the play—than in the individual who produces it. His angle of attack is aesthetically correct; he does not approach literature like a psychoanalyst. Although he affirms that pleasure, not truth, is the actual end of poetry, he insists it be a pleasure wholly limited by the demands of truth, so that the audience may learn to "know themselves." Aristotle felt that the greatest pleasure of all mankind—not only its philosophers—was to be learning something. He relied upon this instinct for learning to convey to audiences, through great drama, the pleasurable recognition of the truths of human existence.

Shakespeare fully shared this theory of *mimesis,* whose success in reflecting reality can best be judged by the poignancy of the emotions roused in the audience. Speaking to the Players through Hamlet, he presents a splendid description of the mimetic reflection of life as the highest form of drama, carefully warning them not to "o'erstep . . . the modesty of nature," for "anything so overdone is from the purpose of playing, whose end . . . is to hold . . . the mirror up to nature. This overdone . . . cannot but make the judicious grieve."

Both comedy *and* tragedy, according to Aristotle, are reflections of life. But since comedy is the portrayal of people as slightly worse than they actually are, and tragedy shows people a little better than their actual selves, the latter becomes the superior dramatic form. Plot is the most important element in tragedy and demands the dramatic unities of action and time, with "a beginning, a middle and an end." An audience enjoys seeing a story more than just looking at characters. What they enjoy most, Aristotle suggests, is a new set of actions. His insistence, nevertheless, that tragedy deal only with certain great houses of antiquity is only an attempt to guarantee that tragedy should not be squandered on unimportant individuals, but should deal with people of a certain magnitude. This view does not lead him to cater to vulgar spectacle, however, and he is aware that a good tragedy is better than its performance, and can even exist, unperformed, in the script.

To Aristotle, tragedy is properly the representation of an action involving a reversal of fortune brought about by some error on the part of the protagonist—"a transformation of the action into its opposite"—the eternal proscription which superior man eternally violates. This "tragic flaw" or "error of judgment or frailty" on the part of a noble character is not one of vice or depravity. Hence the inward resignation with which he willingly accepts the outward penalty of physical suffering for his deeds renders him heroic, or "renowned."

This is the great concept of the *Poetics,* and with it, Aristotle makes one of his greatest contributions not only to theories of poetry and drama, but to the very meaning of human existence. By this elimination of customary social determinants, human acts take on "free" choice for which the *actor* can and must assume responsibility. Concepts of "error" and "wrong" thus assume unambiguous meaning, and ethics becomes possible.

Aristotle's tragic "catharsis" follows a moment of recognition in which a character comes to understand the true meaning of his dilemma and his relation to his fellow-men and the world. In a sense, all mankind today is attempting to draw nearer to this recognition moment, approaching it the hard way through an unparalleled period of dissidence. All contemporary art and thought are groping in the direction of a new humanism which will preserve the great qualitative achievements of the past and offer the conditions to transpose them into the future.

Perhaps, at this writing, the goal is still distant. Culture today suffers from wounds dealt by warped historical compulsions. Yet amidst the turmoil, we can observe the testimony of a new age in the making—the age Aristotle himself dreamed of—in which Homeric laughter at the knowledge of the sadly finite nature of man within the gloriously infinite universe will be rendered easier to bear by the elimination of all earthly forms that still effectively bar mankind from self-determination.

LINCOLN DIAMANT

Washington's Birthday, 1952

POLITICS

Translated by

BENJAMIN JOWETT

BOOK FIRST

I Every state is a community of some kind, and every community is established with a view to some good; for mankind always act in order to obtain that which they think good. But, if all communities aim at some good, the state or political community, which is the highest of all, and which embraces all the rest, aims at good in a greater degree than any other, and at the highest good.

Some people think[1] that the qualifications of a statesman, king, householder, and master are the same, and that they differ, not in kind, but only in the number of their subjects. For example, the ruler over a few is called a master; over more, the manager of a household; over a still larger number, a statesman or king, as if there were no difference between a great household and a small state. The distinction which is made between the king and the statesman is as follows: When the government is personal, the ruler is a king; when, according to the rules of the political science, the citizens rule and are ruled in turn, then he is called a statesman.

But all this is a mistake; for governments differ in kind, as will be evident to any one who considers the matter according to the method[2] which has hitherto guided us. As in other departments of science, so in politics, the compound should always be resolved into the simple elements or least parts of the whole. We must therefore look at the elements of which the state is composed, in order that we may see in what the different kinds of rule differ from one another, and whether any scientific result can be attained about each one of them.

II He who thus considers things in their first growth and origin, whether a state or anything else, will obtain the clearest view of them. In the first place there must be a union of those who cannot exist without each other; namely, of male and female, that the race may continue (and this is a union which is formed, not of deliberate purpose, but because, in common with other animals and with plants, mankind have a natural desire to leave behind

[1] Cp. Plato, *Politicus*, 258 E–259 D.
[2] Cp. Bk. 1, VIII.

them an image of themselves), and of natural ruler and subject, that both may be preserved. For that which can foresee by the exercise of mind is by nature intended to be lord and master, and that which can with its body give effect to such foresight is a subject, and by nature a slave; hence master and slave have the same interest. Now nature has distinguished between the female and the slave. For she is not niggardly, like the smith who fashions the Delphian knife for many uses; she makes each thing for a single use, and every instrument is best made when intended for one and not for many uses. But among barbarians no distinction is made between women and slaves, because there is no natural ruler among them: they are a community of slaves, male and female. Wherefore the poets say—

'It is meet that Hellenes should rule over barbarians';

as if they thought that the barbarian and the slave were by nature one.

Out of these two relationships between man and woman, master and slave, the first thing to arise is the family, and Hesiod is right when he says—

'First house and wife and an ox for the plough',

for the ox is the poor man's slave. The family is the association established by nature for the supply of men's everyday wants, and the members of it are called by Charondas 'companions of the cupboard', and by Epimenides the Cretan, 'companions of the manger.' But when several families are united, and the association aims at something more than the supply of daily needs, the first society to be formed is the village. And the most natural form of the village appears to be that of a colony from the family, composed of the children and grandchildren, who are said to be suckled 'with the same milk'. And this is the reason why Hellenic states were originally governed by kings; because the Hellenes were under royal rule before they came together, as the barbarians still are. Every family is ruled by the eldest, and therefore in the colonies of the family the kingly form of government prevailed because they were of the same blood. As Homer says:[3]

'Each one gives law to his children and to his wives'.

[3] *Od.* ix. 114, quoted by Plato, *Laws*, iii. 680 B, and in *N. Eth.* x. 1180a 28.

For they lived dispersedly, as was the manner in ancient times. Wherefore men say that the Gods have a king, because they themselves either are or were in ancient times under the rule of a king. For they imagine, not only the forms of the Gods, but their ways of life to be like their own.

When several villages are united in a single complete community, large enough to be nearly or quite self-sufficing, the state comes into existence, originating in the bare needs of life, and continuing in existence for the sake of a good life. And therefore, if the earlier forms of society are natural, so is the state, for it is the end of them, and the nature of a thing is its end. For what each thing is when fully developed, we call its nature, whether we are speaking of a man, a horse, or a family. Besides, the final cause and end of a thing is the best, and to be self-sufficing is the end and the best.

Hence it is evident that the state is a creation of nature, and that man is by nature a political animal. And he who by nature and not by mere accident is without a state, is either a bad man or above humanity; he is like the

'Tribeless, lawless, hearthless one',

whom Homer[4] denounces—the natural outcast is forthwith a lover of war; he may be compared to an isolated piece at draughts.

Now, that man is more of a political animal than bees or any other gregarious animals is evident. Nature, as we often say, makes nothing in vain,[5] and man is the only animal whom she has endowed with the gift of speech.[6] And whereas mere voice is but an indication of pleasure or pain, and is therefore found in other animals (for their nature attains to the perception of pleasure and pain and the intimation of them to one another, and no further), the power of speech is intended to set forth the expedient and inexpedient, and therefore likewise the just and the unjust. And it is a characteristic of man that he alone has any sense of good and evil, of just and unjust, and the like, and the association of living beings who have this sense makes a family and a state.

Further, the state is by nature clearly prior to the family and to the individual, since the whole is of necessity prior to the part; for example, if the whole body be destroyed, there will be no foot

[4] *Il.* ix. 63.
[5] Cp. Bk. 1, VIII.
[6] Cp. Bk. 7, XIV.

or hand, except in an equivocal sense, as we might speak of a stone hand; for when destroyed the hand will be no better than that. But things are defined by their working and power; and we ought not to say that they are the same when they no longer have their proper quality, but only that they have the same name. The proof that the state is a creation of nature and prior to the individual is that the individual, when isolated, is not self-sufficing; and therefore he is like a part in relation to the whole. But he who is unable to live in society, or who has no need because he is sufficient for himself, must be either a beast or a god: he is no part of a state. A social instinct is implanted in all men by nature, and yet he who first founded the state was the greatest of benefactors. For man, when perfected, is the best of animals, but, when separated from law and justice, he is the worst of all; since armed injustice is the more dangerous, and he is equipped at birth with arms, meant to be used by intelligence and virtue, which he may use for the worst ends. Wherefore, if he have not virtue, he is the most unholy and the most savage of animals, and the most full of lust and gluttony. But justice is the bond of men in states, for the administration of justice, which is the determination of what is just,[7] is the principle of order in political society.

III Seeing then that the state is made up of households, before speaking of the state we must speak of the management of the household. The parts of household management correspond to the persons who compose the household, and a complete household consists of slaves and freemen. Now we should begin by examining everything in its fewest possible elements; and the first and fewest possible parts of a family are master and slave, husband and wife, father and children. We have therefore to consider what each of these three relations is and ought to be:—I mean the relation of master and servant, the marriage relation (the conjunction of man and wife has no name of its own), and thirdly, the procreative relation (this also has no proper name). And there is another element of a household, the so-called art of getting wealth, which, according to some, is identical with household management, according to others, a principal part of it; the nature of this art will also have to be considered by us.

[7] Cp. *Nic. Eth.* v. 1134ª 31.

Let us first speak of master and slave, looking to the needs of practical life and also seeking to attain some better theory of their relation than exists at present. For some are of opinion that the rule of a master is a science, and that the management of a household, and the mastership of slaves, and the political and royal rule, as I was saying at the outset,[8] are all the same. Others affirm that the rule of a master over slaves is contrary to nature, and that the distinction between slave and freeman exists by law only, and not by nature; and being an interference with nature is therefore unjust.

IV Property is a part of the household, and the art of acquiring property is a part of the art of managing the household; for no man can live well, or indeed live at all, unless he be provided with necessaries. And as in the arts which have a definite sphere the workers must have their own proper instruments for the accomplishment of their work, so it is in the management of a household. Now instruments are of various sorts; some are living, others lifeless; in the rudder, the pilot of a ship has a lifeless, in the look-out man, a living instrument; for in the arts the servant is a kind of instrument. Thus, too, a possession is an instrument for maintaining life. And so, in the arrangement of the family, a slave is a living possession, and property a number of such instruments; and the servant is himself an instrument which takes precedence of all other instruments. For if every instrument could accomplish its own work, obeying or anticipating the will of others, like the statues of Daedalus, or the tripods of Hephaestus, which, says the poet,[9]

'of their own accord entered the assembly of the Gods';

if, in like manner, the shuttle would weave and the plectrum touch the lyre without a hand to guide them, chief workmen would not want servants, nor masters slaves. Here, however, another distinction must be drawn; the instruments commonly so called are instruments of production, whilst a possession is an instrument of action. The shuttle, for example, is not only of use; but something else is made by it, whereas of a garment or of a

[8] Plato in *Pol.* 258 E–259 D, referred to already in Bk. 1, I.
[9] Hom. *Il.* xviii. 376.

bed there is only the use. Further, as production and action are different in kind, and both require instruments, the instruments which they employ must likewise differ in kind. But life is action and not production, and therefore the slave is the minister of action. Again, a possession is spoken of as a part is spoken of; for the part is not only a part of something else, but wholly belongs to it; and this is also true of a possession. The master is only the master of the slave; he does not belong to him, whereas the slave is not only the slave of his master, but wholly belongs to him. Hence we see what is the nature and office of a slave; he who is by nature not his own but another's man, is by nature a slave; and he may be said to be another's man who, being a human being, is also a possession. And a possession may be defined as an instrument of action, separable from the possessor.

V But is there any one thus intended by nature to be a slave, and for whom such a condition is expedient and right, or rather is not all slavery a violation of nature?

There is no difficulty in answering this question, on grounds both of reason and of fact. For that some should rule and others be ruled is a thing not only necessary, but expedient; from the hour of their birth, some are marked out for subjection, others for rule.

And there are many kinds both of rulers and subjects (and that rule is the better which is exercised over better subjects—for example, to rule over men is better than to rule over wild beasts; for the work is better which is executed by better workmen, and where one man rules and another is ruled, they may be said to have a work); for in all things which form a composite whole and which are made up of parts, whether continuous or discrete, a distinction between the ruling and the subject element comes to light. Such a duality exists in living creatures, but not in them only; it originates in the constitution of the universe; even in things which have no life there is a ruling principle, as in a musical mode. But we are wandering from the subject. We will therefore restrict ourselves to the living creature, which, in the first place, consists of soul and body: and of these two, the one is by nature the ruler, and the other the subject. But then we must look for the intentions of nature in things which retain their nature, and not in things which are corrupted. And therefore we must study the man who is in the most perfect state both of body and soul, for in him we shall see the true relation of the two; although in bad or corrupted natures the body will often appear to rule over the soul, because they are in an evil and unnatural condition. At all events we may firstly observe in living creatures both a despotical and a constitutional rule; for the soul rules the body with a despotical rule, whereas the intellect rules the appetites with a constitutional and royal rule. And it is clear that the rule of the soul over the body, and of the mind and the rational element over the passionate, is natural and expedient; whereas the equality of the two or the rule of the inferior is always hurtful. The same holds good of animals in relation to men; for tame animals have a better nature than wild, and all tame animals are better off when they are ruled by man; for then they are preserved. Again, the male is by nature superior, and the female inferior; and the one rules, and the other is ruled; this principle, of necessity, extends to all mankind. Where then there is such a difference as that between soul and body, or between men and animals (as in the case of those whose business is to use their body, and who can do nothing better), the lower sort are by nature slaves, and it is better for them as for all inferiors that they should be under the rule of a master. For he who can be, and therefore is, another's and he who participates in rational principle enough to apprehend, but not to have, such a principle, is a slave by nature. Whereas the lower animals cannot even apprehend a principle; they obey their instincts. And indeed the use made of slaves and of tame animals is not very different; for both with their bodies minister to the needs of life. Nature would like to distinguish between the bodies of freemen and slaves, making the one strong for servile labour, the other upright, and although useless for such services, useful for political life in the arts both of war and peace. But the opposite often happens—that some have the souls and others have the bodies of freemen. And doubtless if men differed from one another in the mere forms of their bodies as much as the statues of the Gods do from men, all would acknowledge that the inferior class should be slaves of the superior. And if this is true of the body, how much more just that a similar distinction should exist in the soul? but the beauty of the body is seen, whereas the beauty of the soul is not seen. It is clear, then, that some men are by nature free, and others slaves, and that for these latter slavery is both expedient and right.

VI But that those who take the opposite view have in a certain way right on their side, may be easily seen. For the words slavery and slave are used in two senses. There is a slave or slavery by law as well as by nature. The law of which I speak is a sort of convention—the law by which whatever is taken in war is supposed to belong to the victors. But this right many jurists impeach, as they would an orator who brought forward an unconstitutional measure: they detest the notion that, because one man has the power of doing violence and is superior in brute strength, another shall be his slave and subject. Even among philosophers there is a difference of opinion. The origin of the dispute, and what makes the views invade each other's territory, is as follows: in some sense virtue, when furnished with means, has actually the greatest power of exercising force: and as superior power is only found where there is superior excellence of some kind, power seems to imply virtue, and the dispute to be simply one about justice (for it is due to one party identifying justice with goodwill,[10] while the other identifies it with the mere rule of the stronger). If these views are thus set out separately, the other views[11] have no force or plausibility against the view that the superior in virtue ought to rule, or be master. Others, clinging, as they think, simply to a principle of justice (for law and custom are a sort of justice), assume that slavery in accordance with the custom of war is justified by law, but at the same moment they deny this. For what if the cause of the war be unjust? And again, no one would ever say that he is a slave who is unworthy to be a slave. Were this the case, men of the highest rank would be slaves and the children of slaves if they or their parents chance to have been taken captive and sold. Wherefore Hellenes do not like to call Hellenes slaves, but confine the term to barbarians. Yet, in using this language, they really mean the natural slave of whom

[10] i. e. mutual goodwill, which is held to be incompatible with the relation of master and slave.

[11] i. e. those stated in ll. 5–12, that the stronger always has, and that he never has, a right to enslave the weaker. Aristotle finds that these views cannot maintain themselves against his intermediate view, that the superior in *virtue* should rule.

we spoke at first;[12] for it must be admitted that some are slaves everywhere, others nowhere. The same principle applies to nobility. Hellenes regard themselves as noble everywhere, and not only in their own country, but they deem the barbarians noble only when at home, thereby implying that there are two sorts of nobility and freedom, the one absolute, the other relative. The Helen of Theodectes says:

'Who would presume to call me servant who am on both sides sprung from the stem of the Gods?'

What does this mean but that they distinguish freedom and slavery, noble and humble birth, by the two principles of good and evil? They think that as men and animals beget men and animals, so from good men a good man springs. But this is what nature, though she may intend it, cannot always accomplish.

We see then that there is some foundation for this difference of opinion, and that all are not either slaves by nature or freemen by nature, and also that there is in some cases a marked distinction between the two classes, rendering it expedient and right for the one to be slaves and the others to be masters: the one practising obedience, the others exercising the authority and lordship which nature intended them to have. The abuse of this authority is injurious to both; for the interests of part and whole,[13] of body and soul, are the same, and the slave is a part of the master, a living but separated part of his bodily frame. Hence, where the relation of master and slave between them is natural they are friends and have a common interest, but where it rests merely on law and force the reverse is true.

VII The previous remarks are quite enough to show that the rule of a master is not a constitutional rule, and that all the different kinds of rule are not, as some affirm, the same with each other.[14] For there is one rule exercised over subjects who are by nature free, another over subjects who are by nature slaves. The rule of a household is a monarchy, for every house is under one head: whereas constitutional rule is a government of freemen and

[12] Chap. V.

[13] Cp. Bk. 1, IV.

[14] Plato, *Polit.* 258 E–259 D, referred to already in Bk. 1, I, IV.

equals. The master is not called a master because he has science,[15] but because he is of a certain character, and the same remark applies to the slave and the freeman. Still there may be a science for the master and science for the slave. The science of the slave would be such as the man of Syracuse taught, who made money by instructing slaves in their ordinary duties. And such a knowledge may be carried further, so as to include cookery and similar menial arts. For some duties are of the more necessary, others of the more honourable sort; as the proverb says, 'slave before slave, master before master'. But all such branches of knowledge are servile. There is likewise a science of the master, which teaches the use of slaves; for the master as such is concerned, not with the acquisition, but with the use of them. Yet this so-called science is not anything great or wonderful; for the master need only know how to order that which the slave must know how to execute. Hence those who are in a position which places them above toil have stewards who attend to their households while they occupy themselves with philosophy or with politics. But the art of acquiring slaves, I mean of justly acquiring them, differs both from the art of the master and the art of the slave, being a species of hunting or war.[16] Enough of the distinction between master and slave.

VIII Let us now inquire into property generally, and into the art of getting wealth, in accordance with our usual method,[17] for a slave has been shown[18] to be a part of property. The first question is whether the art of getting wealth is the same with the art of managing a household or a part of it, or instrumental to it; and if the last, whether in the way that the art of making shuttles is instrumental to the art of weaving, or in the way that the casting of bronze is instrumental to the art of the statuary, for they are not instrumental in the same way, but the one provides tools and the other material; and by material I mean the substratum out of which any work is made; thus wool is the material of the weaver, bronze of the statuary. Now it is easy to see that the art of household management is not identical with the art of getting

[15] *Polit.* 259 c, 293 c.

[16] Cp. Bk. 7, XIV.

[17] Of understanding the whole by the part, Cp. Bk. 1, I.

[18] Chap. IV.

wealth, for the one uses the material which the other provides. For the art which uses household stores can be no other than the art of household management. There is, however, a doubt whether the art of getting wealth is a part of household management or a distinct art. If the getter of wealth has to consider whence wealth and property can be procured, but there are many sorts of property and riches, then are husbandry, and the care and provision of food in general, parts of the wealth-getting art or distinct arts? Again, there are many sorts of food, and therefore there are many kinds of lives both of animals and men; they must all have food, and the differences in their food have made differences in their ways of life. For of beasts, some are gregarious, others are solitary; they live in the way which is best adapted to sustain them, accordingly as they are carnivorous or herbivorous or omnivorous: and their habits are determined for them by nature in such a manner that they may obtain with greater facility the food of their choice. But, as different species have different tastes, the same things are not naturally pleasant to all of them; and therefore the lives of carnivorous or herbivorous animals further differ among themselves. In the lives of men too there is a great difference. The laziest are shepherds, who lead an idle life, and get their subsistence without trouble from tame animals; their flocks having to wander from place to place in search of pasture, they are compelled to follow them, cultivating a sort of living farm. Others support themselves by hunting, which is of different kinds. Some, for example, are brigands, others, who dwell near lakes or marshes or rivers or a sea in which there are fish, are fishermen, and others live by the pursuit of birds or wild beasts. The greater number obtain a living from the cultivated fruits of the soil. Such are the modes of subsistence which prevail among those whose industry springs up of itself, and whose food is not acquired by exchange and retail trade—there is the shepherd, the husbandman, the brigand, the fisherman, the hunter. Some gain a comfortable maintenance out of two employments, eking out the deficiencies of one of them by another: thus the life of a shepherd may be combined with that of a brigand, the life of a farmer with that of a hunter. Other modes of life are similarly combined in any way which the needs of men may require. Property, in the sense of a bare livelihood, seems to be given by nature herself to all, both when they are first born, and when they are grown up.

For some animals bring forth, together with their offspring, so much food as will last until they are able to supply themselves; of this the vermiparous or oviparous animals are an instance; and the viviparous animals have up to a certain time a supply of food for their young in themselves, which is called milk. In like manner we may infer that, after the birth of animals, plants exist for their sake, and that the other animals exist for the sake of man, the tame for use and food, the wild, if not all, at least the greater part of them, for food, and for the provision of clothing and various instruments. Now if nature makes nothing incomplete, and nothing in vain, the inference must be that she has made all animals for the sake of man. And so, in one point of view, the art of war is a natural art of acquisition, for the art of acquisition includes hunting, an art which we ought to practise against wild beasts, and against men who, though intended by nature to be governed, will not submit; for war of such a kind is naturally just.[19]

Of the art of acquisition then there is one kind which by nature is a part of the management of a household, in so far as the art of household management must either find ready to hand, or itself provide, such things necessary to life, and useful for the community of the family or state, as can be stored. They are the elements of true riches; for the amount of property which is needed for a good life is not unlimited, although Solon in one of his poems says that

'No bound to riches has been fixed for man'.

But there is a boundary fixed, just as there is in the other arts; for the instruments of any art are never unlimited, either in number or size, and riches may be defined as a number of instruments to be used in a household or in a state. And so we see that there is a natural art of acquisition which is practised by managers of households and by statesmen, and what is the reason of this.

IX There is another variety of the art of acquisition which is commonly and rightly called an art of wealth-getting, and has in fact suggested the notion that riches and property have no limit. Being nearly connected with the preceding, it is often identified with it. But though they are not very different, neither are they

[19] Cp. Bk. 1, VII; Bk. 7, XIV.

the same. The kind already described is given by nature, the other is gained by experience and art.

Let us begin our discussion of the question with the following considerations:

Of everything which we possess there are two uses: both belong to the thing as such, but not in the same manner, for one is the proper, and the other the improper or secondary use of it. For example, a shoe is used for wear, and is used for exchange; both are uses of the shoe. He who gives a shoe in exchange for money or food to him who wants one, does indeed use the shoe as a shoe, but this is not its proper or primary purpose, for a shoe is not made to be an object of barter. The same may be said of all possessions, for the art of exchange extends to all of them, and it arises at first from what is natural, from the circumstance that some have too little, others too much. Hence we may infer that retail trade is not a natural part of the art of getting wealth; had it been so, men would have ceased to exchange when they had enough. In the first community, indeed, which is the family, this art is obviously of no use, but it begins to be useful when the society increases. For the members of the family originally had all things in common; later, when the family divided into parts, the parts shared in many things, and different parts in different things, which they had to give in exchange for what they wanted, a kind of barter which is still practised among barbarous nations who exchange with one another the necessaries of life and nothing more; giving and receiving wine, for example, in exchange for corn, and the like. This sort of barter is not part of the wealth-getting art and is not contrary to nature, but is needed for the satisfaction of men's natural wants. The other or more complex form of exchange grew, as might have been inferred, out of the simpler. When the inhabitants of one country became more dependent on those of another, and they imported what they needed, and exported what they had too much of, money necessarily came into use. For the various necessaries of life are not easily carried about, and hence men agreed to employ in their dealings with each other something which was intrinsically useful and easily applicable to the purposes of life, for example, iron, silver, and the like. Of this the value was at first measured simply by size and weight, but in process of time they put a stamp upon it, to save the trouble of weighing and to mark the value.

When the use of coin had once been discovered, out of the barter of necessary articles arose the other art of wealth-getting, namely, retail trade; which was at first probably a simple matter, but became more complicated as soon as men learned by experience whence and by what exchanges the greatest profit might be made. Originating in the use of coin, the art of getting wealth is generally thought to be chiefly concerned with it, and to be the art which produces riches and wealth; having to consider how they may be accumulated. Indeed, riches is assumed by many to be only a quantity of coin, because the arts of getting wealth and retail trade are concerned with coin. Others maintain that coined money is a mere sham, a thing not natural, but conventional only, because, if the users substitute another commodity for it, it is worthless, and because it is not useful as a means to any of the necessities of life, and, indeed, he who is rich in coin may often be in want of necessary food. But how can that be wealth of which a man may have a great abundance and yet perish with hunger, like Midas in the fable, whose insatiable prayer turned everything that was set before him into gold?

Hence men seek after a better notion of riches and of the art of getting wealth than the mere acquisition of coin, and they are right. For natural riches and the natural art of wealth-getting are a different thing; in their true form they are part of the management of a household; whereas retail trade is the art of producing wealth, not in every way, but by exchange. And it is thought to be concerned with coin; for coin is the unit of exchange and the measure or limit of it. And there is no bound to the riches which spring from this art of wealth-getting.[20] As in the art of medicine there is no limit to the pursuit of health, and as in the other arts there is no limit to the pursuit of their several ends, for they aim at accomplishing their ends to the uttermost (but of the means there is a limit, for the end is always the limit), so, too, in this art of wealth-getting there is no limit of the end, which is riches of the spurious kind, and the acquisition of wealth. But the art of wealth-getting which consists in household management, on the other hand, has a limit; the unlimited acquisition of wealth is not its business. And, therefore, in one point of view, all riches must have a limit; nevertheless, as a matter of fact, we find the opposite to be the case; for all getters of wealth

[20] Cp. Bk. 1, VIII.

increase their hoard of coin without limit. The source of the confusion is the near connection between the two kinds of wealth-getting; in either, the instrument is the same, although the use is different, and so they pass into one another; for each is a use of the same property, but with a difference: accumulation is the end in the one case, but there is a further end in the other. Hence some persons are led to believe that getting wealth is the object of household management, and the whole idea of their lives is that they ought either to increase their money without limit, or at any rate not to lose it. The origin of this disposition in men is that they are intent upon living only, and not upon living well; and, as their desires are unlimited, they also desire that the means of gratifying them should be without limit. Those who do aim at a good life seek the means of obtaining bodily pleasures; and, since the enjoyment of these appears to depend on property, they are absorbed in getting wealth: and so there arises the second species of wealth-getting. For, as their enjoyment is in excess, they seek an art which produces the excess of enjoyment; and, if they are not able to supply their pleasures by the art of getting wealth, they try other arts, using in turn every faculty in a manner contrary to nature. The quality of courage, for example, is not intended to make wealth, but to inspire confidence; neither is this the aim of the general's or of the physician's art; but the one aims at victory and the other at health. Nevertheless, some men turn every quality or art into a means of getting wealth; this they conceive to be the end, and to the promotion of the end they think all things must contribute.

Thus, then, we have considered the art of wealth-getting which is unnecessary, and why men want it; and also the necessary art of wealth-getting, which we have seen to be different from the other, and to be a natural part of the art of managing a household, concerned with the provision of food, not, however, like the former kind, unlimited, but having a limit.

X And we have found the answer to our original question,[21] Whether the art of getting wealth is the business of the manager of a household and of the statesman or not their business?—viz. that wealth is presupposed by them. For as political science does

[21] Bk. 1, VIII.

not make men, but takes them from nature and uses them, so too nature provides them with earth or sea or the like as a source of food. At this stage begins the duty of the manager of a household, who has to order the things which nature supplies;—he may be compared to the weaver who has not to make but to use wool, and to know, too, what sort of wool is good and serviceable or bad and unserviceable. Were this otherwise, it would be difficult to see why the art of getting wealth is a part of the management of a household and the art of medicine not; for surely the members of a household must have health just as they must have life or any other necessary. The answer is that as from one point of view the master of the house and the ruler of the state have to consider about health, from another point of view not they but the physician; so in one way the art of household management, in another way the subordinate art, has to consider about wealth. But, strictly speaking, as I have already said, the means of life must be provided beforehand by nature; for the business of nature is to furnish food to that which is born, and the food of the offspring is always what remains over of that from which it is produced.[22] Wherefore the art of getting wealth out of fruits and animals is always natural.

There are two sorts of wealth-getting, as I have said[23]; one is a part of household management, the other is retail trade: the former necessary and honourable, while that which consists in exchange is justly censured; for it is unnatural, and a mode by which men gain from one another. The most hated sort, and with the greatest reason, is usury, which makes a gain out of money itself, and not from the natural object of it. For money was intended to be used in exchange, but not to increase at interest. And this term interest,[24] which means the birth of money from money, is applied to the breeding of money because the offspring resembles the parent. Wherefore of all modes of getting wealth this is the most unnatural.

XI Enough has been said about the theory of wealth-getting; we will now proceed to the practical part. The discussion of such matters is not unworthy of philosophy, but to be engaged in them

[22] Cp. Bk. 1, VIII.
[23] Bk. 1, VIII-X.
[24] *tokos*, lit. 'offspring'.

practically is illiberal and irksome. The useful parts of wealth-getting are, first, the knowledge of live-stock—which are most profitable, and where, and how—as, for example, what sort of horses or sheep or oxen or any other animals are most likely to give a return. A man ought to know which of these pay better than others, and which pay best in particular places, for some do better in one place and some in another. Secondly, husbandry, which may be either tillage or planting, and the keeping of bees and of fish, or fowl, or of any animals which may be useful to man. These are the divisions of the true or proper art of wealth-getting and come first. Of the other, which consists in exchange, the first and most important division is commerce (of which there are three kinds—the provision of a ship, the conveyance of goods, exposure for sale—these again differing as they are safer or more profitable), the second is usury, the third, service for hire—of this, one kind is employed in the mechanical arts, the other in unskilled and bodily labour. There is still a third sort of wealth-getting intermediate between this and the first or natural mode which is partly natural, but is also concerned with exchange, viz., the industries that make their profit from the earth, and from things growing from the earth which, although they bear no fruit, are nevertheless profitable; for example, the cutting of timber and all mining. The art of mining, by which minerals are obtained, itself has many branches, for there are various kinds of things dug out of the earth. Of the several divisions of wealth-getting I now speak generally; a minute consideration of them might be useful in practice, but it would be tiresome to dwell upon them at greater length now.

Those occupations are most truly arts in which there is the least element of chance; they are the meanest in which the body is most deteriorated, the most servile in which there is the greatest use of the body, and the most illiberal in which there is the least need of excellence.

Works have been written upon these subjects by various persons; for example, by Chares the Parian, and Apollodorus the Lemnian, who have treated of Tillage and Planting, while others have treated of other branches; any one who cares for such matters may refer to their writings. It would be well also to collect the scattered stories of the ways in which individuals have succeeded in amassing a fortune; for all this is useful to persons who value the art of getting wealth. There is the anecdote of Thales the Milesian and his financial device, which involves a principle of universal application, but is attributed to him on account of his reputation for wisdom. He was reproached for his poverty, which was supposed to show that philosophy was of no use. According to the story, he knew by his skill in the stars while it was yet winter that there would be a great harvest of olives in the coming year; so, having a little money, he gave deposits for the use of all the olive-presses in Chios and Miletus, which he hired at a low price because no one bid against him. When the harvest-time came, and many were wanted all at once and of a sudden, he let them out at any rate which he pleased, and made a quantity of money. Thus he showed the world that philosophers can easily be rich if they like, but that their ambition is of another sort. He is supposed to have given a striking proof of his wisdom, but, as I was saying, his device for getting wealth is of universal application, and is nothing but the creation of a monopoly. It is an art often practised by cities when they are in want of money; they make a monopoly of provisions.

There was a man of Sicily, who, having money deposited with him, bought up all the iron from the iron mines; afterwards, when the merchants from their various markets came to buy, he was the only seller, and without much increasing the price he gained 200 per cent. Which when Dionysius heard, he told him that he might take away his money, but that he must not remain at Syracuse, for he thought that the man had discovered a way of making money which was injurious to his own interests. He made the same discovery as Thales; they both contrived to create a monopoly for themselves. And statesmen as well ought to know these things; for a state is often as much in want of money and of such devices for obtaining it as a household, or even more so; hence some public men devote themselves entirely to finance.

XII Of household management we have seen[25] that there are three parts—one is the rule of a master over slaves, which has been discussed already,[26] another of a father, and the third of a husband. A husband and father, we saw, rules over wife and children, both free, but the rule differs, the rule over his children

[25] Bk. 1, IV.

[26] Bk. 1, IV-VII.

being a royal, over his wife a constitutional rule. For although there may be exceptions to the order of nature, the male is by nature fitter for command than the female, just as the elder and full-grown is superior to the younger and more immature. But in most constitutional states the citizens rule and are ruled by turns, for the idea of a constitutional state implies that the natures of the citizens are equal, and do not differ at all.[27] Nevertheless, when one rules and the other is ruled we endeavour to create a difference of outward forms and names and titles of respect, which may be illustrated by the saying of Amasis about his foot-pan.[28] The relation of the male to the female is of this kind, but there the inequality is permanent. The rule of a father over his children is royal, for he rules by virtue both of love and of the respect due to age, exercising a kind of royal power. And therefore Homer has appropriately called Zeus 'father of Gods and men', because he is the king of them all. For a king is the natural superior of his subjects, but he should be of the same kin or kind with them, and such is the relation of elder and younger, of father and son.

XIII Thus it is clear that household management attends more to men than to the acquisition of inanimate things, and to human excellence more than to the excellence of property which we call wealth, and to the virtue of freemen more than to the virtue of slaves. A question may indeed be raised, whether there is any excellence at all in a slave beyond and higher than merely instrumental and ministerial qualities—whether he can have the virtues of temperance, courage, justice, and the like; or whether slaves possess only bodily and ministerial qualities. And, whichever way we answer the question, a difficulty arises; for, if they have virtue, in what will they differ from freemen? On the other hand, since they are men and share in rational principle, it seems absurd to say that they have no virtue. A similar question may be raised about women and children, whether they too have virtues: ought a woman to be temperate and brave and just, and is a child to be called temperate, and intemperate, or not? So in general we may ask about the natural ruler, and the natural subject, whether they have the same or different virtues. For if a noble nature is equally required in both, why should one of them always rule, and the

[27] Cp. Bk. 2, I; Bk. 3, XVII.

[28] Herod. ii. 172.

other always be ruled? Nor can we say that this is a question of degree, for the difference between ruler and subject is a difference of kind, which the difference of more and less never is. Yet how strange is the supposition that the one ought, and that the other ought not, to have virtue! For if the ruler is intemperate and unjust, how can he rule well? If the subject, how can he obey well? If he be licentious and cowardly, he will certainly not do his duty. It is evident, therefore, that both of them must have a share of virtue, but varying as natural subjects also vary among themselves. Here the very constitution of the soul has shown us the way; in it one part naturally rules, and the other is subject, and the virtue of the ruler we maintain to be different from that of the subject;—the one being the virtue of the rational, and the other of the irrational part. Now, it is obvious that the same principle applies generally, and therefore almost all things rule and are ruled according to nature. But the kind of rule differs;—the freeman rules over the slave after another manner from that in which the male rules over the female, or the man over the child; although the parts of the soul are present in all of them, they are present in different degrees. For the slave has no deliberative faculty at all; the woman has, but it is without authority, and the child has, but it is immature. So it must necessarily be supposed to be with the moral virtues also; all should partake of them, but only in such manner and degree as is required by each for the fulfilment of his duty. Hence the ruler ought to have moral virtue in perfection, for his function, taken absolutely, demands a master artificer, and rational principle is such an artificer; the subjects, on the other hand, require only that measure of virtue which is proper to each of them. Clearly, then, moral virtue belongs to all of them; but the temperance of a man and of a woman, or the courage and justice of a man and of a woman, are not, as Socrates maintained,[29] the same; the courage of a man is shown in commanding, of a woman in obeying. And this holds of all other virtues, as will be more clearly seen if we look at them in detail, for those who say generally that virtue consists in a good disposition of the soul, or in doing rightly, or the like, only deceive themselves. Far better than such definitions is their mode of speaking, who, like Gorgias,[30] enumerate the

[29] Plato, *Meno*, 72 A–73 C.

[30] *Meno*, 71 E, 72 A.

virtues. All classes must be deemed to have their special attributes; as the poet says of women,

'Silence is a woman's glory',

but this is not equally the glory of man. The child is imperfect, and therefore obviously his virtue is not relative to himself alone, but to the perfect man and to his teacher, and in like manner the virtue of the slave is relative to a master. Now we determined[31] that a slave is useful for the wants of life, and therefore he will obviously require only so much virtue as will prevent him from failing in his duty through cowardice or lack of self-control. Some one will ask whether, if what we are saying is true, virtue will not be required also in the artisans, for they often fail in their work through the lack of self-control? But is there not a great difference in the two cases? For the slave shares in his master's life; the artisan is less closely connected with him, and only attains excellence in proportion as he becomes a slave. The meaner sort of mechanic has a special and separate slavery; and whereas the slave exists by nature, not so the shoemaker or other artisan. It is manifest, then, that the master ought to be the source of such excellence in the slave, and not a mere possessor of the art of mastership which trains the slave in his duties.[32] Wherefore they are mistaken who forbid us to converse with slaves and say that we should employ command only,[33] for slaves stand even more in need of admonition than children.

So much for this subject; the relations of husband and wife, parent and child, their several virtues, what in their intercourse with one another is good, and what is evil, and how we may pursue the good and escape the evil, will have to be discussed when we speak of the different forms of government.[34] For, inasmuch as every family is a part of a state, and these relationships are the parts of a family, and the virtue of the part must have regard to the virtue of the whole, women and children must be trained by education with an eye to the constitution,[35] if the virtues of either of them are supposed to make any difference in the virtues

[31] Bk. 1, V, Cf. Bk. 1, XII.
[32] Cp. Bk. 1, VII.
[33] Plato, *Laws, vi.* 777 E.
[34] The question is not actually discussed in the *Politics*.
[35] Cp. Bk. 5, IX; Bk. 8, II.

of the state. And they must make a difference: for the children grow up to be citizens, and half the free persons in a state are women.[36]

Of these matters, enough has been said; of what remains, let us speak at another time. Regarding, then, our present inquiry as complete, we will make a new beginning. And, first, let us examine the various theories of a perfect state.

[36] Plato, *Laws,* vi. 781 A.

BOOK SECOND

I Our purpose is to consider what form of political community is best of all for those who are most able to realize their ideal of life. We must therefore examine not only this but other constitutions, both such as actually exist in well-governed states, and any theoretical forms which are held in esteem; that what is good and useful may be brought to light. And let no one suppose that in seeking for something beyond them we are anxious to make a sophistical display at any cost; we only undertake this inquiry because all the constitutions with which we are acquainted are faulty.

We will begin with the natural beginning of the subject. Three alternatives are conceivable: The members of a state must either have (1) all things or (2) nothing in common, or (3) some things in common and some not. That they should have nothing in common is clearly impossible, for the constitution is a community, and must at any rate have a common place—one city will be in one place, and the citizens are those who share in that one city. But should a well-ordered state have all things, as far as may be, in common, or some only and not others? For the citizens might conceivably have wives and children and property in common, as Socrates proposes in the *Republic* of Plato.[1] Which is better, our present condition, or the proposed new order of society?

II There are many difficulties in the community of women. And the principle on which Socrates rests the necessity of such an institution evidently is not established by his arguments. Further, as a means to the end which he ascribes to the state, the scheme, taken literally, is impracticable, and how we are to interpret it is nowhere precisely stated. I am speaking of the premise from which the argument of Socrates proceeds, 'that the greater the unity of the state the better'. Is it not obvious that a state may at length attain such a degree of unity as to be no longer a state?—since the nature of a state is to be a plurality, and in tending to greater unity, from being a state, it becomes a family, and from being a family, an individual; for the family may be said to be

[1] *Rep.* iv. 423 E, v. 457 C, 462 B.

more than the state, and the individual than the family. So that we ought not to attain this greatest unity even if we could, for it would be the destruction of the state. Again, a state is not made up only of so many men, but of different kinds of men; for similars do not constitute a state. It is not like a military alliance. The usefulness of the latter depends upon its quantity even where there is no difference in quality (for mutual protection is the end aimed at), just as a greater weight of anything is more useful than a less (in like manner, a state differs from a nation, when the nation has not its population organized in villages, but lives an Arcadian sort of life); but the elements out of which a unity is to be formed differ in kind. Wherefore the principle of compensation, as I have already remarked in the *Ethics*,[2] is the salvation of states. Even among freemen and equals this is a principle which must be maintained, for they cannot all rule together, but must change at the end of a year or some other period of time or in some order of succession. The result is that upon this plan they all govern; just as if shoemakers and carpenters were to exchange their occupations, and the same persons did not always continue shoemakers and carpenters. And since it is better that this should be so in politics as well, it is clear that while there should be continuance of the same persons in power where this is possible, yet where this is not possible by reason of the natural equality of the citizens, and at the same time it is just that all should share in the government (whether to govern be a good thing or a bad[3]), an approximation to this is that equals should in turn retire from office and should, apart from official position, be treated alike.[4] Thus the one party rule and the others are ruled in turn, as if they were no longer the same persons. In like manner when they hold office there is a variety in the offices held. Hence it is evident that a city is not by nature one in that sense which some persons affirm; and that what is said to be the greatest good of cities is in reality their destruction; but surely the good of things must be that which preserves them.[5] Again, in another point of view, this extreme unification of the state is clearly not good; for a family is more self-sufficing than an individual, and a city than a family, and a city only comes into being when the community is large

[2] *Nic. Eth.* v. 1132[b] 32.
[3] Cp. Pl. *Rep.* i. 345–6.
[4] Cp. Bk. 1, XII; Bk. 3, XVII.
[5] Cp. Pl. *Rep.* i. 353.

enough to be self-sufficing. If then self-sufficiency is to be desired, the lesser degree of unity is more desirable than the greater.

III But, even supposing that it were best for the community to have the greatest degree of unity, this unity is by no means proved to follow from the fact 'of all men saying "mine" and "not mine" at the same instant of time', which, according to Socrates,[6] is the sign of perfect unity in a state. For the word 'all' is ambiguous. If the meaning be that every individual says 'mine' and 'not mine' at the same time, then perhaps the result at which Socrates aims may be in some degree accomplished; each man will call the same person his own son and the same person his own wife, and so of his property and of all that falls to his lot. This, however, is not the way in which people would speak who had their wives and children in common; they would say 'all' but not 'each'. In like manner their property would be described as belonging to them, not severally but collectively. There is an obvious fallacy in the term 'all': like some other words, 'both', 'odd', 'even', it is ambiguous, and even in abstract argument becomes a source of logical puzzles. That all persons call the same thing mine in the sense in which each does so may be a fine thing, but it is impracticable; or if the words are taken in the other sense, such a unity in no way conduces to harmony. And there is another objection to the proposal. For that which is common to the greatest number has the least care bestowed upon it. Every one thinks chiefly of his own, hardly at all of the common interest; and only when he is himself concerned as an individual. For besides other considerations, everybody is more inclined to neglect the duty which he expects another to fulfil; as in families many attendants are often less useful than a few. Each citizen will have a thousand sons who will not be his sons individually, but anybody will be equally the son of anybody, and will therefore be neglected by all alike. Further, upon this principle, every one will use the word 'mine' of one who is prospering or the reverse,[7] however small a fraction he may himself be of the whole number; the same boy will be 'my son', 'so and so's son', the son of each of the thousand, or whatever be the number of the citizens; and even about this he will

[6] Pl. *Rep.* v. 462 C.

[7] Cp. *Rep.* v. 463 E.

not be positive; for it is impossible to know who chanced to have a child, or whether, if one came into existence, it has survived. But which is better—for each to say 'mine' in this way, making a man the same relation to two thousand or ten thousand citizens, or to use the word 'mine' in the ordinary and more restricted sense? For usually the same person is called by one man his own son whom another calls his own brother or cousin or kinsman—blood relation or connexion by marriage either of himself or of some relation of his, and yet another his clansman or tribesman; and how much better is it to be the real cousin of somebody than to be a son after Plato's fashion! Nor is there any way of preventing brothers and children and fathers and mothers from sometimes recognizing one another; for children are born like their parents, and they will necessarily be finding indications of their relationship to one another. Geographers declare such to be the fact; they say that in part of Upper Libya, where the women are common, nevertheless the children who are born are assigned to their respective fathers on the ground of their likeness. And some women, like the females of other animals—for example, mares and cows—have a strong tendency to produce offspring resembling their parents, as was the case with the Pharsalian mare called Honest.

IV Other evils, against which it is not easy for the authors of such a community to guard, will be assaults and homicides, voluntary as well as involuntary, quarrels and slanders, all which are most unholy acts when committed against fathers and mothers and near relations, but not equally unholy when there is no relationship. Moreover, they are much more likely to occur if the relationship is unknown, and, when they have occurred, the customary expiations of them cannot be made. Again, how strange it is that Socrates,[8] after having made the children common, should hinder lovers from carnal intercourse only, but should permit love and familiarities between father and son or between brother and brother, than which nothing can be more unseemly, since even without them love of this sort is improper. How strange, too, to forbid intercourse for no other reason than the

[8] *Rep.* iii. 403 A–C.

violence of the pleasure, as though the relationship of father and son or of brothers with one another made no difference.

This community of wives and children seems better suited to the husbandmen than to the guardians, for if they have wives and children in common, they will be bound to one another by weaker ties, as a subject class should be, and they will remain obedient and not rebel.[9] In a word, the result of such a law would be just the opposite of that which good laws ought to have, and the intention of Socrates in making these regulations about women and children would defeat itself. For friendship we believe to be the greatest good of states[10] and the preservative of them against revolutions; neither is there anything which Socrates so greatly lauds as the unity of the state which he and all the world declare to be created by friendship. But the unity which he commends[11] would be like that of the lovers in the *Symposium*,[12] who, as Aristophanes says, desire to grow together in the excess of their affection, and from being two to become one, in which case one or both would certainly perish. Whereas in a state having women and children common, love will be watery; and the father will certainly not say 'my son', or the son 'my father'.[13] As a little sweet wine mingled with a great deal of water is imperceptible in the mixture, so, in this sort of community, the idea of relationship which is based upon these names will be lost; there is no reason why the so-called father should care about the son, or the son about the father, or brothers about one another. Of the two qualities which chiefly inspire regard and affection—that a thing is your own and that it is your only one—neither can exist in such a state as this.

Again, the transfer of children as soon as they are born from the rank of husbandmen or of artisans to that of guardians, and from the rank of guardians into a lower rank,[14] will be very difficult to arrange; the givers or transferrers cannot but know whom they are giving and transferring, and to whom. And the previously mentioned[15] evils, such as assaults, unlawful loves, homicides, will happen more often amongst those who are transferred to the lower classes, or who have a place assigned to them among

[9] Cp. Bk. 7, X.
[10] Cp. *Nic. Eth.* viii. 1155ᵃ 22.
[11] Cp. II.
[12] *Symp.* 191 A, 192 C.
[13] Cp. III.
[14] *Rep.* iii. 415 B.
[15] IV.

the guardians; for they will no longer call the members of the class they have left brothers, and children, and fathers, and mothers, and will not, therefore, be afraid of committing any crimes by reason of consanguinity. Touching the community of wives and children, let this be our conclusion.

V Next let us consider what should be our arrangements about property: should the citizens of the perfect state have their possessions in common or not? This question may be discussed separately from the enactments about women and children. Even supposing that the women and children belong to individuals, according to the custom which is at present universal, may there not be an advantage in having and using possessions in common? Three cases are possible: (1) the soil may be appropriated, but the produce may be thrown for consumption into the common stock; and this is the practice of some nations. Or (2), the soil may be common, and may be cultivated in common, but the produce divided among individuals for their private use; this is a form of common property which is said to exist among certain barbarians. Or (3), the soil and the produce may be alike common.

When the husbandmen are not the owners, the case will be different and easier to deal with; but when they till the ground for themselves the question of ownership will give a world of trouble. If they do not share equally in enjoyments and toils, those who labour much and get little will necessarily complain of those who labour little and receive or consume much. But indeed there is always a difficulty in men living together and having all human relations in common, but especially in their having common property. The partnerships of fellow-travellers are an example to the point; for they generally fall out over everyday matters and quarrel about any trifle which turns up. So with servants: we are most liable to take offense at those with whom we most frequently come into contact in daily life.

These are only some of the disadvantages which attend the community of property; the present arrangement, if improved as it might be by good customs and laws, would be far better, and would have the advantages of both systems. Property should be in a certain sense common, but, as a general rule, private; for, when everyone has a distinct interest,[16] men will not complain of one another, and they will make more progress, because every one will be attending to his own business. And yet by reason of goodness, and in respect of use, 'Friends', as the proverb says, will have all things common.'[17] Even now there are traces of such a principle, showing that it is not impracticable, but, in well-ordered states, exists already to a certain extent and may be carried further. For, although every man has his own property, some things he will place at the disposal of his friends, while of others he shares the use with them. The Lacedaemonians, for example, use one another's slaves, and horses, and dogs, as if they were their own; and when they lack provisions on a journey, they appropriate what they find in the fields throughout the country. It is clearly better that property should be private, but the use of it common; and the special business of the legislator is to create in men this benevolent disposition. Again, how immeasurably greater is the pleasure, when a man feels a thing to be his own; for surely the love of self[18] is a feeling implanted by nature and not given in vain, although selfishness is rightly censured; this, however, is not the mere love of self, but the love of self in excess, like the miser's love of money; for all, or almost all, men love money and other such objects in a measure. And further, there is the greatest pleasure in doing a kindness or service to friends or guests or companions, which can only be rendered when a man has private property. These advantages are lost by excessive unification of the state. The exhibition of two virtues, besides, is visibly annihilated in such a state: first, temperance towards women (for it is an honourable action to abstain from another's wife for temperance sake), secondly, liberality in the matter of property. No one, when men have all things in common, will any longer set an example of liberality or do any liberal action; for liberality consists in the use which is made of property.[19]

Such legislation may have a specious appearance of benevolence; men readily listen to it, and are easily induced to believe that in some wonderful manner everybody will become everybody's friend, especially when some one[20] is heard denouncing

[16] Cp. *Rep.* ii. 374. [17] Cp. *Rep.* iv. 424 A. [18] Cp. *Nic. Eth.* ix. 8.
[19] Cp. *Nic. Eth.* iv. 1119b 22. [20] *Rep.* v. 464, 465.

the evils now existing in states, suits about contracts, convictions for perjury, flatteries of rich men and the like, which are said to arise out of the possession of private property. These evils, however, are due to a very different cause—the wickedness of human nature. Indeed, we see that there is much more quarrelling among those who have all things in common, though there are not many of them when compared with the vast numbers who have private property.

Again, we ought to reckon, not only the evils from which the citizens will be saved, but also the advantages which they will lose. The life which they are to lead appears to be quite impracticable. The error of Socrates must be attributed to the false notion of unity from which he starts.[21] Unity there should be, both of the family and of the state, but in some respects only. For there is a point at which a state may attain such a degree of unity as to be no longer a state, or at which, without actually ceasing to exist, it will become an inferior state, like harmony passing into unison, or rhythm which has been reduced to a single foot. The state, as I was saying, is a plurality,[22] which should be united and made into a community by education; and it is strange that the author of a system of education which he thinks will make the state virtuous, should expect to improve his citizens by regulations of this sort, and not by philosophy or by customs and laws, like those which prevail at Sparta and Crete respecting common meals, whereby the legislator has made property common. Let us remember that we should not disregard the experience of ages; in the multitude of years these things, if they were good, would certainly not have been unknown; for almost everything has been found out, although sometimes they are not put together; in other cases men do not use the knowledge which they have. Great light would be thrown on this subject if we could see such a form of government in the actual process of construction; for the legislator could not form a state at all without distributing and dividing its constituents into associations for common meals, and into phratries and tribes. But all this legislation ends only in forbidding agriculture to the guardians, a prohibition which the Lacedaemonians try to enforce already.

But, indeed, Socrates has not said, nor is it easy to decide, what in such a community will be the general form of the state. The

[21] Cp. II.

[22] Cp. Bk. 2, I.

citizens who are not guardians are the majority, and about them nothing has been determined: are the husbandmen, too, to have their property in common? Or is each individual to have his own? and are the wives and children to be individual or common? If, like the guardians, they are to have all things in common, in what do they differ from them, or what will they gain by submitting to their government? Or, upon what principle would they submit, unless indeed the governing class adopt the ingenious policy of the Cretans, who give their slaves the same institutions as their own, but forbid them gymnastic exercises and the possession of arms. If, on the other hand, the inferior classes are to be like other cities in respect of marriage and property, what will be the form of the community? Must it not contain two states in one,[23] each hostile to the other? He makes the guardians into a mere occupying garrison, while the husbandmen and artisans and the rest are the real citizens. But if so the suits and quarrels, and all the evils which Socrates affirms[24] to exist in other states, will exist equally among them. He says indeed that, having so good an education, the citizens will not need many laws, for example laws about the city or about the markets[25]; but then he confines his education to the guardians. Again, he makes the husbandmen owners of the property upon condition of their paying a tribute.[26] But in that case they are likely to be much more unmanageable and conceited than the Helots, or Penestae, or slaves in general.[27] And whether community of wives and property be necessary for the lower equally with the higher class or not, and the questions akin to this, what will be the education, form of government, laws of the lower class, Socrates has nowhere determined: neither is it easy to discover this, nor is their character of small importance if the common life of the guardians is to be maintained.

Again, if Socrates makes the women common, and retains private property, the men will see to the fields, but who will see to the house? And who will do so if the agricultural class have both their property and their wives in common? Once more: it is absurd to argue, from the analogy of the animals, that men and women should follow the same pursuits,[28] for animals have not to manage a household. The government, too, as constituted by Socrates, contains elements of danger; for he makes the same

[23] Cp. *Rep.* iv. 422 E. [24] *Rep.* v. 464, 465. [25] *Rep.* iv. 425 D.
[26] *Rep.* v. 464 C. [27] Cp. Bk. 2, VIII. [28] Cp. *Rep.* v. 451 D.

persons always rule. And if this is often a cause of disturbance among the meaner sort, how much more among high-spirited warriors? But that the persons whom he makes rulers must be the same is evident; for the gold which the God mingles in the souls of men is not at one time given to one, at another time to another, but always to the same: as he says, 'God mingles gold in some, and silver in others, from their very birth; but brass and iron in those who are meant to be artisans and husbandmen.'[29] Again, he deprives the guardians even of happiness, and says that the legislator ought to make the whole state happy.[30] But the whole cannot be happy unless most, or all, or some of its parts enjoy happiness.[31] In this respect happiness is not like the even principle in numbers, which may exist only in the whole, but in neither of the parts; not so happiness. And if the guardians are not happy, who are? Surely not the artisans, or the common people. The Republic of which Socrates discourses has all these difficulties, and others quite as great.

VI The same, or nearly the same, objections apply to Plato's later work, the *Laws*, and therefore we had better examine briefly the constitution which is therein described. In the *Republic*, Socrates has definitely settled in all a few questions only; such as the community of women and children, the community of property, and the constitution of the state. The population is divided into two classes—one of husbandmen, and the other of warriors[32]; from this latter is taken a third class of counsellors and rulers of the state.[33] But Socrates has not determined whether the husbandmen and artisans are to have a share in the government, and whether they, too, are to carry arms and share in military service, or not. He certainly thinks[34] that the women ought to share in the education of the guardians, and to fight by their side. The remainder of the work is filled up with digressions foreign to the main subject, and with discussions about the education of the guardians. In the *Laws* there is hardly anything but laws; not much is said about the constitution. This, which he had intended to make more of the ordinary type, he gradually brings

[29] Cp. *Rep.* iii. 415 A.
[30] *Rep.* iv. 419, 420.
[31] Cp. Bk. 7, IX.
[32] *Rep.* ii. 373 E.
[33] *Rep.* iii. 412 B.
[34] *Rep.* v. 451 E.

round to the other or ideal form. For with the exception of the community of women and property, he supposes everything to be the same in both states; there is to be the same education; the citizens of both are to live free from servile occupations, and there are to be common meals in both. The only difference is that in the *Laws*, the common meals are extended to women,[35] and the warriors number 5000,[36] but in the *Republic* only 1000.[37]

The discourses of Socrates are never commonplace; they always exhibit grace and originality and thought; but perfection in everything can hardly be expected. We must not overlook the fact that the number of 5000 citizens, just now mentioned, will require a territory as large as Babylon, or some other huge site, if so many persons are to be supported in idleness, together with their women and attendants, who will be a multitude many times as great. In framing an ideal we may assume what we wish, but should avoid impossibilities.[38]

It is said that the legislator ought to have his eye directed to two points—the people and the country.[39] But neighbouring countries also must not be forgotten by him,[40] firstly because the state for which he legislates is to have a political and not an isolated life.[41] For a state must have such a military force as will be serviceable against her neighbours, and not merely useful at home. Even if the life of action is not admitted to be the best, either for individuals or states,[42] still a city should be formidable to enemies, whether invading or retreating.

There is another point: Should not the amount of property be defined in some way which differs from this by being clearer? For Socrates says that a man should have so much property as will enable him to live temperately,[43] which is only a way of saying 'to live well'; this is too general a conception. Further, a man may live temperately and yet miserably. A better definition would be that a man must have so much property as will enable him to live not only temperately but liberally[44]; if the two are parted, liberality will combine with luxury; temperance will be associated with toil. For liberality and temperance are the only eligible qualities which have to do with the use of property. A

[35] *Laws*, vi. 780 E.
[36] *Laws*, v. 737 E.
[37] *Rep.* iv. 423 A.
[38] Cp. Bk. 7, III.
[39] Perhaps *Laws*, iv. 704–709, and v. 747 D.
[40] Cp. Bk. 2, VII.
[41] Cp. Bk. 7, VI.
[42] Cp. Bk. 7, II and III.
[43] *Laws*, v. 737 D.
[44] Cp. Bk. 7, V.

man cannot use property with mildness or courage, but temperately and liberally he may; and therefore the practice of these virtues is inseparable from property. There is an inconsistency, too, in equalizing the property and not regulating the number of the citizens[45]; the population is to remain unlimited, and he thinks that it will be sufficiently equalized by a certain number of mar riages being unfruitful, however many are born to others, because he finds this to be the case in existing states. But greater care will be required than now; for among ourselves, whatever may be the number of citizens, the property is always distributed among them, and therefore no one is in want; but, if the property were incapable of division as in the Laws, the supernumeraries, whether few or many, would get nothing. One would have thought that it was even more necessary to limit population than property; and that the limit should be fixed by calculating the chances of mortality in the children, and of sterility in married persons. The neglect of this subject, which in existing states is so common, is a never-failing cause of poverty among the citizens; and poverty is the parent of revolution and crime. Pheidon the Corinthian, who was one of the most ancient legislators, thought that the families and the number of citizens ought to remain the same, although originally all the lots may have been of different sizes: but in the *Laws* the opposite principle is maintained. What in our opinion is the right arrangement will have to be explained hereafter.[46]

There is another omission in the *Laws:* Socrates does not tell us how the rulers differ from their subjects; he only says that they should be related as the warp and the woof, which are made out of different wools.[47] He allows that a man's whole property may be increased fivefold,[48] but why should not his land also increase to a certain extent? Again, will the good management of a household be promoted by his arrangement of homesteads? For he assigns to each individual two homesteads in separate places,[49] and it is difficult to live in two houses.

The whole system of government tends to be neither democ-

[45] But see *Laws*, v. 740 B–741 A.

[46] Cp. Bk. 7, V, X, XVI; but the promise is hardly fulfilled.

[47] *Laws*, v. 734 E, 735 A.

[48] *Laws*, v. 744 E.

[49] *Laws*, v. 745 C, but Cp. infra, Bk. 7, X.

racy nor oligarchy, but something in a mean between them, which is usually called a polity, and is composed of the heavy-armed soldiers. Now, if he intended to frame a constitution which would suit the greatest number of states, he was very likely right, but not if he meant to say that this constitutional form came nearest to his first or ideal state; for many would prefer the Lacedaemonian, or, possibly, some other more aristocratic government. Some, indeed, say that the best constitution is a combination of all existing forms, and they praise the Lacedaemonian[50] because it is made up of oligarchy, monarchy, and democracy, the king forming the monarchy, and the council of elders the oligarchy, while the democratic element is represented by the Ephors; for the Ephors are selected from the people. Others, however, declare the Ephoralty to be a tyranny, and find the element of democracy in the common meals and in the habits of daily life. In the *Laws*[51] it is maintained that the best constitution is made up of democracy and tyranny, which are either not constitutions at all, or are the worst of all. But they are nearer the truth who combine many forms; for the constitution is better which is made up of more numerous elements. The constitution proposed in the *Laws* has no element of monarchy at all; it is nothing but oligarchy and democracy, leaning rather to oligarchy. This is seen in the mode of appointing magistrates[52]; for although the appointment of them by lot from among those who have been already selected combines both elements, the way in which the rich are compelled by law to attend the assembly[53] and vote for magistrates or discharge other political duties, while the rest may do as they like, and the endeavour[54] to have the greater number of the magistrates appointed out of the richer classes and the highest officers selected from those who have the greatest incomes, both these are oligarchical features. The oligarchical principle prevails also in the choice of the council,[55] for all are compelled to choose, but the compulsion extends only to the choice out of the first class, and of an equal number out of the second class and out of the third class, but not in this latter case

[50] Cp. Bk. 4, VIII, IX.
[51] iii. 693 D, 701 E, iv. 710, vi. 756 E.
[52] *Laws*, vi. 756, 763 E, 765.
[53] *Laws*, vi. 764 A; and *Pol.* Bk. 4, VIII, XIV.
[54] *Laws*, vi. 763 D E.
[55] *Laws*, vi. 756 B–E.

to all the voters but to those of the first three classes; and the selection of candidates out of the fourth class is only compulsory on the first and second. Then, from the persons so chosen, he says that there ought to be an equal number of each class selected. Thus a preponderance will be given to the better sort of people, who have the larger incomes, because many of the lower classes, not being compelled, will not vote. These considerations, and others which will be adduced[56] when the time comes for examining similar polities, tend to show that states like Plato's should not be composed of democracy and monarchy. There is also a danger in electing the magistrates out of a body who are themselves elected[57]; for, if but a small number choose to combine, the elections will always go as they desire. Such is the constitution which is described in the *Laws.*

VII Other constitutions have been proposed; some by private persons, others by philosophers and statesmen, which all come nearer to established or existing ones than either of Plato's. No one else has introduced such novelties as the community of women and children, or public tables for women: other legislators begin with what is necessary. In the opinion of some, the regulation of property is the chief point of all, that being the question upon which all revolutions turn. This danger was recognized by Phaleas of Chalcedon, who was the first to affirm that the citizens of a state ought to have equal possessions. He thought that in a new colony the equalization might be accomplished without difficulty, not so easily when a state was already established; and that then the shortest way of compassing the desired end would be for the rich to give and not to receive marriage portions, and for the poor not to give but to receive them.

Plato in the *Laws*[58] was of opinion that, to a certain extent, accumulation should be allowed, forbidding, as I have already observed,[59] any citizen to possess more than five times the minimum qualification. But those who make such laws should remember what they are apt to forget[60]—that the legislator who

[56] Bk. 4, XI, XII.
[57] *Laws,* vi. 753 D.
[58] v. 744 E.
[59] Bk. 2, VI.
[60] Cp. Bk. 2, VI.

fixes the amount of property should also fix the number of children; for, if the children are too many for the property, the law must be broken. And, besides the violation of the law, it is a bad thing that many from being rich should become poor; for men of ruined fortunes are sure to stir up revolutions. That the equalization of property exercises an influence on political society was clearly understood even by some of the old legislators. Laws were made by Solon and others prohibiting an individual from possessing as much land as he pleased; and there are other laws in states which forbid the sale of property: among the Locrians, for example, there is a law that a man is not to sell his property unless he can prove unmistakably that some misfortune has befallen him. Again, there have been laws which enjoin the preservation of the original lots. Such a law existed in the island of Leucas, and the abrogation of it made the constitution too democratic, for the rulers no longer had the prescribed qualification. Again, where there is equality of property, the amount may be either too large or too small, and the possessor may be living either in luxury or penury. Clearly, then, the legislator ought not only to aim at the equalization of properties, but at moderation in their amount. Further, if he prescribe this moderate amount equally to all, he will be no nearer the mark; for it is not the possessions but the desires of mankind which require to be equalized,[61] and this is impossible, unless a sufficient education is provided by the laws. But Phaleas will probably reply that this is precisely what he means; and that, in his opinion, there ought to be in states, not only equal property, but equal education. Still he should tell precisely what he means; and that, in his opinion, there ought to be in having one and the same for all, if it is of a sort that predisposes men to avarice, or ambition, or both. Moreover, civil troubles arise, not only out of the inequality of property, but out of the inequality of honour, though in opposite ways. For the common people quarrel about the inequality of property, the higher class about the equality of honour; as the poet says—

'The bad and good alike in honour share.'[62]

There are crimes of which the motive is want; and for these Phaleas expects to find a cure in the equalization of property,

[61] Cp. Bk. 2, V.

[62] *Il.* ix. 319.

which will take away from a man the temptation to be a highwayman, because he is hungry or cold. But want is not the sole incentive to crime; men also wish to enjoy themselves and not to be in a state of desire—they wish to cure some desire, going beyond the necessities of life, which preys upon them; nay, this is not the only reason—they may desire superfluities in order to enjoy pleasures unaccompanied with pain, and therefore they commit crimes.

Now what is the cure of these three disorders? Of the first, moderate possessions and occupation; of the second, habits of temperance; as to the third, if any desire pleasures which depend on themselves, they will find the satisfaction of their desires nowhere but in philosophy; for all other pleasures we are dependent on others. The fact is that the greatest crimes are caused by excess and not by necessity. Men do not become tyrants in order that they may not suffer cold; and hence great is the honour bestowed, not on him who kills a thief, but on him who kills a tyrant. Thus we see that the institutions of Phaleas avail only against petty crimes.

There is another objection to them. They are chiefly designed to promote the internal welfare of the state. But the legislator should consider also its relation to neighbouring nations, and to all who are outside of it.[63] The government must be organized with a view to military strength; and of this he has said not a word. And so with respect to property: there should not only be enough to supply the internal wants of the state, but also to meet dangers coming from without. The property of the state should not be so large that more powerful neighbours may be tempted by it, while the owners are unable to repel the invaders; nor yet so small that the state is unable to maintain a war even against states of equal power, and of the same character. Phaleas has not laid down any rule; but we should bear in mind that abundance of wealth is an advantage. The best limit will probably be, that a more powerful neighbour must have no inducement to go to war with you by reason of the excess of your wealth, but only such as he would have had if you had possessed less. There is a story that Eubulus, when Autophradates was going to besiege Atarneus, told him to consider how long the operation would

[63] Cp. Bk. 2, VI.

take, and then reckon up the cost which would be incurred in the time. 'For', said he, 'I am willing for a smaller sum than that to leave Atarneus at once'. These words of Eubulus made an impression on Autophradates, and he desisted from the siege.

The equalization of property is one of the things that tend to prevent the citizens from quarrelling. Not that the gain in this direction is very great. For the nobles will be dissatisfied because they think themselves worthy of more than an equal share of honours; and this is often found to be a cause of sedition and revolution.[64] And the avarice of mankind is insatiable; at one time two obols was pay enough; but now, when this sum has become customary, men always want more and more without end; for it is of the nature of desire not to be satisfied, and most men live only for the gratification of it. The beginning of reform is not so much to equalize property as to train the nobler sort of natures not to desire more, and to prevent the lower from getting more; that is to say, they must be kept down, but not ill-treated. Besides, the equalization proposed by Phaleas is imperfect; for he only equalizes land, whereas a man may be rich also in slaves, and cattle, and money, and in the abundance of what are called his movables. Now either all these things must be equalized, or some limit must be imposed on them, or they must all be let alone. It would appear that Phaleas is legislating for a small city only, if, as he supposes, all the artisans are to be public slaves and not to form a supplementary part of the body of citizens. But if there is a law that artisans are to be public slaves, it should only apply to those engaged on public works, as at Epidamnus, or at Athens on the plan which Diophantus once introduced.

From these observations any one may judge how far Phaleas was wrong or right in his ideas.

VIII Hippodamus, the son of Euryphon, a native of Miletus, the same who invented the art of planning cities, and who also laid out the Piraeus—a strange man, whose fondness for distinction led him into a general eccentricity of life, which made some think him affected (for he would wear flowing hair and expensive ornaments; but these were worn on a cheap but warm garment

[64] Cp. l. 1.

both in winter and summer); he, besides aspiring to be an adept in the knowledge of nature, was the first person not a statesman who made inquiries about the best form of government.

The city of Hippodamus was composed of 10,000 citizens divided into three parts—one of artisans, one of husbandmen, and a third of armed defenders of the state. He also divided the land into three parts, one sacred, one public, the third private:—the first was set apart to maintain the customary worship of the gods, the second was to support the warriors, the third was the property of the husbandmen. He also divided laws into three classes, and no more, for he maintained that there are three subjects of lawsuits—insult, injury, and homicide. He likewise instituted a single final court of appeal, to which all causes seeming to have been improperly decided might be referred; this court he formed of elders chosen for the purpose. He was further of opinion that the decisions of the courts ought not to be given by the use of a voting pebble, but that every one should have a tablet on which he might not only write a simple condemnation, or leave the tablet blank for a simple acquittal; but, if he partly acquitted and partly condemned, he was to distinguish accordingly. To the existing law he objected that it obliged the judges to be guilty of perjury, whichever way they voted. He also enacted that those who discovered anything for the good of the state should be honoured; and he provided that the children of citizens who died in battle should be maintained at the public expense, as if such an enactment had never been heard of before, yet it actually exists at Athens and in other places. As to the magistrates, he would have them all elected by the people, that is, by the three classes already mentioned, and those who were elected were to watch over the interests of the public, of strangers, and of orphans. These are the most striking points in the constitution of Hippodamus. There is not much else.

The first of these proposals to which objection may be taken is the threefold division of the citizens. The artisans, and the husbandmen, and the warriors, all have a share in the government. But the husbandmen have no arms, and the artisans neither arms nor land, and therefore they become all but slaves of the warrior class. That they should share in all the offices is an impossibility; for generals and guardians of the citizens, and nearly all the principal magistrates, must be taken from the class of those who carry arms. Yet, if the two other classes have no share in the government, how can they be loyal citizens? It may be said that those who have arms must necessarily be masters of both the other classes, but this is not so easily accomplished unless they are numerous; and if they are, why should the other classes share in the government at all, or have power to appoint magistrates? Further, what use are farmers to the city? Artisans there must be, for these are wanted in every city, and they can live by their craft, as elsewhere; and the husbandmen too, if they really provided the warriors with food, might fairly have a share in the government. But in the republic of Hippodamus they are supposed to have land of their own, which they cultivate for their private benefit. Again, as to this common land out of which the soldiers are maintained, if they are themselves to be the cultivators of it, the warrior class will be identical with the husbandmen, although the legislator intended to make a distinction between them. If, again, there are to be other cultivators distinct both from the husbandmen, who have land of their own, and from the warriors, they will make a fourth class, which has no place in the state and no share in anything. Or, if the same persons are to cultivate their own lands, and those of the public as well, they will have a difficulty in supplying the quantity of produce which will maintain two households: and why, in this case, should there be any division, for they might find food themselves and give to the warriors from the same land and the same lots? There is surely a great confusion in all this.

Neither is the law to be commended which says that the judges, when a simple issue is laid before them, should distinguish in their judgement; for the judge is thus converted into an arbitrator. Now, in an arbitration, although the arbitrators are many, they confer with one another about the decision, and therefore they can distinguish; but in courts of law this is impossible, and, indeed, most legislators take pains to prevent the judges from holding any communication with one another. Again, will there not be confusion if the judge thinks that damages should be given, but not so much as the suitor demands? He asks, say, for twenty minae, and the judge allows him ten minae (or in general the suitor asks for more and the judge allows less), while another judge allows five, another four minae. In this way they will go on splitting up the damages, and some will grant the whole and others nothing: how is the final reckoning to be taken? Again, no one contends that he who votes for a simple acquittal or condemnation perjures himself, if the indictment has been laid in an unqualified form; and this is just, for the judge who acquits does not decide that the defendant owes nothing, but that he does not owe the twenty minae. He only is guilty of perjury who thinks that the defendant ought not to pay twenty minae, and yet condemns him.

To honour those who discover anything which is useful to the state is a proposal which has a specious sound, but cannot safely be enacted by law, for it may encourage informers, and perhaps even lead to political commotions. This question involves another. It has been doubted whether it is or is not expedient to make any changes in the laws of a country, even if another law be better. Now, if all changes are inexpedient, we can hardly assent to the proposal of Hippodamus; for, under pretence of doing a public service, a man may introduce measures which are really destructive to the laws or to the constitution. But, since we have touched upon this subject, perhaps we had better go a little into detail, for, as I was saying, there is a difference of opinion, and it may sometimes seem desirable to make changes. Such changes in the other arts and sciences have certainly been beneficial; medicine, for example, and gymnastic, and every other art and craft have departed from traditional usage. And, if politics be an art, change must be necessary in this as in any other art. That improvement has occurred is shown by the fact that old customs are exceedingly simple and barbarous. For the ancient Hellenes went about armed and bought their brides of each other. The remains of ancient laws which have come down to us are quite absurd; for example, at Cumae there is a law about murder, to the effect that if the accuser produce a certain number of witnesses from among his own kinsmen, the accused shall be held guilty. Again, men in general desire the good, and not merely what their fathers had. But the primeval inhabitants, whether they were born of the earth or were the survivors of some destruction, may be supposed to have been no better than ordinary or even foolish people among ourselves (such is certainly the tradition[65] concerning the earth-born men); and it would be ridiculous to rest contented with

[65] Cp. Plato, *Laws*, iii. 677 B; *Polit.* 274 C; *Tim.* 22 D.

their notions. Even when laws have been written down, they ought not always to remain unaltered. As in other sciences, so in politics, it is impossible that all things should be precisely set down in writing; for enactments must be universal, but actions are concerned with particulars.[66] Hence we infer that sometimes and in certain cases laws may be changed; but when we look at the matter from another point of view, great caution would seem to be required. For the habit of lightly changing the laws is an evil, and, when the advantage is small, some errors both of lawgivers and rulers had better be left; the citizen will not gain so much by making the change as he will lose by the habit of disobedience. The analogy of the arts[67] is false; a change in a law is a very different thing from a change in an art. For the law has no power to command obedience except that of habit, which can only be given by time, so that a readiness to change from old to new laws enfeebles the power of the law. Even if we admit that the laws are to be changed, are they all to be changed, and in every state? And are they to be changed by anybody who likes, or only by certain persons? These are very important questions; and therefore we had better reserve the discussion of them to a more suitable occasion.[68]

IX In the governments of Lacedaemon and Crete, and indeed in all governments, two points have to be considered: first, whether any particular law is good or bad, when compared with the perfect state; secondly, whether it is or is not consistent with the idea and character which the lawgiver has set before his citizens. That in a well-ordered state the citizens should have leisure and not have to provide for their daily wants is generally acknowledged, but there is a difficulty in seeing how this leisure is to be attained. The Thessalian Penestae have often risen against their masters, and the Helots in like manner against the Lacedaemonians, for whose misfortunes they are always lying in wait. Nothing, however, of this kind has as yet happened to the Cretans; the reason probably is that the neighbouring cities, even when at war with one another, never form an alliance

[66] Cp. Plato, *Polit.* 295 A.
[67] Bk. 2, VIII.
[68] These questions are not actually discussed in the *Politics*.

with rebellious serfs, rebellions not being for their interest, since they themselves have a dependent population.[69] Whereas all the neighbours of the Lacedaemonians, whether Argives, Messenians, or Arcadians, were their enemies. In Thessaly, again, the original revolt of the slaves occurred because the Thessalians were still at war with the neighbouring Achaeans, Perrhaebians and Magnesians. Besides, if there were no other difficulty, the treatment or management of slaves is a troublesome affair; for, if not kept in hand, they are insolent, and think that they are as good as their masters, and, if harshly treated, they hate and conspire against them. Now it is clear that when these are the results the citizens of a state have not found out the secret of managing their subject population.

Again, the license of the Lacedaemonian women defeats the intention of the Spartan constitution, and is adverse to the happiness of the state. For, a husband and a wife being each a part of every family, the state may be considered as about equally divided into men and women; and, therefore, in those states in which the condition of the women is bad, half the city[70] may be regarded as having no laws. And this is what has actually happened at Sparta; the legislator wanted to make the whole state hardy and temperate, and he has carried out his intention in the case of the men, but he has neglected the women, who live in every sort of intemperance and luxury. The consequence is that in such a state wealth is too highly valued, especially if the citizens fall under the dominion of their wives, after the manner of most warlike races, except the Celts and a few others who openly approve of male loves. The old mythologer would seem to have been right in uniting Ares and Aphrodite, for all warlike races are prone to the love either of men or of women. This was exemplified among the Spartans in the days of their greatness; many things were managed by their women. But what difference does it make whether women rule, or the rulers are ruled by women? The result is the same. Even in regard to courage, which is of no use in daily life, and is needed only in war, the influence of the Lacedaemonian women has been most mischievous. The evil showed itself in the Theban invasion, when, unlike the women in other cities, they were utterly useless and caused more confusion than the enemy. This license of the Lacedaemonian

[69] Cp. Bk. 2, IX.

[70] Cp. Bk. 1, XIII.

women existed from the earliest times, and was only what might be expected. For, during the wars of the Lacedaemonians, first against the Argives, and afterwards against the Arcadians and Messenians, the men were long away from home, and, on the return of peace, they gave themselves into the legislator's hand, already prepared by the discipline of a soldier's life (in which there are many elements of virtue), to receive his enactments. But, when Lycurgus, as tradition says, wanted to bring the women under his laws, they resisted, and he gave up the attempt. These then are the causes of what then happened, and this defect in the constitution is clearly to be attributed to them. We are not, however, considering what is or is not to be excused, but what is right or wrong, and the disorder of the women, as I have already said,[71] not only gives an air of indecorum to the constitution considered in itself, but tends in a measure to foster avarice.

The mention of avarice naturally suggests a criticism on the inequality of property. While some of the Spartan citizens have quite small properties, others have very large ones; hence the land has passed into the hands of a few. And this is due also to faulty laws; for, although the legislator rightly holds up to shame the sale or purchase of an inheritance, he allows anybody who likes to give or bequeath it. Yet both practices lead to the same result. And nearly two-fifths of the whole country are held by women; this is owing to the number of heiresses and to the large dowries which are customary. It would surely have been better to have given no dowries at all, or, if any, but small or moderate ones. As the law now stands, a man may bestow his heiress on any one whom he pleases, and, if he die intestate, the privilege of giving her away descends to his heir.[72] Hence, although the country is able to maintain 1500 cavalry and 30,000 hoplites, the whole number of Spartan citizens[73] fell below 1000. The result proves the faulty nature of their laws respecting property; for the city sank under a single defeat; the want of men was their ruin. There is a tradition that, in the days of their ancient kings, they were in the habit of giving the rights of citizenship to strangers, and therefore, in spite of their long wars, no lack of population was experienced by them; indeed, at one time Sparta is said to have numbered not less than 10,000 citizens. Whether this state-

[71] Bk. 2, IX.
[72] i. e. to the person who 'inherits' the heiress.
[73] At the time of the Theban invasion.

ment is true or not, it would certainly have been better to have maintained their numbers by the equalization of property. Again, the law which relates to the procreation of children is adverse to the correction of this inequality. For the legislator, wanting to have as many Spartans as he could, encouraged the citizens to have large families; and there is a law at Sparta that the father of three sons shall be exempt from military service, and he who has four from all the burdens of the state. Yet it is obvious that, if there were many children, the land being distributed as it is, many of them must necessarily fall into poverty.

The Lacedaemonian constitution is defective in another point; I mean the Ephoralty. This magistracy has authority in the highest matters, but the Ephors are chosen from the whole people, and so the office is apt to fall into the hands of very poor men, who, being badly off, are open to bribes. There have been many examples at Sparta of this evil in former times; and quite recently, in the matter of the Andrians, certain of the Ephors who were bribed did their best to ruin the state. And so great and tyrannical is their power, that even the kings have been compelled to court them, so that, in this way as well, together with the royal office, the whole constitution has deteriorated, and from being an aristocracy has turned into a democracy. The Ephoralty certainly does keep the state together; for the people are contented when they have a share in the highest office, and the result, whether due to the legislator or to chance, has been advantageous. For if a constitution is to be permanent, all the parts of the state must wish that it should exist and the same arrangements be maintained. This is the case at Sparta, where the kings desire its permanence because they have due honour in their own persons; the nobles because they are represented in the council of elders (for the office of elder is a reward of virtue); and the people, because all are eligible to the Ephoralty. The election of Ephors out of the whole people is perfectly right, but ought not to be carried on in the present fashion, which is too childish. Again, they have the decision of great causes, although they are quite ordinary men, and therefore they should not determine them merely on their own judgement, but according to written rules, and to the laws. Their way of life, too, is not in accordance with the spirit of the constitution—they have a deal too much license; whereas, in the case of the other citizens, the excess of strictness is so intolerable that they run away from the law into the secret indulgence of sensual pleasures.

Again, the council of elders is not free from defects. It may be said that the elders are good men and well trained in manly virtue; and that, therefore, there is an advantage to the state in having them. But that judges of important causes should hold office for life is a disputable thing, for the mind grows old as well as the body. And when men have been educated in such a manner that even the legislator himself cannot trust them, there is real danger. Many of the elders are well known to have taken bribes and to have been guilty of partiality in public affairs. And therefore they ought not to be irresponsible; yet at Sparta they are so. But (it may be replied), 'All magistracies are accountable to the Ephors.' Yes, but this prerogative is too great for them, and we maintain that the control should be exercised in some other manner. Further, the mode in which the Spartans elect their elders is childish; and it is improper that the person to be elected should canvass for the office; the worthiest should be appointed, whether he chooses or not. And here the legislator clearly indicates the same intention which appears in other parts of his constitution; he would have his citizens ambitious, and he has reckoned upon this quality in the election of the elders; for no one would ask to be elected if he were not. Yet ambition and avarice, almost more than any other passions, are the motives of crime.

Whether kings are or are not an advantage to states, I will consider at another time[74]; they should at any rate be chosen, not as they are now, but with regard to their personal life and conduct. The legislator himself obviously did not suppose that he could make them really good men; at least he shows a great distrust of their virtue. For this reason the Spartans used to join enemies with them in the same embassy, and the quarrels between the kings were held to be conservative of the state.

Neither did the first introducer of the common meals, called 'phiditia', regulate them well. The entertainment ought to have been provided at the public cost, as in Crete[75]; but among the Lacedaemonians every one is expected to contribute, and some of them are too poor to afford the expense; thus the intention of the legislator is frustrated. The common meals were meant to be

[74] Bk. 3, XIV–XVII.

[75] Cp. Bk. 2, X.

a popular institution, but the existing manner of regulating them is the reverse of popular. For the very poor can scarcely take part in them; and, according to ancient custom, those who cannot contribute are not allowed to retain their rights of citizenship.

The law about the Spartan admirals has often been censured, and with justice; it is a source of dissension, for the kings are perpetual generals, and this office of admiral is but the setting up of another king.

The charge which Plato brings, in the *Laws*,[76] against the intention of the legislator, is likewise justified; the whole constitution has regard to one part of virtue only—the virtue of the soldier, which gives victory in war. So long as they were at war, therefore, their power was preserved, but when they had attained empire they fell,[77] for of the arts of peace they knew nothing, and had never engaged in any employment higher than war. There is another error, equally great, into which they have fallen. Although they truly think that the goods for which men contend are to be acquired by virtue rather than by vice, they err in supposing that these goods are to be preferred to the virtue which gains them.

Once more: the revenues of the state are ill-managed; there is no money in the treasury, although they are obliged to carry on great wars, and they are unwilling to pay taxes. The greater part of the land being in the hands of the Spartans, they do not look closely into one another's contributions. The result which the legislator has produced is the reverse of beneficial; for he has made his city poor, and his citizens greedy.

Enough respecting the Spartan constitution, of which these are the principal defects.

X The Cretan constitution nearly resembles the Spartan, and in some few points is quite as good; but for the most part less perfect in form. The older constitutions are generally less elaborate than the later, and the Lacedaemonian is said to be, and probably is, in a very great measure, a copy of the Cretan. According to tradition, Lycurgus, when he ceased to be the guardian of King Charillus, went abroad and spent most of his time in Crete. For the two countries are nearly connected; the Lyctians are a

[76] *Laws*, i. 625 E, 630.

[77] Cp. Bk. 7, XIV.

colony of the Lacedaemonians, and the colonists, when they came to Crete, adopted the constitution which they found existing among the inhabitants. Even to this day the Perioeci, or subject population of Crete, are governed by the original laws which Minos is supposed to have enacted. The island seems to be intended by nature for dominion in Hellas, and to be well situated; it extends right across the sea, around which nearly all the Hellenes are settled; and while one end is not far from the Peloponnese, the other almost reaches to the region of Asia about Triopium and Rhodes. Hence Minos acquired the empire of the sea, subduing some of the islands and colonizing others; at last he invaded Sicily, where he died near Camicus.

The Cretan institutions resemble the Lacedaemonian. The Helots are the husbandmen of the one, the Perioeci of the other, and both Cretans and Lacedaemonians have common meals, which were anciently called by the Lacedaemonians not 'phiditia' but 'andria'; and the Cretans have the same word, the use of which proves that the common meals originally came from Crete. Further, the two constitutions are similar; for the office of the Ephors is the same as that of the Cretan Cosmi, the only difference being that whereas the Ephors are five, the Cosmi are ten in number. The elders, too, answer to the elders in Crete, who are termed by the Cretans the council. And the kingly office once existed in Crete, but was abolished, and the Cosmi have now the duty of leading them in war. All classes share in the ecclesia, but it can only ratify the decrees of the elders and the Cosmi.

The common meals of Crete are certainly better managed than the Lacedaemonian; for in Lacedaemon every one pays so much per head, or, if he fails, the law, as I have already explained,[78] forbids him to exercise the rights of citizenship. But in Crete they are of a more popular character. There, of all the fruits of the earth and cattle raised on the public lands, and of the tribute which is paid by the Perioeci, one portion is assigned to the gods and to the service of the state, and another to the common meals, so that men, women, and children are all supported out of a common stock.[79] The legislator has many ingenious ways of securing moderation in eating, which he conceives to be a gain; he likewise encourages the separation of men from women, lest they should have too many children, and the companionship of men

[78] Bk. 2, IX.

[79] Bk. 7, X.

with one another—whether this is a good or bad thing I shall have an opportunity of considering at another time.[80] But that the Cretan common meals are better ordered than the Lacedaemonian there can be no doubt.

On the other hand, the Cosmi are even a worse institution than the Ephors, of which they have all the evils without the good. Like the Ephors, they are any chance persons, but in Crete this is not counterbalanced by a corresponding political advantage. At Sparta every one is eligible, and the body of the people, having a share in the highest office, want the constitution to be permanent.[81] But in Crete the Cosmi are elected out of certain families, and not out of the whole people, and the elders out of those who have been Cosmi.

The same criticism may be made about the Cretan, which has been already made about the Lacedaemonian elders.[82] Their irresponsibility and life tenure is too great a privilege, and their arbitrary power of acting upon their own judgement, and dispensing with written law, is dangerous. It is no proof of the goodness of the institution that the people are not discontented at being excluded from it. For there is no profit to be made out of the office as out of the Ephoralty, since, unlike the Ephors, the Cosmi, being in an island, are removed from temptation.

The remedy by which they correct the evil of this institution is an extraordinary one, suited rather to a close oligarchy than to a constitutional state. For the Cosmi are often expelled by a conspiracy of their own colleagues, or of private individuals; and they are allowed also to resign before their term of office has expired. Surely all matters of this kind are better regulated by law than by the will of man, which is a very unsafe rule. Worst of all is the suspension of the office of Cosmi, a device to which the nobles often have recourse when they will not submit to justice. This shows that the Cretan government, although possessing some of the characteristics of a constitutional state, is really a close oligarchy.

The nobles have a habit, too, of setting up a chief; they get together a party among the common people and their own friends and then quarrel and fight with one another. What is this but the temporary destruction of the state and dissolution of society? A

[80] The question is nowhere discussed by Aristotle.

[81] Cp. *supra*, Bk. 2, IX.

[82] Bk. 2, IX.

city is in a dangerous condition when those who are willing are also able to attack her. But, as I have already said,[83] the island of Crete is saved by her situation; distance has the same effect as the Lacedaemonian prohibition of strangers; and the Cretans have no foreign dominions. This is the reason why the Perioeci are contented in Crete, whereas the Helots are perpetually revolting. But when lately foreign invaders found their way into the island, the weakness of the Cretan constitution was revealed. Enough of the government of Crete.

XI The Carthaginians are also considered to have an excellent form of government, which differs from that of any other state in several respects, though it is in some very like the Lacedaemonian. Indeed, all three states—the Lacedaemonian, the Cretan, and the Carthaginian—nearly resemble one another, and are very different from any others. Many of the Carthaginian institutions are excellent. The superiority of their constitution is proved by the fact that the common people remain loyal to the constitution; the Carthaginians have never had any rebellion worth speaking of, and have never been under the rule of a tyrant.

Among the points in which the Carthaginian constitution resembles the Lacedaemonian are the following:—The common tables of the clubs answer to the Spartan phiditia, and their magistracy of the 104 to the Ephors; but, whereas the Ephors are any chance persons, the magistrates of the Carthaginians are elected according to merit—this is an improvement. They have also their kings and their gerusia, or council of elders, who correspond to the kings and elders of Sparta. Their kings, unlike the Spartan, are not always of the same family, nor that an ordinary one, but if there is some distinguished family they are selected out of it and not appointed by seniority—this is far better. Such officers have great power, and therefore, if they are persons of little worth, do a great deal of harm, and they have already done harm at Lacedaemon.

Most of the defects or deviations from the perfect state, for which the Carthaginian constitution would be censured, apply equally to all the forms of government which we have mentioned. But of the deflections from aristocracy and constitutional govern-

[83] Bk. 2, IX.

ment, some incline more to democracy and some to oligarchy. The kings and elders, if unanimous, may determine whether they will or will not bring a matter before the people, but when they are not unanimous, the people decide on such matters as well. And whatever the kings and elders bring before the people is not only heard but also determined by them, and any one who likes may oppose it; now this is not permitted in Sparta and Crete. That the magistracies of five who have under them many important matters should be co-opted, that they should choose the supreme council of 100, and should hold office longer than other magistrates (for they are virtually rulers both before and after they hold office)—these are oligarchical features; their being without salary and not elected by lot, and any similar points, such as the practice of having all suits tried by the magistrates,[84] and not some by one class of judges or jurors and some by another, as at Lacedaemon, are characteristic of aristocracy. The Carthaginian constitution deviates from aristocracy and inclines to oligarchy, chiefly on a point where popular opinion is on their side. For men in general think that magistrates should be chosen not only for their merit, but for their wealth: a man, they say, who is poor cannot rule well—he has not the leisure. If, then, election of magistrates for their wealth be characteristic of oligarchy, and election for merit of aristocracy, there will be a third form under which the constitution of Carthage is comprehended; for the Carthaginians choose their magistrates, and particularly the highest of them—their kings and generals—with an eye both to merit and to wealth.

But we must acknowledge that, in thus deviating from aristocracy, the legislator has committed an error. Nothing is more absolutely necessary than to provide that the highest class, not only when in office, but when out of office, should have leisure and not disgrace themselves in any way; and to this his attention should be first directed. Even if you must have regard to wealth, in order to secure leisure, yet it is surely a bad thing that the greatest offices, such as those of kings and generals, should be bought. The law which allows this abuse makes wealth of more account than virtue, and the whole state becomes avaricious. For, whenever the chiefs of the state deem anything honourable, the other citizens are sure to follow their example; and, where virtue

[84] Cp. Bk. 3, II.

has not the first place, their aristocracy cannot be firmly established. Those who have been at the expense of purchasing their places will be in the habit of repaying themselves; and it is absurd to suppose that a poor and honest man will be wanting to make gains, and that a lower stamp of man who has incurred a great expense will not. Wherefore they should rule who are able to rule best. And even if the legislator does not care to protect the good from poverty, he should at any rate secure leisure for them when in office.[85]

It would seem also to be a bad principle that the same person should hold many offices, which is a favourite practice among the Carthaginians, for one business is better done by one man.[86] The legislator should see to this and should not appoint the same person to be a flute-player and a shoemaker. Hence, where the state is large, it is more in accordance both with constitutional and with democratic principles that the offices of state should be distributed among many persons. For, as I said,[87] this arrangement is fairer to all, and any action familiarized by repetition is better and sooner performed. We have a proof in military and naval matters; the duties of command and of obedience in both these services extend to all.

The government of the Carthaginians is oligarchical, but they successfully escape the evils of oligarchy by enriching one portion of the people after another by sending them to their colonies. This is their panacea and the means by which they give stability to the state. Accident favours them, but the legislator should be able to provide against revolution without trusting to accidents. As things are, if any misfortune occurred, and the bulk of the subjects revolted, there would be no way of restoring peace by legal methods.

Such is the character of the Lacedaemonian, Cretan, and Carthaginian constitutions, which are justly celebrated.

XII Of those who have treated of governments, some have never taken any part at all in public affairs, but have passed their lives in a private station; about most of them, what was worth telling has been already told.[88] Others have been lawgivers, either in

[85] Cp. Bk. 2, VIII.
[86] Cp. Plato, *Rep.* ii. 374 A.
[87] Bk. 2, II.
[88] I–VIII.

their own or in foreign cities, whose affairs they have administered; and of these some have only made laws, others have framed constitutions; for example, Lycurgus and Solon did both. Of the Lacedaemonian constitution I have already spoken.[89] As to Solon, he is thought by some to have been a good legislator, who put an end to the exclusiveness of the oligarchy, emancipated the people, established the ancient Athenian democracy, and harmonized the different elements of the state. According to their view, the council of Areopagus was an oligarchical element, the elected magistracy, aristocratical, and the courts of law, democratical. The truth seems to be that the council and the elected magistracy existed before the time of Solon, and were retained by him, but that he formed the courts of law out of all the citizens, thus creating the democracy, which is the very reason why he is sometimes blamed. For in giving the supreme power to the law courts, which are elected by lot, he is thought to have destroyed the non-democratic element. When the law courts grew powerful, to please the people who were now playing the tyrant the old constitution was changed into the existing democracy. Ephialtes and Pericles curtailed the power of the Areopagus; Pericles also instituted the payment of the juries, and thus every demagogue in turn increased the power of the democracy until it became what we now see. All this is true; it seems, however, to be the result of circumstances, and not to have been intended by Solon. For the people, having been instrumental in gaining the empire of the sea in the Persian War,[90] began to get a notion of itself, and followed worthless demagogues, whom the better class opposed. Solon, himself, appears to have given the Athenians only that power of electing to offices and calling to account the magistrates which was absolutely necessary[91]; for without it they would have been in a state of slavery and enmity to the government. All the magistrates he appointed from the notables and the men of wealth, that is to say, from the pentacosio-medimni, or from the class called zeugitae, or from a third class of so-called knights or cavalry. The fourth class were labourers who had no share in any magistracy.

Mere legislators were Zaleucus, who gave laws to the Epizephyrian Locrians, and Charondas, who legislated for his own

[89] IX.
[90] Cp. Bk. 5, IV; 8, VI.
[91] Cp. Bk. 3, XI.

city of Catana, and for the other Chalcidian cities in Italy and Sicily. Some people attempt to make out that Onomacritus was the first person who had any special skill in legislation, and that he, although a Locrian by birth, was trained in Crete, where he lived in the exercise of his prophetic art; that Thales was his companion, and that Lycurgus and Zaleucus were disciples of Thales, as Charondas was of Zaleucus. But their account is quite inconsistent with chronology.

There was also Philolaus, the Corinthian, who gave laws to the Thebans. This Philolaus was one of the family of the Bacchiadae, and a lover of Diocles, the Olympic victor, who left Corinth in horror of the incestuous passion which his mother Halcyone had conceived for him, and retired to Thebes, where the two friends together ended their days. The inhabitants still point out their tombs, which are in full view of one another, but one is visible from the Corinthian territory, the other not. Tradition says the two friends arranged them thus, Diocles out of horror at his misfortunes, so that the land of Corinth might not be visible from his tomb; Philolaus that it might. This is the reason why they settled at Thebes, and so Philolaus legislated for the Thebans, and, besides some other enactments, gave them laws about the procreation of children, which they call the 'Laws of Adoption'. These laws were peculiar to him, and were intended to preserve the number of the lots.

In the legislation of Charondas there is nothing remarkable, except the suits against false witnesses. He is the first who instituted denunciation for perjury. His laws are more exact and more precisely expressed than even those of our modern legislators.

(Characteristic of Phaleas is the equalization of property; of Plato, the community of women, children, and property, the common meals of women, and the law about drinking, that the sober shall be masters of the feast[92]; also the training of soldiers to acquire by practice equal skill with both hands, so that one should be as useful as the other.[93])

Draco has left laws, but he adapted them to a constitution which already existed, and there is no peculiarity in them which is worth mentioning, except the greatness and severity of the punishments.

[92] Cp. *Laws*, i. 640 D, ii. 671 D–672 A.
[93] Cp. *Laws*, vii. 794 D.

Pittacus, too, was only a lawgiver, and not the author of a constitution; he has a law which is peculiar to him, that, if a drunken man do something wrong, he shall be more heavily punished than if he were sober[94]; he looked not to the excuse which might be offered for the drunkard, but only to expediency, for drunken more often than sober people commit acts of violence.

Androdamas of Rhegium gave laws to the Chalcidians of Thrace. Some of them relate to homicide, and to heiresses; but there is nothing remarkable in them.

And here let us conclude our inquiry into the various constitutions which either actually exist, or have been devised by theorists.

[94] Cp. *Nic. Eth.* 1113^b 31.

BOOK THIRD

I He who would inquire into the essence and attributes of various kinds of governments must first of all determine 'What is a state?' At present this is a disputed question. Some say that the state has done a certain act; others, no, not the state,[1] but the oligarchy or the tyrant. And the legislator or statesman is concerned entirely with the state; a constitution or government being an arrangement of the inhabitants of a state. But a state is composite, like any other whole made up of many parts;—these are the citizens, who compose it. It is evident, therefore, that we must begin by asking, Who is the citizen, and what is the meaning of the term? For here again there may be a difference of opinion. He who is a citizen in a democracy will often not be a citizen in an oligarchy. Leaving out of consideration those who have been made citizens, or who have obtained the name of citizen in any other accidental manner, we may say, first, that a citizen is not a citizen because he lives in a certain place, for resident aliens and slaves share in the place; nor is he a citizen who has no legal right except that of suing and being sued; for this right may be enjoyed under the provisions of a treaty. Nay, resident aliens in many places do not possess even such rights completely, for they are obliged to have a patron, so that they do but imperfectly participate in citizenship, and we call them citizens only in a qualified sense, as we might apply the term to children who are too young to be on the register, or to old men who have been relieved from state duties. Of these we do not say quite simply that they are citizens, but add in the one case that they are not of age, and in the other, that they are past the age, or something of that sort; the precise expression is immaterial, for our meaning is clear. Similar difficulties to those which I have mentioned may be raised and answered about deprived citizens and about exiles. But the citizen whom we are seeking to define is a citizen in the strictest sense, against whom no such exception can be taken, and his special characteristic is that he shares in the administration of justice, and in offices. Now of offices some are discontinuous, and the same persons are not allowed to hold them twice, or can only hold them after a fixed interval; others have no limit of time—for

[1] Cp. Bk. 3, III.

example, the office of dicast or ecclesiast.[2] It may, indeed, be argued that these are not magistrates at all, and that their functions give them no share in the government. But surely it is ridiculous to say that those who have the supreme power do not govern. Let us not dwell further upon this, which is a purely verbal question; what we want is a common term including both dicast and ecclesiast. Let us, for the sake of distinction, call it 'indefinite office', and we will assume that those who share in such office are citizens. This is the most comprehensive definition of a citizen, and best suits all those who are generally so called.

But we must not forget that things of which the underlying principles differ in kind, one of them being first, another second, another third, have, when regarded in this relation, nothing, or hardly anything, worth mentioning in common. Now we see that governments differ in kind, and that some of them are prior and that others are posterior; those which are faulty or perverted are necessarily posterior to those which are perfect. (What we mean by perversion will be hereafter explained.[3]) The citizen then of necessity differs under each form of government; and our definition is best adapted to the citizen of a democracy; but not necessarily to other states. For in some states the people are not acknowledged, nor have they any regular assembly, but only extraordinary ones; and suits are distributed by sections among the magistrates. At Lacedaemon, for instance, the Ephors determine suits about contracts, which they distribute among themselves, while the elders are judges of homicide, and other causes are decided by other magistrates. A similar principle prevails at Carthage[4]; there certain magistrates decide all causes. We may, indeed, modify our definition of the citizen so as to include these states. In them it is the holder of a definite, not of an indefinite office, who legislates and judges, and to some or all such holders of definite offices is reserved the right of deliberating or judging about some things or about all things. The conception of the citizen now begins to clear up.

He who has the power to take part in the deliberative or judicial administration of any state is said by us to be a citizen of that

[2] 'Dicast' = juryman and judge in one: 'ecclesiast' = member of the ecclesia or assembly of the citizens.

[3] Cp. Bk. 3, VII.

[4] Cp. Bk. 2, XI.

state; and, speaking generally, a state is a body of citizens sufficing for the purposes of life.

II But in practice a citizen is defined to be one of whom both the parents are citizens; others insist on going further back; say to two or three or more ancestors. This is a short and practical definition; but there are some who raise the further question: How this third or fourth ancestor came to be a citizen? Gorgias of Leontini, partly because he was in a difficulty, partly in irony, said—'Mortars are what is made by the mortar-makers, and the citizens of Larissa are those who are made by the magistrates[5]; for it is their trade to make Larissaeans.' Yet the question is really simple, for, if according to the definition just given they shared in the government, they were citizens. This is a better definition than the other. For the words, 'born of a father or mother who is a citizen', cannot possibly apply to the first inhabitants or founders of a state.

There is a greater difficulty in the case of those who have been made citizens after a revolution, as by Cleisthenes at Athens after the expulsion of the tyrants, for he enrolled in tribes many metics, both strangers and slaves. The doubt in these cases is, not who is, but whether he who is ought to be a citizen; and there will still be a furthering the state, whether a certain act is or is not an act of the state; for what ought not to be is what is false. Now, there are some who hold office, and yet ought not to hold office, whom we describe as ruling, but ruling unjustly. And the citizen was defined[6] by the fact of his holding some kind of rule or office—he who holds a judicial or legislative office fulfils our definition of a citizen. It is evident, therefore, that the citizens about whom the doubt has arisen must be called citizens.

III Whether they ought to be so or not is a question which is bound up with the previous inquiry.[7] For a parallel question is raised respecting the state, whether a certain act is or is not an

[5] An untranslatable play upon the word *demiourgos,* which means either 'a magistrate' or 'an artisan'.

[6] Bk. 3, I.

[7] Cp. Bk. 2, XII.

act of the state; for example, in the transition from an oligarchy or a tyranny to a democracy. In such cases persons refuse to fulfil their contracts or any other obligations, on the ground that the tyrant, and not the state, contracted them; they argue that some constitutions are established by force, and not for the sake of the common good. But this would apply equally to democracies, for they too may be founded on violence, and then the acts of the democracy will be neither more nor less acts of the state in question than those of an oligarchy or of a tyranny. This question runs up into another:—on what principle shall we ever say that the state is the same, or different? It would be a very superficial view which considered only the place and the inhabitants (for the soil and the population may be separated, and some of the inhabitants may live in one place and some in another). This, however, is not a very serious difficulty; we need only remark that the word 'state' is ambiguous.[8]

It is further asked: When are men, living in the same place, to be regarded as a single city—what is the limit? Certainly not the wall of the city, for you might surround all Peloponnesus with a wall. Like this, we may say, is Babylon,[9] and every city that has the compass of a nation rather than a city; Babylon, they say, had been taken for three days before some part of the inhabitants became aware of the fact. This difficulty may, however, with advantage be deferred[10] to another occasion; the statesman has to consider the size of the state, and whether it should consist of more than one nation or not.

Again, shall we say that while the race of inhabitants, as well as their place of abode, remain the same, the city is also the same, although the citizens are always dying and being born, as we call rivers and fountains the same, although the water is always flowing away and coming again? Or shall we say that the generations of men, like the rivers, are the same, but that the state changes? For, since the state is a partnership, and is a partnership of citizens in a constitution, when the form of the government changes, and becomes different, then it may be supposed that the state is

[8] i. e. *Polis* means both 'state' and 'city'.

[9] Cp. Bk. 2, VI.

[10] The size of the state is discussed in Bk. 7, IV-VI; the question whether it should consist of more than one nation is barely touched upon, in Bk. 5, III.

no longer the same, just as a tragic differs from a comic chorus, although the members of both may be identical. And in this manner we speak of every union or composition of elements as different when the form of their composition alters; for example, a scale containing the same sounds is said to be different, accordingly as the Dorian or the Phrygian mode is employed. And if this is true it is evident that the sameness of the state consists chiefly in the sameness of the constitution, and it may be called or not called by the same name, whether the inhabitants are the same or entirely different. It is quite another question, whether a state ought or ought not to fulfil engagements when the form of government changes.

IV There is a point nearly allied to the preceding: Whether the virtue of a good man and a good citizen is the same or not.[11] But, before entering on this discussion, we must certainly first obtain some general notion of the virtue of the citizen. Like the sailor, the citizen is a member of a community. Now, sailors have different functions, for one of them is a rower, another a pilot, and a third a look-out man, a fourth is described by some similar term; and while the precise definition of each individual's virtue applies exclusively to him, there is, at the same time, a common definition applicable to them all. For they have all of them a common object, which is safety in navigation. Similarly, one citizen differs from another, but the salvation of the community is the common business of them all. This community is the constitution; the virtue of the citizen must therefore be relative to the constitution of which he is a member. If, then, there are many forms of government, it is evident that there is not one single virtue of the good citizen which is perfect virtue. But we say that the good man is he who has one single virtue which is perfect virtue. Hence it is evident that the good citizen need not of necessity possess the virtue which makes a good man.

The same question may also be approached by another road, from a consideration of the best constitution. If the state cannot be entirely composed of good men, and yet each citizen is expected to do his own business well, and must therefore have virtue, still, inasmuch as all the citizens cannot be alike, the virtue

[11] Cp. *Nic. Eth.* v. 1130b 28.

of the citizen and of the good man cannot coincide. All must have the virtue of the good citizen—thus, and thus only, can the state be perfect; but they will not have the virtue of a good man, unless we assume that in the good state all the citizens must be good.

Again, the state, as composed of unlikes, may be compared to the living being: as the first elements into which a living being is resolved are soul and body, as soul is made up of rational principle and appetite, the family of husband and wife, property of master and slave, so of all these, as well as other dissimilar elements, the state is composed; and, therefore, the virtue of all the citizens cannot possibly be the same, any more than the excellence of the leader of a chorus is the same as that of the performer who stands by his side. I have said enough to show why the two kinds of virtue cannot be absolutely and always the same.

But will there then be no case in which the virtue of the good citizen and the virtue of the good man coincide? To this we answer that the good *ruler* is a good and wise man, and that he who would be a statesman must be a wise man. And some persons say that even the education of the ruler should be of a special kind; for are not the children of kings instructed in riding and military exercises? As Euripides says:

'No subtle arts for me, but what the state requires'.

As though there were a special education needed by a ruler. If then the virtue of a good ruler is the same as that of a good man, and we assume further that the subject is a citizen as well as the ruler, the virtue of the good citizen and the virtue of the good man cannot be absolutely the same, although in some cases they may; for the virtue of a ruler differs from that of a citizen. It was the sense of this difference which made Jason say that 'he felt hungry when he was not a tyrant', meaning that he could not endure to live in a private station. But, on the other hand, it may be argued that men are praised for knowing both how to rule and how to obey, and he is said to be a citizen of approved virtue who is able to do both. Now if we suppose the virtue of a good man to be that which rules, and the virtue of the citizen to include ruling and obeying, it cannot be said that they are equally worthy of praise. Since, then, it is sometimes thought that the ruler and the ruled must learn different things and not the same, but that the citizen must know and share in them both, the inference is obvious. There is, indeed, the rule of a master, which is concerned with menial offices[12]—the master need not know how to perform these, but may employ others in the execution of them: the other would be degrading; and by the other I mean the power actually to do menial duties, which vary much in character and are executed by various classes of slaves, such, for example, as handicraftsmen, who, as their name signifies, live by the labour of their hands:—under these the mechanic is included. Hence in ancient times, and among some nations, the working classes had no share in the government—a privilege which they only acquired under the extreme democracy. Certainly the good man and the statesman and the good citizen ought not to learn the crafts of inferiors except for their own occasional use[13]; if they habitually practice them, there will cease to be a distinction between master and slave.

This is not the rule of which we are speaking; but there is a rule of another kind, which is exercised over freemen and equals by birth—a constitutional rule, which the ruler must learn by obeying, as he would learn the duties of a general of cavalry by being under the orders of a general of cavalry, or the duties of a general of infantry by being under the orders of a general of infantry, and by having had the command of a regiment and of a company. It has been well said that 'he who has never learned to obey cannot be a good commander'. The two are not the same, but the good citizen ought to be capable of both; he should know how to govern like a freeman, and how to obey like a freeman—these are the virtues of a citizen. And, although the temperance and justice of a ruler are distinct from those of a subject, the virtue of a good man will include both; for the virtue of the good man who is free and also a subject, e. g. his justice, will not be one but will comprise distinct kinds, the one qualifying him to rule, the other to obey, and differing as the temperance and courage of men and women differ.[14] For a man would be thought a coward if he had no more courage than a courageous woman, and a woman would be thought loquacious if she imposed no more restraint on her conversation than the good man; and indeed their part in the management of the household is different, for the duty of the one is to acquire, and of the other to preserve. Prac-

[12] Cp. Bk. 1, VII.
[13] Cp. Bk. 8, II.
[14] Cp. Bk. 1, XIII.

tical wisdom only is characteristic of the ruler[15]: it would seem that all other virtues must equally belong to ruler and subject. The virtue of the subject is certainly not wisdom, but only true opinion; he may be compared to the maker of the flute, while his master is like the flute-player or user of the flute.[16]

From these considerations may be gathered the answer to the question, whether the virtue of the good man is the same as that of the good citizen, or different, and how far the same, and how far different.[17]

V There still remains one more question about the citizen: Is he only a true citizen who has a share of office, or is the mechanic to be included? If they who hold no office are to be deemed citizens, not every citizen can have this virtue of ruling and obeying; for this man is a citizen. And if none of the lower class are citizens, in which part of the state are they to be placed? For they are not resident aliens, and they are not foreigners. May we not reply, that as far as this objection goes there is no more absurdity in excluding them than in excluding slaves and freedmen from any of the above-mentioned classes? It must be admitted that we cannot consider all those to be citizens who are necessary to the existence of the state; for example, children are not citizens equally with grown-up men, who are citizens absolutely, but children, not being grown up, are only citizens on a certain assumption.[18] Nay, in ancient times, and among some nations, the artisan class *were* slaves or foreigners, and therefore the majority of them are so now. The best form of state will not admit them to citizenship; but if they are admitted, then our definition of the virtue of a citizen will not apply to every citizen, nor to every free man as such, but only to those who are freed from necessary services. The necessary people are either slaves who minister to the wants of individuals, or mechanics and labourers who are the servants of the community. These reflections carried a little further will explain their position; and indeed what has been said already[19] is of itself, when understood, explanation enough.

[15] Cp. *Rep.* iv. 428.
[16] Cp. *Rep.* x. 601 D, E.
[17] Cp. Bk. 3, V, XVII; Bk. 4, VIII; Bk. 7, XIV.
[18] *sc.* that they grow up to be men.
[19] Bk. 3, I.

Since there are many forms of government there must be many varieties of citizens, and especially of citizens who are subjects; so that under some governments the mechanic and the labourer will be citizens, but not in others, as, for example, in aristocracy or the so-called government of the best (if there be such an one), in which honours are given according to virtue and merit; for no man can practise virtue who is living the life of a mechanic or labourer. In oligarchies the qualification for office is high, and therefore no labourer can ever be a citizen; but a mechanic may, for an actual majority of them are rich. At Thebes[20] there was a law that no man could hold office who had not retired from business for ten years. But in many states the law goes to the length of admitting aliens; for in some democracies a man is a citizen though his mother only be a citizen; and a similar principle is applied to illegitimate children; the law is relaxed when there is a dearth of population. But when the number of citizens increases, first the children of a male or a female slave are excluded; then those whose mothers only are citizens; and at last the right of citizenship is confined to those whose fathers and mothers are both citizens.

Hence, as is evident, there are different kinds of citizens; and he is a citizen in the highest sense who shares in the honours of the state. Compare Homer's words 'like some dishonoured stranger'[21]; he who is excluded from the honours of the state is no better than an alien. But when this exclusion is concealed, then the object is that the privileged class may deceive their fellow inhabitants.

As to the question whether the virtue of the good man is the same as that of the good citizen, the considerations already adduced prove that in some states the good man and the good citizen are the same, and in others different. When they are the same it is not every citizen who is a good man, but only the statesman and those who have or may have, alone or in conjunction with others, the conduct of public affairs.

VI Having determined these questions, we have next to consider whether there is only one form of government or many, and if

[20] Cp. Bk. 6, VI.

[21] Achilles complains of Agamemnon's so treating him, *Il.* ix. 648, xvi. 59.

many, what they are, and how many, and what are the differences between them.

A constitution is the arrangement of magistracies in a state,[22] especially of the highest of all. The government is everywhere sovereign in the state, and the constitution is in fact the government. For example, in democracies the people are supreme, but in oligarchies, the few; and, therefore, we say that these two forms of government also are different: and so in other cases.

First, let us consider what is the purpose of a state, and how many forms of government there are by which human society is regulated. We have already said, in the first part of this treatise,[23] when discussing household management and the rule of a master, that man is by nature a political animal. And therefore, men, even when they do not require one another's help, desire to live together; not but that they are also brought together by their common interests in proportion as they severally attain to any measure of well-being. This is certainly the chief end, both of individuals and of states. And also for the sake of mere life (in which there is possibly some noble element so long as the evils of existence do not greatly overbalance the good) mankind meet together and maintain the political community. And we all see that men cling to life even at the cost of enduring great misfortune, seeming to find in life a natural sweetness and happiness.

There is no difficulty in distinguishing the various kinds of authority; they have been often defined already in discussions outside the school. The rule of a master, although the slave by nature and the master by nature have in reality the same interests, is nevertheless exercised primarily with a view to the interest of the master, but accidentally considers the slave, since, if the slave perish, the rule of the master perishes with him. On the other hand, the government of a wife and children and of a household, which we have called household management, is exercised in the first instance for the good of the governed or for the common good of both parties, but essentially for the good of the governed, as we see to be the case in medicine, gymnastic, and the arts in general, which are only accidentally concerned with the good of the artists themselves.[24] For there is no reason why the trainer may not sometimes practise gymnastics, and the

[22] Cp. Bk. 2, XII; 4, I.

[23] Cp. Bk. 1, II.

[24] Cp. Pl. *Rep.* i. 341 D.

helmsman is always one of the crew. The trainer or the helmsman considers the good of those committed to his care. But, when he is one of the persons taken care of, he accidentally participates in the advantage, for the helmsman is also a sailor, and the trainer becomes one of those in training. And so in politics: when the state is framed upon the principle of equality and likeness, the citizens think that they ought to hold office by turns. Formerly, as is natural, every one would take his turn of service; and then again, somebody else would look after his interest, just as he, while in office, had looked after theirs.[25] But nowadays, for the sake of the advantage which is to be gained from the public revenues and from office, men want to be always in office. One might imagine that the rulers, being sickly, were only kept in health while they continued in office; in that case we may be sure that they would be hunting after places. The conclusion is evident: that governments which have a regard to the common interest are constituted in accordance with strict principles of justice, and are therefore true forms; but those which regard only the interest of the rulers are all defective and perverted forms, for they are despotic, whereas a state is a community of freemen.

VII Having determined these points, we have next to consider how many forms of government there are, and what they are; and in the first place what are the true forms, for when they are determined the perversions of them will at once be apparent. The words constitution and government have the same meaning, and the government, which is the supreme authority in states, must be in the hands of one, or of a few, or of the many. The true forms of government, therefore, are those in which the one, or the few, or the many, govern with a view to the common interest; but governments which rule with a view to the private interest, whether of the one, or of the few, or of the many, are perversions.[26] For the members of a state, if they are truly citizens, ought to participate in its advantages. Of forms of government in which one rules, we call that which regards the common interests, kingship or royalty; that in which more than one, but not many, rule, aristocracy; and it is so called, either because the rulers are the best men, or because they have at heart the best interests of

[25] Cp. Bk. 2, I.

[26] Cp. *Nic. Eth.* viii. 10.

the state and of the citizens. But when the citizens at large administer the state for the common interest, the government is called by the generic name—a constitution. And there is a reason for this use of language. One man or a few may excel in virtue; but as the number increases it becomes more difficult for them to attain perfection in every kind of virtue, though they may in military virtue, for this is found in the masses. Hence in a constitutional government the fighting-men have the supreme power, and those who possess arms are the citizens.

Of the above-mentioned forms, the perversions are as follows:—of royalty, tyranny; of aristocracy, oligarchy; of constitutional government, democracy. For tyranny is a kind of monarchy which has in view the interest of the monarch only; oligarchy has in view the interest of the wealthy; democracy, of the needy: none of them the common good of all.

VIII But there are difficulties about these forms of government, and it will therefore be necessary to state a little more at length the nature of each of them. For he who would make a philosophical study of the various sciences, and does not regard practice only, ought not to overlook or omit anything, but to set forth the truth in every particular. Tyranny, as I was saying, is monarchy exercising the rule of a master over the political society; oligarchy is when men of property have the government in their hands; democracy, the opposite, when the indigent, and not the men of property, are the rulers. And here arises the first of our difficulties, and it relates to the distinction just drawn. For democracy is said to be the government of the many. But what if the many are men of property and have the power in their hands? In like manner oligarchy is said to be the government of the few; but what if the poor are fewer than the rich, and have the power in their hands because they are stronger? In these cases the distinction which we have drawn between these different forms of government would no longer hold good.

Suppose, once more, that we add wealth to the few and poverty to the many, and name the governments accordingly—an oligarchy is said to be that in which the few and the wealthy, and a democracy that in which the many and the poor are the rulers—there will still be a difficulty. For, if the only forms of government are the ones already mentioned, how shall we describe those other governments also just mentioned by us, in which the rich are the more numerous and the poor are the fewer, and both govern in their respective states?

The argument seems to show that, whether in oligarchies or in democracies, the number of the governing body, whether the greater number, as in a democracy, or the smaller number, as in an oligarchy, is an accident due to the fact that the rich everywhere are few, and the poor numerous. But if so, there is a misapprehension of the causes of the difference between them. For the real difference between democracy and oligarchy is poverty and wealth. Wherever men rule by reason of their wealth, whether they be few or many, that is an oligarchy, and where the poor rule, that is a democracy. But as a fact the rich are few and the poor many; for few are well-to-do, whereas freedom is enjoyed by all, and wealth and freedom are the grounds on which the oligarchical and democratical parties respectively claim power in the state.

IX Let us begin by considering the common definitions of oligarchy and democracy, and what is justice oligarchical and democratical. For all men cling to justice of some kind, but their conceptions are imperfect and they do not express the whole idea. For example, justice is thought by them to be, and is, equality, not, however, for all, but only for equals. And inequality is thought to be, and is, justice; neither is this for all, but only for unequals. When the persons are omitted, then men judge erroneously. The reason is that they are passing judgement on themselves, and most people are bad judges in their own case. And whereas justice implies a relation to persons as well as to things, and a just distribution, as I have already said in the *Ethics*,[27] implies the same ratio between the persons and between the things, they agree about the equality of the things, but dispute about the equality of the persons, chiefly for the reason which I have just given—because they are bad judges in their own affairs; and secondly, because both the parties to the argument are speaking of a limited and partial justice, but imagine themselves to be speaking of absolute justice. For the one party, if

[27] v. 1131a 15.

they are unequal in one respect, for example wealth, consider themselves to be unequal in all; and the other party, if they are equal in one respect, for example free birth, consider themselves to be equal in all. But they leave out the capital point. For if men met and associated out of regard to wealth only, their share in the state would be proportioned to their property, and the oligarchical doctrine would then seem to carry the day. It would not be just that he who paid one mina should have the same share of a hundred minae, whether of the principal or of the profits, as he who paid the remaining ninety-nine. But a state exists for the sake of a good life, and not for the sake of life only: if life only were the object, slaves and brute animals might form a state, but they cannot, for they have no share in happiness or in a life of free choice. Nor does a state exist for the sake of alliance and security from injustice, nor yet for the sake of exchange and mutual intercourse; for then the Tyrrhenians and the Carthaginians, and all who have commercial treaties with one another,[28] would be the citizens of one state. True, they have agreements about imports, and engagements that they will do no wrong to one another, and written articles of alliance. But there are no magistracies common to the contracting parties who will enforce their engagements; different states have each their own magistracies. Nor does one state take care that the citizens of the other are such as they ought to be, nor see that those who come under the terms of the treaty do no wrong or wickedness at all, but only that they do no injustice to one another. Whereas, those who care for good government take into consideration virtue and vice in states. Whence it may be further inferred that virtue must be the care of a state which is truly so called, and not merely enjoys the name: for without this end the community becomes a mere alliance which differs only in place from alliances of which the members live apart; and law is only a convention, 'a surety to one another of justice,' as the sophist Lycophron says, and has no real power to make the citizens good and just.

This is obvious; for suppose distinct places, such as Corinth and Megara, to be brought together so that their walls touched, still they would not be one city, not even if the citizens had the right to intermarry, which is one of the rights peculiarly charac-

[28] Cp. Bk. 3, I.

teristic of states. Again, if men dwelt at a distance from one another, but not so far off as to have no intercourse, and there were laws among them that they should not wrong each other in their exchanges, neither would this be a state. Let us suppose that one man is a carpenter, another a husbandman, another a shoemaker, and so on, and that their number is ten thousand: nevertheless, if they have nothing in common but exchange, alliance, and the like, that would not constitute a state. Why is this? Surely not because they are at a distance from one another: for even supposing that such a community were to meet in one place, but that each man had a house of his own, which was in a manner his state, and that they made alliance with one another, but only against evil doers, still an accurate thinker would not deem this to be a state, if their intercourse with one another was of the same character after as before their union. It is clear then that a state is not a mere society, having a common place, established for the prevention of mutual crime and for the sake of exchange.[29] These are conditions without which a state cannot exist; but all of them together do not constitute a state, which is a community of families and aggregations of families in well-being, for the sake of a perfect and self-sufficing life. Such a community can only be established among those who live in the same place and intermarry. Hence arises in cities family connexions, brotherhoods, common sacrifices, amusements which draw men together. But these are created by friendship, for the will to live together is friendship. The end of the state is the good life, and these are the means towards it. And the state is the union of families and villages in a perfect and self-sufficing life, by which we mean a happy and honourable life.[30]

Our conclusion, then, is that political society exists for the sake of noble actions, and not of mere companionship. Hence they who contribute most to such a society have a greater share in it than those who have the same or a greater freedom or nobility of birth but are inferior to them in political virtue; or than those who exceed them in wealth but are surpassed by them in virtue.

From what has been said it will be clearly seen that all the partisans of different forms of government speak of a part of justice only.

[29] Cp. *Protag.* 322 B.

[30] Cp. Bk. 1, II. *Nic. Eth.* i. 1097^{b} 6.

X There is also a doubt as to what is to be the supreme power in the state:—Is it the multitude? Or the wealthy? Or the good? Or the one best man? Or a tyrant? Any of these alternatives seems to involve disagreeable consequences. If the poor, for example, because they are more in number, divide among themselves the property of the rich—is not this unjust? No, by heaven (will be the reply), for the supreme authority justly willed it. But if this is not injustice, pray what is? Again, when in the first division all has been taken, and the majority divide anew the property of the minority, is it not evident, if this goes on, that they will ruin the state? Yet surely, virtue is not the ruin of those who possess her, nor is justice destructive of a state; and therefore this law of confiscation clearly cannot be just. If it were, all the acts of a tyrant must of necessity be just; for he only coerces other men by superior power, just as the multitude coerce the rich. But is it just then that the few and the wealthy should be the rulers? And what if they, in like manner, rob and plunder the people—is this just? If so, the other case will likewise be just. But there can be no doubt that all these things are wrong and unjust.

Then ought the good to rule and have supreme power? But in that case everybody else, being excluded from power, will be dishonoured. For the offices of a state are posts of honour; and if one set of men always holds them, the rest must be deprived of them. Then will it be well that the one best man should rule? Nay, that is still more oligarchical, for the number of those who are dishonoured is thereby increased. Some one may say that it is bad in any case for a man, subject as he is to all the accidents of human passion, to have the supreme power, rather than the law. But what if the law itself be democratical or oligarchical, how will that help us out of our difficulties?[31] Not at all; the same consequences[32] will follow.

XI Most of these questions may be reserved for another occasion.[33] The principle that the multitude ought to be supreme rather than the few best is one that is maintained, and, though not free from difficulty, yet seems to contain an element of truth. For the many, of whom each individual is but an ordinary person,

[31] Cp. Bk. 3, XII. [32] Cp. ll. 11–34. [33] XII–XVII, Bk. 4, 6.

when they meet together may very likely be better than the few good, if regarded not individually but collectively, just as a feast to which many contribute is better than a dinner provided out of a single purse. For each individual among the many has a share of virtue and prudence, and when they meet together, they become in a manner one man, who has many feet, and hands, and senses; that is a figure of their mind and disposition. Hence the many are better judges than a single man of music and poetry; for some understand one part, and some another, and among them they understand the whole. There is a similar combination of qualities in good men, who differ from any individual of the many, as the beautiful are said to differ from those who are not beautiful, and works of art from realities, because in them the scattered elements are combined, although, if taken separately, the eye of one person or some other feature in another person would be fairer than in the picture. Whether this principle can apply to every democracy, and to all bodies of men, is not clear. Or rather, by heaven, in some cases it is impossible of application; for the argument would equally hold about brutes; and wherein, it will be asked, do some men differ from brutes? But there may be bodies of men about whom our statement is nevertheless true. And if so, the difficulty which has been already raised,[34] and also another which is akin to it–viz. what power should be assigned to the mass of freemen and citizens, who are not rich and have no personal merit–are both solved. There is still a danger in allowing them to share the great offices of state, for their folly will lead them into error, and their dishonesty into crime. But there is a danger also in not letting them share, for a state in which many poor men are excluded from office will necessarily be full of enemies. The only way of escape is to assign to them some deliberative and judicial functions. For this reason Solon[35] and certain other legislators give them the power of electing to offices, and of calling the magistrates to account, but they do not allow them to hold office singly. When they meet together their perceptions are quite good enough, and combined with the better class they are useful to the state (just as impure food when mixed with what is pure sometimes makes the entire mass more wholesome than a small quantity of the pure would be), but each

[34] X.

[35] Cp. Bk. 2, XII.

individual, left to himself, forms an imperfect judgement. On the other hand, the popular form of government involves certain difficulties. In the first place, it might be objected that he who can judge of the healing of a sick man would be one who could himself heal his disease, and make him whole—that is, in other words, the physician; and so in all professions and arts. As, then, the physician ought to be called to account by physicians, so ought men in general to be called to account by their peers. But physicians are of three kinds:—there is the ordinary practitioner, and there is the physician of the higher class, and thirdly the intelligent man who has studied the art: in all arts there is such a class; and we attribute the power of judging to them quite as much as to professors of the art. Secondly, does not the same principle apply to elections? For a right election can only be made by those who have knowledge; those who know geometry, for example, will chose a geometrician rightly, and those who know how to steer, a pilot; and, even if there be some occupations and arts in which private persons share in the ability to choose, they certainly cannot choose better than those who know. So that, according to this argument, neither the election of magistrates, nor the calling of them to account, should be entrusted to the many. Yet possibly these objections are to a great extent met by our old answer,[36] that if the people are not utterly degraded, although individually they may be worse judges than those who have special knowledge—as a body they are as good or better. Moreover, there are some arts whose products are not judged of solely, or best, by the artists themselves, namely those arts whose products are recognized even by those who do not possess the art; for example, the knowledge of the house is not limited to the builder only; the user, or, in other words, the master, of the house will be even a better judge than the builder, just as the pilot will judge better of a rudder than the carpenter, and the guest will judge better of a feast than the cook.

This difficulty seems now to be sufficiently answered, but there is another akin to it. That inferior persons should have authority in greater matters than the good would appear to be a strange thing, yet the election and calling to account of the magistrates is the greatest of all. And these, as I was saying,[37] are functions

[36] Bk. 3, X.

[37] Bk. 3, XI.

which in some states are assigned to the people, for the assembly is supreme in all such matters. Yet persons of any age, and having but a small property qualification, sit in the assembly and deliberate and judge, although for the great officers of state, such as treasurers and generals, a high qualification is required. This difficulty may be solved in the same manner as the preceding, and the present practice of democracies may be really defensible. For the power does not reside in the dicast, or senator, or ecclesiast, but in the court, and the senate, and the assembly, of which individual senators, or ecclesiasts, or dicasts, are only parts or members. And for this reason the many may claim to have a higher authority than the few; for the people, and the senate, and the courts consist of many persons, and their property collectively is greater than the property of one or of a few individuals holding great offices. But enough of this.

The discussion of the first question[38] shows nothing so clearly as that laws, when good, should be supreme; and that the magistrate or magistrates should regulate those matters only on which the laws are unable to speak with precision owing to the difficulty of any general principle embracing all particulars.[39] But what are good laws has not yet been clearly explained; the old difficulty remains.[40] The goodness or badness, justice or injustice, of laws varies of necessity with the constitutions of states. This, however, is clear, that the laws must be adapted to the constitutions. But if so, true forms of government will of necessity have just laws, and perverted forms of government will have unjust laws.

XII In all sciences and arts the end is a good, and the greatest good and in the highest degree a good in the most authoritative of all[41]—this is the political science of which the good is justice, in other words, the common interest. All men think justice to be a sort of equality; and to a certain extent[42] they agree in the philosophical distinctions which have been laid down by us about Ethics.[43] For they admit that justice is a thing and has a relation to persons, and that equals ought to have equality. But there still

[38] X.
[39] Cp. *Nic. Eth.* v. 1137[b] 19.
[40] Cp. Bk. 3, X.
[41] Cp. Bk. 1, I; *N. Eth.* i. 1094[a] 1.
[42] Cp. Bk. 3, IX.
[43] Cp. *Nic. Eth.* V. 3.

remains a question: equality or inequality of what? Here is a difficulty which calls for political speculation. For very likely some persons will say that offices of state ought to be unequally distributed according to superior excellence, in whatever respect, of the citizen, although there is no other difference between him and the rest of the community; for that those who differ in any one respect have different rights and claims. But, surely, if this is true, the complexion or height of a man, or any other advantage, will be a reason for his obtaining a greater share of political rights. The error here lies upon the surface, and may be illustrated from the other arts and sciences. When a number of flute-players are equal in their art, there is no reason why those of them who are better born should have better flutes given to them; for they will not play any better on the flute, and the superior instrument should be reserved for him who is the superior artist. If what I am saying is still obscure, it will be made clearer as we proceed. For if there were a superior flute-player who was far inferior in birth and beauty, although either of these may be a greater good than the art of flute-playing, and may excel flute-playing in a greater ratio than he excels the others in his art, still he ought to have the best flutes given to him, unless the advantages of wealth and birth contribute to excellence in flute-playing, which they do not. Moreover, upon this principle any good may be compared with any other. For if a given height may be measured against wealth and against freedom, height in general may be so measured. Thus if A excels in height more than B in virtue, even if virtue in general excels height still more, all goods will be commensurable; for if a certain amount is better than some other, it is clear that some other will be equal. But since no such comparison can be made, it is evident that there is good reason why in politics men do not ground their claim to office on every sort of inequality any more than in the arts. For if some be slow, and others swift, that is no reason why the one should have little and the others much; it is in gymnastic contests that such excellence is rewarded. Whereas the rival claims of candidates for office can only be based on the possession of elements which enter into the composition of a state. And therefore the noble, or free-born, or rich, may with good reason claim office; for holders of offices must be freemen and tax-payers: a state can be no more composed entirely of poor men than entirely of slaves. But if wealth and freedom are necessary elements, justice and valour are equally so[44]; for without the former qualities a state cannot exist at all, without the latter not well.

XIII If the existence of the state is alone to be considered, then it would seem that all, or some at least, of these claims are just; but, if we take into account a good life, then, as I have already said,[45] education and virtue have superior claims. As, however, those who are equal in one thing ought not to have an equal share in all, nor those who are unequal in one thing to have an unequal share in all, it is certain that all forms of government which rest on either of these principles are perversions. All men have a claim in a certain sense, as I have already admitted,[46] but all have not an absolute claim. The rich claim because they have a greater share in the land, and land is the common element of the state; also they are generally more trustworthy in contracts. The free claim under the same title as the noble; for they are nearly akin. For the noble are citizens in a truer sense than the ignoble, and good birth is always valued in a man's own home and country.[47] Another reason is, that those who are sprung from better ancestors are likely to be better men, for nobility is excellence of race. Virtue, too, may be truly said to have a claim, for justice has been acknowledged by us to be a social[48] virtue, and it implies all others.[49] Again, the many may urge their claim against the few; for, when taken collectively, and compared with the few, they are stronger and richer and better. But, what if the good, the rich, the noble, and the other classes who make up a state, are all living together in the same city, will there, or will there not, be any doubt who shall rule?—No doubt at all in determining who ought to rule in each of the above-mentioned forms of government. For states are characterized by differences in their governing bodies—one of them has a government of the rich, another of the virtuous, and so on. But a difficulty arises when all these elements co-exist. How are we to decide? Suppose the virtuous to be very few in number: may we consider their numbers in relation to their duties, and ask whether they are enough to administer the

[44] Cp. Bk. 4, IV.
[45] Cp. Bk. 3, X.
[46] Bk. 3, IX.
[47] Cp. Bk. 1, VI.
[48] Cp. Bk. 1, II.
[49] Cp. *N. Eth.* v. 1129b 25.

state, or so many as will make up a state? Objections may be urged against all the aspirants to political power. For those who found their claims on wealth or family might be thought to have no basis of justice; on this principle, if any one person were richer than all the rest, it is clear that he ought to be ruler of them. In like manner he who is very distinguished by his birth ought to have the superiority over all those who claim on the ground that they are freeborn. In an aristocracy, or government of the best, a like difficulty occurs about virtue; for if one citizen be better than the other members of the government, however good they may be, he too, upon the same principle of justice, should rule over them. And if the people are to be supreme because they are stronger than the few, then if one man, or more than one, but not a majority, is stronger than the many, they ought to rule, and not the many.

All these considerations appear to show that none of the principles on which men claim to rule and to hold all other men in subjection to them are strictly right. To those who claim to be masters of the government on the ground of their virtue or their wealth, the many might fairly answer that they themselves are often better and richer than the few—I do not say individually, but collectively. And another ingenious objection which is sometimes put forward may be met in a similar manner. Some persons doubt whether the legislator who desires to make the justest laws ought to legislate with a view to the good of the higher classes or of the many, when the case which we have mentioned occurs.[50] Now what is just or right is to be interpreted in the sense of 'what is equal'; and that which is right in the sense of being equal is to be considered with reference to the advantage of the state, and the common good of the citizens. And a citizen is one who shares in governing and being governed. He differs under different forms of government, but in the best state he is one who is able and willing to be governed and to govern with a view to the life of virtue.

If, however, there be some one person, or more than one, although not enough to make up the full complement of a state, whose virtue is so pre-eminent that the virtues or the political capacity of all the rest admit of no comparison with his or theirs, he or they can be no longer regarded as part of a state; for justice

[50] i. e. when the many collectively are better than the few.

will not be done to the superior, if he is reckoned only as the equal of those who are so far inferior to him in virtue and in political capacity. Such an one may truly be deemed a God among men. Hence we see that legislation is necessarily concerned only with those who are equal in birth and in capacity; and that for men of pre-eminent virtue there is no law—they are themselves a law. Any one would be ridiculous who attempted to make laws for them: they would probably retort what, in the fable of Antisthenes, the lions said to the hares,[51] when in the council of the beasts the latter began haranguing and claiming equality for all. And for this reason democratic states have instituted ostracism; equality is above all things their aim, and therefore they ostracized and banished from the city for a time those who seemed to predominate too much through their wealth, or the number of their friends, or through any other political influence. Mythology tells us that the Argonauts left Heracles behind for a similar reason; the ship Argo would not take him because she feared that he would have been too much for the rest of the crew. Wherefore those who denounce tyranny and blame the counsel which Periander gave to Thrasybulus cannot be held altogether just in their censure. The story is that Periander, when the herald was sent to ask counsel of him, said nothing, but only cut off the tallest ears of corn till he had brought the field to a level. The herald did not know the meaning of the action, but came and reported what he had seen to Thrasybulus, who understood that he was to cut off the principal men in the state[52]; and this is a policy not only expedient for tyrants or in practice confined to them, but equally necessary in oligarchies and democracies. Ostracism[53] is a measure of the same kind, which acts by disabling and banishing the most prominent citizens. Great powers do the same to whole cities and nations, as the Athenians did to the Samians, Chians, and Lesbians; no sooner had they obtained a firm grasp of the empire, than they humbled their allies contrary to treaty; and the Persian king has repeatedly crushed the Medes, Babylonians, and other nations, when their spirit has been stirred by the recollection of their former greatness.

The problem is a universal one, and equally concerns all forms

[51] i. e. 'where are your claws and teeth?'
[52] Cp. Bk. 5, X.
[53] Cp. Bk. 5, III.

of government, true as well as false; for, although perverted forms with a view to their own interests may adopt this policy, those which seek the common interest do so likewise. The same thing may be observed in the arts and sciences[54]; for the painter will not allow the figure to have a foot which, however beautiful, is not in proportion, nor will the ship-builder allow the stern or any other part of the vessel to be unduly large, any more than the chorus-master will allow any one who sings louder or better than all the rest to sing in the choir. Monarch, too, may practise compulsion and still live in harmony with their cities, if their own government is for the interest of the state. Hence where there is an acknowledged superiority the argument in favour of ostracism is based upon a kind of political justice. It would certainly be better that the legislator should from the first so order his state as to have no need of such a remedy. But if the need arises, the next best thing is that he should endeavour to correct the evil by this or some similar measure. The principle, however, has not been fairly applied in states; for, instead of looking to the good of their own constitution, they have used ostracism for factious purposes. It is true that under perverted forms of government, and from their special point of view, such a measure is just and expedient, but it is also clear that it is not absolutely just. In the perfect state there would be great doubts about the use of it, not when applied to excess in strength, wealth, popularity, or the like, but when used against some one who is pre-eminent in virtue —what is to be done with him? Mankind will not say that such an one is to be expelled and exiled; on the other hand, he ought not to be a subject—that would be as if mankind should claim to rule over Zeus, dividing his offices among them. The only alternative is that all should joyfully obey such a ruler, according to what seems to be the order of nature, and that men like him should be kings in their state for life.

XIV The preceding discussion, by a natural transition, leads to the consideration of royalty, which we admit to be one of the true forms of government. Let us see whether in order to be well governed a state or country should be under the rule of a king or under some other form of government; and whether monarchy,

[54] Cp. Bk. 5, III, V; Bk. 7, IV; *Rep.* iv. 420.

although good for some, may not be bad for others. But first we must determine whether there is one species of royalty or many. It is easy to see that there are many, and that the manner of government is not the same in all of them.

Of royalties according to law, (1) the Lacedaemonian is thought to answer best to the true pattern; but there the royal power is not absolute, except when the kings go on an expedition, and then they take the command. Matters of religion are likewise committed to them. The kingly office is in truth a kind of generalship, irresponsible and perpetual. The king has not the power of life and death, except in a specified case, as for instance, in ancient times, he had it when upon a campaign, by right of force. This custom is described in Homer. ForAgamemnon is patient when he is attacked in the assembly, but when the army goes out to battle he has the power even of life and death. Does he not say?—'When I find a man skulking apart from the battle, nothing shall save him from the dogs and vultures, for in my hands is death.'[55]

This, then, is one form of royalty—a generalship for life: and of such royalties some are hereditary and others elective.

(2) There is another sort of monarchy not uncommon among the barbarians, which nearly resembles tyranny. But this is both legal and hereditary. For barbarians, being more servile in character than Hellenes, and Asiatics than Europeans, do not rebel against a despotic government. Such royalties have the nature of tyrannies because the people are by nature slaves[56]; but there is no danger of their being overthrown, for they are hereditary and legal. Wherefore also their guards are such as a king and not such as a tyrant would employ, that is to say, they are composed of citizens, whereas the guards of tyrants are mercenaries.[57] For kings rule according to law over voluntary subjects, but tyrants over involuntary; and the one are guarded by their fellow-citizens, the others are guarded against them.

These are two forms of monarchy, and there was a third (3) which existed in ancient Hellas, called an Aesymnetia or dictatorship. This may be defined generally as an elective tyranny, which, like the barbarian monarchy, is legal, but differs from it in not being hereditary. Sometimes the office was held for life, sometimes for a term of years, or until certain duties had been per-

[55] *Il.* ii. 391–393.
[56] Cp. Bk. 1, II.
[57] Cp. Bk. 5, X.

formed. For example, the Mytilenaeans elected Pittacus leader against the exiles, who were headed by Antimenides and Alcaeus the poet. And Alcaeus himself shows in one of his banquet odes that they chose Pittacus tyrant, for he reproaches his fellow-citizens for 'having made the low-born Pittacus tyrant of the spiritless and ill-fated city, with one voice shouting his praises'.

These forms of government have always had the character of tyrannies, because they possess despotic power; but inasmuch as they are elective and acquiesced in by their subjects, they are kingly.

(4) There is a fourth species of kingly rule—that of the heroic times—which was hereditary and legal, and was exercised over willing subjects. For the first chiefs were benefactors of the people[58] in arts or arms; they either gathered them into a community, or procured land for them; and thus they became kings of voluntary subjects, and their power was inherited by their descendants. They took the command in war and presided over the sacrifices, except those which required a priest. They also decided causes either with or without an oath; and when they swore, the form of the oath was the stretching out of their sceptre. In ancient times their power extended continuously to all things whatsoever, in city and country, as well as in foreign parts; but at a later date they relinquished several of these privileges, and others the people took from them, until in some states nothing was left to them but the sacrifices; and where they retained more of the reality they had only the right of leadership in war beyond the border.

These, then, are the four kinds of royalty. First the monarchy of the heroic ages; this was exercised over voluntary subjects, but limited to certain functions; the king was a general and a judge, and had the control of religion. The second is that of the barbarians, which is an hereditary despotic government in accordance with law. A third is the power of the so-called Aesymnete or Dictator; this is an elective tyranny. The fourth is the Lacedaemonian, which is in fact a generalship, hereditary and perpetual. These four forms differ from one another in the manner which I have described.

(5) There is a fifth form of kingly rule in which one has the disposal of all, just as each nation or each state has the disposal of

[58] Cp. Bk. 5, X.

public matters; this form corresponds to the control of a household. For as household management is the kingly rule of a house, so kingly rule is the household management of a city, or of a nation, or of many nations.

XV Of these forms we need only consider two, the Lacedaemonian and the absolute royalty; for most of the others lie in a region between them, having less power than the last, and more than the first. Thus the inquiry is reduced to two points: first, is it advantageous to the state that there should be a perpetual general, and if so, should the office be confined to one family, or open to the citizens in turn? Secondly, is it well that a single man should have the supreme power in all things? The first question falls under the head of laws rather than of constitutions; for perpetual generalship might equally exist under any form of government, so that this matter may be dismissed for the present.[59] The other kind of royalty is a sort of constitution; this we have now to consider, and briefly to run over the difficulties involved in it. We will begin by inquiring whether it is more advantageous to be ruled by the best man or by the best laws.[60]

The advocates of royalty maintain that the laws speak only in general terms, and cannot provide for circumstances; and that for any science to abide by written rules is absurd. In Egypt the physician is allowed to alter his treatment after the fourth day, but if sooner, he takes the risk. Hence it is clear that a government acting according to written laws is plainly not the best. Yet surely the ruler cannot dispense with the general principle which exists in law, and this is a better ruler which is free from passion than that in which it is innate. Whereas the law is passionless, passion must ever sway the heart of man. Yes, it may be replied, but then on the other hand an individual will be better able to deliberate in particular cases.

The best man, then, must legislate, and laws must be passed, but these laws will have no authority when they miss the mark, though in all other cases retaining their authority. But when the law cannot determine a point at all, or not well, should the one best man or should all decide? According to our present practice assemblies meet, sit in judgement, deliberate, and decide, and their

[59] It is not discussed later.

[60] Cp. Plato, *Polit.* 294 A–295 C.

judgements all relate to individual cases. Now any member of the assembly, taken separately, is certainly inferior to the wise man. But the state is made up of many individuals. And as a feast to which all the guests contribute is better than a banquet furnished by a single man,[61] so a multitude is a better judge of many things than any individual.

Again, the many are more incorruptible than the few; they are like the greater quantity of water which is less easily corrupted than a little. The individual is liable to be overcome by anger or by some other passion, and then his judgement is necessarily perverted; but it is hardly to be supposed that a great number of persons would all get into a passion and go wrong at the same moment. Let us assume that they are the freemen, and that they never act in violation of the law, but fill up the gaps which the law is obliged to leave. Or, if such virtue is scarcely attainable by the multitude, we need only suppose that the majority are good man and good citizens, and ask which will be the more incorruptible, the one good ruler, or the many who are all good? Will not the many? But, you will say, there may be parties among them, whereas the one man is not divided against himself. To which we may answer that their character is as good as his. If we call the rule of many men, who are all of them good, aristocracy, and the rule of one man royalty, then aristocracy will be better for states than royalty, whether the government is supported by force or not,[62] provided only that a number of men equal in virtue can be found.

The first governments were kingships, probably for this reason, because of old, when cities were small, men of eminent virtue were few. Further, they were made kings because they were benefactors,[63] and benefits can only be bestowed by good men. But when many persons equal in merit arose, no longer enduring the pre-eminence of one, they desired to have a commonwealth, and set up a constitution. The ruling class soon deteriorated and enriched themselves out of the public treasury; riches became the path to honour, and so oligarchies naturally grew up. These passed into tyrannies and tyrannies into democracies; for love of gain in the ruling classes was always tending to diminish their number, and so to strengthen the masses, who in the end set upon their masters and established democracies. Since cities have in-

[61] Cp. Bk. 3, X. [62] Cp. l. 30. [63] Cp. Bk. 3, XIV.

creased in size, no other form of government appears to be any longer even easy to establish.[64]

Even supposing the principle to be maintained that kingly power is the best thing for states, how about the family of the king? Are his children to succeed him? If they are no better than anybody else, that will be mischievous. But, says the lover of royalty, the king, though he might, will not hand on his power to his children. That, however, is hardly to be expected, and is too much to ask of human nature. There is also a difficulty about the force which he is to employ; should a king have guards about him by whose aid he may be able to coerce the refractory? If not, how will he administer his kingdom? Even if he be the lawful sovereign who does nothing arbitrarily or contrary to law, still he must have some force wherewith to maintain the law. In the case of a limited monarchy there is not much difficulty in answering this question; the king must have such force as will be more than a match for one or more individuals, but not so great as that of the people. The ancients observe this principle when they have guards to any one whom they appointed dictator or tyrant. Thus, when Dionysius asked the Syracusans to allow him guards, somebody advised that they should give him only such a number.

XVI At this place in the discussion there impends the inquiry respecting the king who acts solely according to his own will; he has now to be considered. The so-called limited monarchy, or kingship according to law, as I have already remarked,[65] is not a distinct form of government, for under all governments, as, for example, in a democracy or aristocracy, there may be a general holding office for life, and one person is often made supreme over the administration of a state. A magistracy of this kind exists at Epidamnus,[66] and also at Opus, but in the latter city has a more limited power. Now, absolute monarchy, or the arbitrary rule of a sovereign over all the citizens, in a city which consists of equals, is thought by some to be quite contrary to nature; it is argued that those who are by nature equals must have the same natural right and worth, and that for unequals to have an equal share, or for equals to have an uneven share, in the offices of state, is as bad

[64] Cp. Bk. 4, VI, XIII.

[65] Bk. 3, XV.

[66] Cp. Bk. 5, I.

as for different bodily constitutions to have the same food and clothing. Wherefore it is thought to be just that among equals every one be ruled as well as rule, and therefore that all should have their turn. We thus arrive at law; for an order of succession implies law. And the rule of the law, it is argued, is preferable to that of any individual. On the same principle, even if it be better for certain individuals to govern, they should be made only guardians and ministers of the law. For magistrates there must be—this is admitted; but then men say that to give authority to any one man when all are equal is unjust. Nay, there may indeed be cases which the law seems unable to determine, but in such cases can a man? Nay, it will be replied, the law trains officers for this express purpose, and appoints them to determine matters which are left undecided by it, to the best of their judgement. Further, it permits them to make any amendment of the existing laws which experience suggests. Therefore he who bids the law rule may be deemed to bid God and Reason alone rule, but he who bids man rule adds an element of the beast; for desire is a wild beast, and passion perverts the minds of rulers, even when they are the best of men. The law is reason unaffected by desire. We are told[67] that a patient should call in a physician; he will not get better if he is doctored out of a book. But the parallel of the arts is clearly not in point; for the physician does nothing contrary to rule from motives of friendship; he only cures a patient and takes a fee; whereas magistrates do many things from spite and partiality. And, indeed, if a man suspected the physician of being in league with his enemies to destroy him for a bribe, he would rather have recourse to the book. But certainly physicians, when they are sick, call in other physicians, and training-masters, when they are in training, other training-masters, as if they could not judge truly about their own case and might be influenced by their feelings. Hence it is evident that in seeking for justice men seek for the mean or neutral,[68] for the law is the mean. Again, customary laws have more weight, and relate to more important matters, than written laws, and a man may be a safer ruler than the written law, but not safer than the customary law.

Again, it is by no means easy for one man to superintend many things; he will have to appoint a number of subordinates, and what difference does it make whether these subordinates always

[67] Cp. Bk. 3, XV, *Polit.* 296 B.

[68] Cp. *Nic. Eth.* v. 1132ª 22.

existed or were appointed by him because he needed them? If, as I said before,[69] the good man has a right to rule because he is better, still two good men are better than one: this is the old saying—

'two going together',[70]

and the prayer of Agamemnon—

'would that I had ten such counsellors!'[71]

And at this day there are magistrates, for example judges, who have authority to decide some matters which the law is unable to determine, since no one doubts that the law would command and decide in the best manner whatever it could. But some things can, and other things cannot, be comprehended under the law, and this is the origin of the vexed question whether the best law or the best man should rule. For matters of detail about which men deliberate cannot be included in legislation. Nor does any one deny that the decision of such matters must be left to man, but it is argued that there should be many judges, and not one only. For every ruler who has been trained by the law judges well; and it would surely seem strange that a person should see better with two eyes, or hear better with two ears, or act better with two hands or feet, than many with many; indeed, it is already the practice of kings to make to themselves many eyes and ears and hands and feet. For they make colleagues of those who are the friends of themselves and their governments. They must be friends of the monarch and of his government; if not his friends, they will not do what he wants; but friendship implies likeness and equality; and, therefore, if he thinks that his friends ought to rule, he must think that those who are equal to himself and like himself ought to rule equally with himself. These are the principal controversies relating to monarchy.

XVII But may not all this be true in some cases and not in others? for there is by nature both a justice and an advantage appropriate to the rule of a master, another to kingly rule, another to constitutional rule; but there is none naturally appropriate to

[69] Bk. 3, XIII. [70] *Il.* x. 224. [71] *Il.* ii. 372.

tyranny, or to any other perverted form of government; for these come into being contrary to nature. Now, to judge at least from what has been said, it is manifest that, where men are alike and equal, it is neither expedient nor just that one man should be lord of all, whether there are laws, or whether there are no laws, but he himself is in the place of law. Neither should a good man be lord over good men, nor a bad man over bad; nor, even if he excels in virtue, should he have a right to rule, unless in a particular case, at which I have already hinted, and to which I will once more recur.[72] But first of all, I must determine what natures are suited for government by a king, and what for an aristocracy, and what for a constitutional government.

A people who are by nature capable of producing a race superior in the virtue needed for political rule are fitted for kingly government; and a people submitting to be ruled as freemen by men whose virtue renders them capable of political command are adapted for an aristocracy; while the people who are suited for constitutional freedom are those among whom there naturally exists a warlike multitude[73] able to rule and to obey in turn by a law which gives office to the well-to-do according to their desert. But when a whole family, or some individual, happens to be so pre-eminent in virtue as to surpass all others, then it is just that they should be the royal family and supreme over all, or that this one citizen should be king of the whole nation. For, as I said before,[74] to give them authority is not only agreeable to that ground of right which the founders of all states, whether aristocratical, or oligarchical, or again democratical, are accustomed to put forward (for these all recognize the claim of excellence, although not the same excellence), but accords with the principle already laid down. For surely it would not be right to kill, or ostracize, or exile such a person, or require that he should take his turn in being governed. The whole is naturally superior to the part, and he who has this pre-eminence is in the relation of a whole to a part. But if so, the only alternative is that he should have the supreme power, and that mankind should obey him, not in turn, but always. These are the conclusions at which we arrive respecting royalty and its various forms, and this is the answer to the

[72] Bk. 3, XIII, XVII.
[73] Cp. Bk. 3, VII.
[74] Bk. 3, XIII.

question, whether it is or is not advantageous to states, and to which, and how.

XVIII We maintain[75] that the true forms of government are three, and that the best must be that which is administered by the best, and in which there is one man, or a whole family, or many persons, excelling all the others together in virtue, and both rulers and subjects are fitted, the one to rule, the others to be ruled, in such a manner as to attain the most eligible life. We showed at the commencement of our inquiry[76] that the virtue of the good man is necessarily the same as the virtue of the citizen of the perfect state. Clearly then in the same manner, and by the same means through which a man becomes truly good, he will frame a state that is to be ruled by an aristocracy or by a king, and the same education and the same habits will be found to make a good man and a man fit to be a statesman or a king.

Having arrived at these conclusions, we must proceed to speak of the perfect state, and describe how it comes into being and is established.

[75] Cp. Bk. 3, VII. [76] IV, V.

BOOK FOURTH

I In all arts and sciences which embrace the whole of any subject, and do not come into being in a fragmentary way, it is the province of a single art or science to consider all that appertains to a single subject. For example, the art of gymnastic considers not only the suitableness of different modes of training to different bodies (2), but what sort is absolutely the best (1); (for the absolutely best must suit that which is by nature best and best furnished with the means of life), and also what common form of training is adapted to the great majority of men (4). And if a man does not desire the best habit of body, or the greatest skill in gymnastics, which might be attained by him, still the trainer or the teacher of gymnastic should be able to impart any lower degree of either (3). The same principle equally holds in medicine and ship-building, and the making of clothes, and in the arts generally.[1]

Hence it is obvious that government too is the subject of a single science, which has to consider what government is best and of what sort it must be, to be most in accordance with our aspirations, if there were no external impediment, and also what kind of government is adapted to particular states. For the best is often unattainable, and therefore the true legislator and statesman ought to be acquainted, not only with (1) that which is best in the abstract, but also with (2) that which is best relatively to circumstances. We should be able further to say how a state may be constituted under any given conditions (3); both how it is originally formed and, when formed, how it may be longest preserved; the supposed state being so far from having the best constitution that it is unprovided even with the conditions necessary for the best; neither is it the best under the circumstances, but of an inferior type.

He ought, moreover, to know (4) the form of government which is best suited to states in general; for political writers, although they have excellent ideas, are often unpractical. We should consider, not only what form of government is best, but also what is possible and what is easily attainable by all. There are some who would have none but the most perfect; for this many natural ad-

[1] The numbers in this paragraph are made to correspond with the numbers in the next.

vantages are required. Others, again, speak of a more attainable form, and, although they reject the constitution under which they are living, they extol some one in particular, for example the Lacedaemonian.[2] Any change of government which has to be introduced should be one which men, starting from their existing constitutions, will be both willing and able to adopt, since there is quite as much trouble in the reformation of an old constitution as in the establishment of a new one, just as to unlearn is as hard as to learn. And therefore, in addition to the qualifications of the statesman already mentioned, he should be able to find remedies for the defects of existing constitutions, as has been said before.[3] This he cannot do unless he knows how many forms of government there are. It is often supposed that there is only one kind of democracy and one of oligarchy. But this is a mistake; and, in order to avoid such mistakes, we must ascertain what differences there are in the constitutions of states, and in how many ways they are combined. The same political insight will enable a man to know which laws are the best, and which are suited to different constitutions; for the laws are, and ought to be, relative to the constitution, and not the constitution to the laws. A constitution is the organization of offices in a state, and determines what is to be the governing body, and what is the end of each community. But laws are not to be confounded with the principles of the constitution; they are the rules according to which the magistrates should administer the state, and proceed against offenders. So that we must know the varieties, and the number of varieties, of each form of government, if only with a view to making laws. For the same laws cannot be equally suited to all oligarchies or to all democracies, since there is certainly more than one form both of democracy and of oligarchy.

II In our original discussion[4] about governments we divided them into three true forms: kingly rule, aristocracy, and constitutional government, and three corresponding perversions—tyranny, oligarchy, and democracy. Of kingly rule and of aristocracy, we have already spoken,[5] for the inquiry into the perfect state is the same thing with the discussion of the two forms thus

[2] Cp. Bk. 2, VI.

[3] Cp. Bk. 3, XVIII.

[4] Bk. 3, VII; Cp. *Nic. Eth.* viii. 10.

[5] 3, XIV–XVIII.

named, since both imply a principle of virtue provided with external means. We have already determined in what aristocracy and kingly rule differ from one another, and when the latter should be established.[6] In what follows we have to describe the so-called constitutional government, which bears the common name of all constitutions, and the other forms, tyranny, oligarchy, and democracy.

It is obvious which of the three perversions is the worst, and which is the next in badness. That which is the perversion of the first and most divine is necessarily the worst. And just as a royal rule, if not a mere name, must exist by virtue of some great personal superiority in the king,[7] so tyranny, which is the worst of governments, is necessarily the farthest removed from a well-constituted form; oligarchy is little better, for it is a long way from aristocracy, and democracy is the most tolerable of the three.

A writer[8] who preceded me has already made these distinctions, but his point of view is not the same as mine. For he lays down the principle that when all the constitutions are good (the oligarchy and the rest being virtuous), democracy is the worst, but the best when all are bad. Whereas we maintain that they are in any case defective, and that one oligarchy is not to be accounted better than another, but only less bad.

Not to pursue this question further at present, let us begin by determining (1)[9] how many varieties of constitution there are (since of democracy and oligarchy there are several): (2)[10] what constitution is the most generally acceptable, and what is eligible in the next degree after the perfect state; and besides this what other there is which is aristocratical and well-constituted, and at the same time adapted to states in general; (3)[11] of the other forms of government to whom each is suited. For democracy may meet the needs of some better than oligarchy, and conversely. In the next place (4)[12] we have to consider in what manner a man ought to proceed who desires to establish some one among these various forms, whether of democracy or of oligarchy; and lastly, (5)[13] having briefly discussed these subjects to the best of our

[6] Bk. 3, VII; Bk. 3, XV, XVII.
[7] Cp. Bk. 3; XIII, XVII, XVIII; Bk. 5, X; Bk. 7, III.
[8] Plato, *Polit.* 302 E, 303 A.
[9] III–X. [10] XI. [11] XII.
[12] Bk. 6, I–VII. [13] Bk. 5.

power, we will endeavour to ascertain the modes of ruin and preservation both of constitutions generally and of each separately, and to what causes they are to be attributed.

III The reason why there are many forms of government is that every state contains many elements. In the first place we see that all states are made up of families, and in the multitude of citizens there must be some rich and some poor, and some in a middle condition; the rich are heavy-armed, and the poor not. Of the common people, some are husbandmen, and some traders, and some artisans. There are also among the notables differences of wealth and property—for example, in the number of horses which they keep, for they cannot afford to keep them unless they are rich. And therefore in old times the cities whose strength lay in their cavalry were oligarchies, and they used cavalry in wars against their neighbours; as was the practice of the Eretrians and Chalcidians, and also of the Magnesians on the river Maeander, and of other peoples in Asia. Besides differences of wealth there are differences of rank and merit, and there are some other elements which were mentioned by us when in treating of aristocracy we enumerated the essentials of a state.[14] Of these elements, sometimes all, sometimes the lesser and sometimes the greater number, have a share in the government. It is evident then that there must be many forms of government, differing in kind, since the parts of which they are composed differ from each other in kind. For a constitution is an organization of offices, which all the citizens distribute among themselves, according to the power which different classes possess, for example the rich or the poor, or according to some principle of equality which includes both. There must therefore be as many forms of government as there are modes of arranging the offices, according to the superiorities and differences of the parts of the state.

There are generally thought to be two principal forms: as men say of the winds that there are but two—north and south, and that the rest of them are only variations of these, so of governments there are said to be only two forms—democracy and oligarchy. For aristocracy is considered to be a kind of oligarchy, as being the rule of a few, and the so-called constitutional government to

[14] Bk. 3, XIII; Bk. 7, VIII, IX.

be really a democracy, just as among the winds we make the west a variation of the north, and the east of the south wind. Similarly of musical modes there are said to be two kinds, the Dorian and the Phrygian; the other arrangements of the scale are comprehended under one or other of these two. About forms of government this is a very favourite notion. But in either case the better and more exact way is to distinguish, as I have done,[15] the one or two which are true forms, and to regard the others as perversions, whether of the most perfectly attempered mode or of the best form of government: we may compare the severer and more overpowering modes to the oligarchical forms, and the more relaxed and gentler ones to the democratic.

IV It must not be assumed, as some are fond of saying, that democracy is simply that form of government in which the greater number are sovereign,[16] for in oligarchies, and indeed in every government, the majority rules; nor again is oligarchy that form of government in which a few are sovereign. Suppose the whole population of a city to be 1300, and that of these 1000 are rich, and do not allow the remaining 300 who are poor, but free, and in all other respects their equals, a share of the government—no one will say that this is a democracy. In like manner, if the poor were few and the masters of the rich who outnumber them, no one would ever call such a government, in which the rich majority have no share of office, an oligarchy. Therefore we should rather say that democracy is the form of government in which the free are rulers, and oligarchy in which the rich; it is only an accident that the free are the many and the rich are the few. Otherwise a government in which the offices were given according to stature, as is said to be the case in Ethiopia, or according to beauty, would be an oligarchy; for the number of tall or good-looking men is small. And yet oligarchy and democracy are not sufficiently distinguished merely by these two characteristics of wealth and freedom. Both of them contain many other elements, and therefore we must carry our analysis further, and say that the government is not a democracy in which the freemen, being few in number,

[15] Cp. Bk. 4, I; Bk. 8, V, VII.
[16] Cp. Bk. 3, VII.

rule over the many who are not free, as at Apollonia, on the Ionian Gulf, and at Thera; (for in each of these states the nobles, who were also the earliest settlers, were held in chief honour, although they were but a few out of many). Neither is it a democracy when the rich have the government because they exceed in number; as was the case formerly at Colophon, where the bulk of the inhabitants were possessed of large property before the Lydian War. But the form of government is a democracy when the free, who are also poor and the majority, govern, and an oligarchy when the rich and the noble govern, they being at the same time few in number.

I have said that there are many forms of government, and have explained to what causes the variety is due. Why there are more than those already mentioned,[17] and what they are, and whence they arise, I will now proceed to consider, starting from the principle already admitted,[18] which is that every state consists, not of one, but of many parts. If we were going to speak of the different species of animals, we should first of all determine the organs which are indispensable to every animal, as for example some organs of sense and the instruments of receiving and digesting food, such as the mouth and the stomach, besides organs of locomotion. Assuming now that there are only so many kinds of organs, but that there may be differences in them—I mean different kinds of mouths, and stomachs, and perceptive and locomotive organs—the possible combinations of these differences will necessarily furnish many varieties of animals. (For animals cannot be the same which have different kinds of mouths or of ears.) And when all the combinations are exhausted, there will be as many sorts of animals as there are combinations of the necessary organs. The same, then, is true of the forms of government which have been described; states, as I have repeatedly said,[19] are composed, not of one, but of many elements. One element is the food-producing class, who are called husbandmen; a second, the class of mechanics who practise the arts without which a city cannot exist;—of these arts some are absolutely necessary, others con-

[17] i. e. democracy and oligarchy, Cp. Bk. 4, III.
[18] Bk. 4, II.
[19] Bk. 2, I; Bk. 3, XII; Bk. 4, II, III, IV. Cp. Bk. 3, IV.

tribute to luxury or to the grace of life. The third class is that of traders, and by traders I mean those who are engaged in buying and selling, whether in commerce or in retail trade. A fourth class is that of the serfs or labourers. The warriors make up the fifth class, and they are as necessary as any of the others, if the country is not to be the slave of every invader. For how can a state which has any title to the name be of a slavish nature? The state is independent and self-sufficing, but a slave is the reverse of independent. Hence we see that this subject, though ingeniously, has not been satisfactorily treated in the *Republic*.[20] Socrates says that a state is made up of four sorts of people who are absolutely necessary; these are a weaver, a husbandman, a shoemaker, and a builder; afterwards, finding that they are not enough, he adds a smith, and again a herdsman, to look after the necessary animals; then a merchant, and then a retail trader. All these together form the complement of the first state, as if a state were established merely to supply the necessaries of life, rather than for the sake of the good, or stood equally in need of shoemakers and of husbandmen. But he does not admit into the state a military class until the country has increased in size, and is beginning to encroach on its neighbour's land, whereupon they go to war. Yet even amongst his four original citizens, or whatever be the number of those whom he associates in the state, there must be some one who will dispense justice and determine what is just. And as the soul may be said to be more truly part of an animal than the body, so the higher parts of states, that is to say, the warrior class, the class engaged in the administration of justice, and that engaged in deliberation, which is the special business of political common sense—these are more essential to the state than the parts which minister to the necessaries of life. Whether their several functions are the functions of different citizens, or of the same—for it may often happen that the same persons are both warriors and husbandmen—is immaterial to the argument. The higher as well as the lower elements are to be equally considered parts of the state, and if so, the military element at any rate must be included. There are also the wealthy who minister to the state with their property; these form the seventh class. The eighth class is that of magistrates and of officers; for the state cannot exist

[20] *Rep.* ii. 369.

without rulers. And therefore some must be able to take office and to serve the state, either always or in turn. There only remains the class of those who deliberate and who judge between disputants; we were just now distinguishing them. If presence of all these elements, and their fair and equitable organization, is necessary to states, then there must also be persons who have the ability of statesmen. Different functions appear to be often combined in the same individual; for example, the warrior may also be a husbandman, or an artisan; or, again, the counsellor a judge. And all claim to possess political ability, and think that they are quite competent to fill most offices. But the same persons cannot be rich and poor at the same time. For this reason the rich and the poor are regarded in an especial sense as parts of a state. Again, because the rich are generally few in number, while the poor are many, they appear to be antagonistic, and as the one or the other prevails they form the government. Hence arises the common opinion that there are two kinds of government—democracy and oligarchy.

I have already explained[21] that there are many forms of constitution, and to what causes the variety is due. Let me now show that there are different forms both of democracy and oligarchy, as will indeed be evident from what has preceded. For both in the common people and in the notables various classes are included; of the common people, one class are husbandmen, another artisans; another traders, who are employed in buying and selling; another are the seafaring class, whether engaged in war or in trade, as ferrymen or as fishermen. (In many places any one of these classes forms quite a large population; for example, fishermen at Tarentum and Byzantium, crews of triremes at Athens, merchant seamen at Aegina and Chios, ferrymen at Tenedos.) To the classes already mentioned may be added day-labourers, and those who, owing to their needy circumstances, have no leisure, or those who are not of free birth on both sides; and there may be other classes as well. The notables again may be divided according to their wealth, birth, virtue, education, and similar differences.

Of forms of democracy first comes that which is said to be based strictly on equality. In such a democracy the law says that it is just for the poor to have no more advantage than the rich;

[21] Cp. Bk. 3, VI.

and that neither should be masters, but both equal. For if liberty and equality, as is thought by some, are chiefly to be found in democracy, they will be best attained when all persons alike share in the government to the utmost. And since the people are the majority, and the opinion of the majority is decisive, such a government must necessarily be a democracy. Here then is one sort of democracy. There is another, in which the magistrates are elected according to a certain property qualification, but a low one; he who has the required amount of property has a share in the government, but he who loses his property loses his rights. Another kind is that in which all the citizens who are under no disqualification share in the government, but still the law is supreme. In another, everybody, if he be only a citizen, is admitted to the government, but the law is supreme as before. A fifth form of democracy, in other respects, the same, is that in which, not the law, but the multitude, have the supreme power, and supersede the law by their decrees. This is a state of affairs brought about by the demagogues. For in democracies which are subject to the law the best citizens hold the first place, and there are no demagogues; but where the laws are not supreme, there demagogues spring up. For the people becomes a monarch, and is many in one; and the many have the power in their hands, not as individuals, but collectively. Homer says that 'it is not good to have a rule of many',[22] but whether he means this corporate rule, or the rule of many individuals, is uncertain. At all events this sort of democracy, which is now a monarch, and no longer under the control of law, seeks to exercise monarchical sway, and grows into a despot; the flatterer is held in honour; this sort of democracy being relatively to other democracies what tyranny is to other forms of monarchy. The spirit of both is the same, and they alike exercise a despotic rule over the better citizens. The decrees of the demos correspond to the edicts of the tyrant; and the demagogue is to the one what the flatterer is to the other. Both have great power;—the flatterer with the tyrant, the demagogue with democracies of the kind which we are describing. The demagogues make the decrees of the people override the laws, by referring all things to the popular assembly. And therefore they grow great, because the people have all things in their hands, and they hold in their hands the votes of the people, who

[22] *Il.* ii. 204.

are too ready to listen to them. Further, those who have any complaint to bring against the magistrates say, 'let the people be judges'; the people are too happy to accept the invitation; and so the authority of every office is undermined. Such a democracy is fairly open to the objection that it is not a constitution at all; for where the laws have no authority, there is no constitution. The law ought to be supreme over all, and the magistracies should judge of particulars, and only this should be considered a constitution. So that if democracy be a real form of government, the sort of system in which all things are regulated by decrees is clearly not even a democracy in the true sense of the word, for decrees relate only to particulars.[23]

These then are the different kinds of democracy.

V Of oligarchies, too, there are different kinds:—one where the property qualification for office is such that the poor, although they form the majority, have no share in the government, yet he who acquires a qualification may obtain a share. Another sort is when there is a qualification for office, but a high one, and the vacancies in the governing body are filled by co-optation. If the election is made out of all the qualified persons, a constitution of this kind inclines to an aristocracy, if out of a privileged class, to an oligarchy. Another sort of oligarchy is when the son succeeds the father. There is a fourth form, likewise hereditary, in which the magistrates are supreme and not the law. Among oligarchies this is what tyranny is among monarchies, and the last-mentioned form of democracy among democracies; and in fact this sort of oligarchy receives the name of a dynasty (or rule of powerful families).

These are the different sorts of oligarchies and democracies. It should however be remembered that in many states[24] the constitution which is established by law, although not democratic, owing to the education and habits of the people may be administered democratically, and conversely in other states the established constitution may incline to democracy, but may be administered in an oligarchical spirit. This most often happens after a revolution: for governments do not change at once; at first the dominant party are content with encroaching a little upon

[23] Cp. *Nic. Eth.* v. 1137ᵇ 27.

[24] Cp. Bk. 5, I.

their opponents. The laws which existed previously continue in force, but the authors of the revolution have the power in their hands.

VI From what has been already said we may safely infer that there are so many different kinds of democracies and of oligarchies. For it is evident that either all the classes whom we mentioned[25] must share in the government, or some only and not others. When the class of husbandmen and of those who possess moderate fortunes have the supreme power, the government is administered according to law. For the citizens being compelled to live by their labour have no leisure; and so they set up the authority of the law, and attend assemblies only when necessary. They all obtain a share in the government when they have acquired the qualification which is fixed by the law—the absolute exclusion of any class would be a step towards oligarchy; hence all who have acquired the property qualification are admitted to a share in the constitution. But leisure cannot be provided for them unless there are revenues to support them. This is one sort of democracy, and these are the causes which give birth to it. Another kind is based on the distinction which naturally comes next in order; in this, every one to whose birth there is no objection is eligible, but actually shares in the government only if he can find leisure. Hence in such a democracy the supreme power is vested in the laws, because the state has no means of paying the citizens. A third kind is when all freemen have a right to share in the government, but do not actually share, for the reason which has been already given; so that in this form again the law must rule. A fourth kind of democracy is that which comes latest in the history of states. In our own day, when cities have far outgrown their original size, and their revenues have increased, all the citizens have a place in the government, through the great preponderance of the multitude; and they all, including the poor who receive pay, and therefore have leisure to exercise their rights, share in the administration. Indeed, when they are paid, the common people have the most leisure, for they are not hindered by the care of their property, which often fetters the rich, who are thereby prevented from taking part in the assembly or in the courts, and so

[25] Bk. 4, IV.

the state is governed by the poor, who are a majority, and not by the laws. So many kinds of democracies there are, and they grow out of these necessary causes.

Of oligarchies, one form is that in which the majority of the citizens have some property, but not very much; and this is the first form, which allows to any one who obtains the required amount the right of sharing in the government. The sharers in the government being a numerous body, it follows that the law must govern, and not individuals. For in proportion as they are further removed from a monarchical form of government, and in respect of property have neither so much as to be able to live without attending to business, nor so little as to need state support, they must admit the rule of law and not claim to rule themselves. But if the men of property in the state are fewer than in the former case, and own more property, there arises a second form of oligarchy. For the stronger they are, the more power they claim, and having this object in view, they themselves select those of the other classes who are to be admitted to the government; but, not being as yet strong enough to rule without the law, they make the law represent their wishes.[26] When this power is intensified by a further diminution of their numbers and increase of their property, there arises a third and further stage of oligarchy, in which the governing class keep the offices in their own hands, and the law ordains that the son shall succeed the father. When, again, the rulers have great wealth and numerous friends, this sort of family despotism approaches a monarchy; individuals rule and not the law. This is the fourth sort of oligarchy, and is analogous to the last sort of democracy.

VII There are still two forms besides democracy and oligarchy; one of them is universally recognized and included among the four principal forms of government, which are said to be (1) monarchy, (2) oligarchy, (3) democracy, and (4) the so-called aristocracy or government of the best. But there is also a fifth, which retains the generic name of polity or constitutional government; this is not common, and therefore has not been noticed by writers who attempt to enumerate the different kinds of gov-

[26] i. e. they make a law that the governing class shall have the power of co-optation from other classes.

ernment; like Plato,[27] in their books about the state, they recognize four only. The term 'aristocracy' is rightly applied to the form of government which is described in the first part of our treatise[28]; for that only can be rightly called aristocracy which is a government formed of the best men absolutely, and not merely of men who are good when tried by any given standard. In the perfect state the good man is absolutely the same as the good citizen; whereas in other states the good citizen is only good relatively to his own form of government. But there are some states differing from oligarchies and also differing from the so-called polity or constitutional government; these are termed aristocracies, and in them magistrates are certainly chosen, both according to their wealth and according to their merit. Such a form of government differs from each of the two just now mentioned, and is termed an aristocracy. For indeed in states which do not make virtue the aim of the community, men of merit and reputation for virtue may be found. And so where a government has regard to wealth, virtue, and numbers, as at Carthage,[29] that is aristocracy; and also where it has regard only to two out of the three, as at Lacedaemon, to virtue and numbers, and the two principles of democracy and virtue temper each other. There are these two forms of aristocracy in addition to the first and perfect state, and there is a third form, viz. the constitutions which incline more than the so-called polity towards oligarchy.

VIII I have yet to speak of the so-called polity and of tyranny. I put them in this order, not because a polity or constitutional government is to be regarded as a perversion any more than the above-mentioned aristocracies. The truth is, that they all fall short of the most perfect form of government, and so they are reckoned among perversions, and the really perverted forms are perversions of these, as I said in the original discussion.[30] Last of all I will speak of tyranny, which I place last in the series because I am inquiring into the constitutions of states, and this is the very reverse of a constitution.

Having explained why I have adopted this order, I will proceed to consider constitutional government; of which the nature

[27] *Rep.* viii, ix.
[28] Bk. 3, VII, XV, Cp. Bk. 7, VIII.
[29] Cp. Bk. 2, XI.
[30] Bk. 3, VII.

will be clearer now that oligarchy and democracy have been defined. For polity or constitutional government may be described generally as a fusion of oligarchy and democracy; but the term is usually applied to those forms of government which incline towards democracy, and the term aristocracy to those which incline towards oligarchy, because birth and education are commonly the accompaniments of wealth. Moreover, the rich already possess the external advantages the want of which is a temptation to crime, and hence they are called noblemen and gentlemen. And inasmuch as aristocracy seeks to give predominance to the best of the citizens, people say also of oligarchies that they are composed of noblemen and gentlemen. Now it appears to be an impossible thing that the state which is governed not by the best citizens but by the worst should be well-governed, and equally impossible that the state which is ill-governed should be governed by the best. But we must remember that good laws, if they are not obeyed, do not constitute good government. Hence there are two parts of good government; one is the actual obedience of citizens to the laws, the other part is the goodness of the laws which they obey; they may obey bad laws as well as good. And there may be a further subdivision; they may obey either the best laws which are attainable to them, or the best absolutely.

The distribution of offices according to merit is a special characteristic of aristocracy, for the principle of an aristocracy is virtue, as wealth is of an oligarchy, and freedom of a democracy. In all of them there of course exists the right of the majority, and whatever seems good to the majority of those who share in the government has authority. Now in most states the form called polity exists, for the fusion goes no further than the attempt to unite the freedom of the poor and the wealth of the rich, who commonly take the place of the noble. But as there are three grounds on which men claim an equal share in the government, freedom, wealth, and virtue (for the fourth or good birth is the result of the two last, being only ancient wealth and virtue), it is clear that the admixture of the two elements, that is to say, of the rich and poor, is to be called a polity or constitutional government; and the union of the three is to be called aristocracy or the government of the best, and more than any other form of government, except the true and ideal, has a right to this name.

Thus far I have shown the existence of forms of states other than monarchy, democracy, and oligarchy, and what they are, and in what aristocracies differ from one another, and polities from aristocracies—that the two latter are not very unlike is obvious.

IX Next we have to consider how by the side of oligarchy and democracy the so-called polity or constitutional government springs up, and how it should be organized. The nature of it will be at once understood from a comparison of oligarchy and democracy; we must ascertain their different characteristics, and taking a portion from each, put the two together, like the parts of an indenture. Now there are three modes in which fusions of government may be affected. In the first mode we must combine the laws made by both governments, say concerning the administration of justice. In oligarchies they impose a fine on the rich if they do not serve as judges, and to the poor they give no pay; but in democracies they give pay to the poor and do not fine the rich. Now (1) the union of these two modes[31] is a common or middle term between them, and is therefore characteristic of a constitutional government, for it is a combination of both. This is one mode of uniting the two elements. Or (2) a mean may be taken between the enactments of the two: thus democracies require no property qualification, or only a small one, from members of the assembly, oligarchies a high one; here neither of these is the common term, but a mean between them. (3) There is a third mode, in which something is borrowed from the oligarchical and something from the democratical principle. For example, the appointment of magistrates by lot is thought to be democratical, and the election of them oligarchical; democratical again when there is no property qualification, oligarchical when there is. In the aristocratical or constitutional state, one element will be taken from each—from oligarchy the principle of electing to offices, from democracy the disregard of qualification. Such are the various modes of combination.

There is a true union of oligarchy and democracy when the same state may be termed either a democracy or an oligarchy; those who use both names evidently feel that the fusion is complete. Such a fusion there is also in the mean; for both extremes

[31] Cp. Bk. 4, XII.

appear in it. The Lacedaemonian constitution, for example, is often described as a democracy, because it has many democratical features. In the first place the youth receive a democratical education. For the sons of the poor are brought up with the sons of the rich, who are educated in such a manner as to make it possible for the sons of the poor to be educated like them. A similar equality prevails in the following period of life, and when the citizens are grown up to manhood the same rule is observed; there is no distinction between the rich and poor. In like manner they all have the same food at their public tables, and the rich wear only such clothing as any poor man can afford. Again, the people elect to one of the two greatest offices of state, and in the other they share[32]; for they elect the Senators and share in the Ephoralty. By others the Spartan constitution is said to be an oligarchy, because it has many oligarchical elements. That all offices are filled by election and none by lot, is one of these oligarchical characteristics; that the power of inflicting death or banishment rests with a few persons is another; and there are others. In a well attempted polity there should appear to be both elements and yet neither; also the government should rely on itself, and not on foreign aid, and on itself not through the good will of a majority—they might be equally well-disposed when there is a vicious form of government—but through the general willingness of all classes in the state to maintain the constitution.

Enough of the manner in which a constitutional government, and in which the so-called aristocracies ought to be framed.

X Of the nature of tyranny I have still to speak, in order that it may have its place in our inquiry (since even tyranny is reckoned by us to be a form of government), although there is not much to be said about it. I have already in the former part of this treatise[33] discussed royalty or kingship according to the most usual meaning of the term, and considered whether it is or is not advantageous to states, and what kind of royalty should be established, and from what source, and how.

When speaking of royalty we also spoke[34] of two forms of tyranny, which are both according to law, and therefore easily pass into royalty. Among Barbarians there are elected monarchs

[32] Cp. Bk. 2, IX. [33] Bk. 3, XIV–XVII. [34] Bk. 3, XIV.

who exercise a despotic power; despotic rulers were also elected in ancient Hellas, called Aesymnetes or dictators. These monarchies, when compared with one another, exhibit certain differences. And they are, as I said before,[35] royal, in so far as the monarch rules according to law over willing subjects; but they are tyrannical in so far as he is despotic and rules according to his own fancy. There is also a third kind of tyranny, which is the most typical form, and is the counterpart of the perfect monarchy. This tyranny is just that arbitrary power of an individual which is responsible to no one, and governs all alike, whether equals or better, with a view to its own advantage, not to that of its subjects, and therefore against their will. No freeman, if he can escape from it, will endure such a government.

The kinds of tyranny are such and so many, and for the reasons which I have given.

XI We have now to inquire what is the best constitution for most states, and the best life for most men, neither assuming a standard of virtue which is above ordinary persons, nor an education which is exceptionally favoured by nature and circumstances, nor yet an ideal state which is an aspiration only, but having regard to the life in which the majority are able to share, and to the form of government which states in general can attain. As to those aristocracies, as they are called, of which we were just now speaking,[36] they either lie beyond the possibilities of the greater number of states, or they approximate to the so-called constitutional government, and therefore need no separate discussion. And in fact the conclusion at which we arrive respecting all these forms rests upon the same grounds. For if what was said in the *Ethics*[37] is true, that the happy life is the life according to virtue lived without impediment, and that virtue is a mean, then the life which is in a mean, and in a mean attainable by every one, must be the best. And the same principles of virtue and vice are characteristic of cities and of constitutions; for the constitution is in a figure the life of the city.

[35] Bk. 3, XIV.
[36] Bk. 4, VIII.
[37] *Nic. Eth.* i. 1098^a 16. vii. 1153^b 10, x. 1177^a 12.

Now in all states there are three elements: one class is very rich, another very poor, and a third in a mean. It is admitted that moderation and the mean are best, and therefore it will clearly be best to possess the gifts of fortune in moderation; for in that condition of life men are most ready to follow rational principle. But he who greatly excels in beauty, strength, birth, or wealth, or on the other hand who is very poor, or very weak, or very much disgraced, finds it difficult to follow rational principle.[38] Of these two the one sort grow into violent and great criminals, the others into rogues and petty rascals. And two sorts of offences correspond to them, the one committed from violence, the other from roguery. Again, the middle class is least likely to shrink from rule, or to be over-ambitious for it; both of which are injuries to the state. Again, those who have too much of the goods of fortune, strength, wealth, friends, and the like, are neither willing nor able to submit to authority. The evil begins at home; for when they are boys, by reason of the luxury in which they are brought up,[39] they never learn, even at school, the habit of obedience. On the other hand, the very poor, who are in the opposite extreme, are too degraded. So that the one class cannot obey, and can only rule despotically; the other knows not how to command and must be ruled like slaves. Thus arises a city, not of freemen, but of masters and slaves, the one despising, the other envying; and nothing can be more fatal to friendship and good fellowship in states than this: for good fellowship springs from friendship; when men are at enmity with one another, they would rather not even share the same path. But a city ought to be composed, as far as possible, of equals and similars; and these are generally the middle classes. Wherefore the city which is composed of middle-class citizens is necessarily best constituted in respect of the elements of which we say the fabric of the state naturally consists.[40] And this is the class of citizens which is most secure in a state, for they do not, like the poor, covet their neighbours' goods; nor do others covet theirs, as the poor covet the goods of the rich; and as they neither plot against others, nor are themselves plotted against, they pass through life safely. Wisely then did Phocylides pray—'Many things are best in the mean; I desire to be of a middle condition in my city.'

[38] Cp. Pl. *Rep.* iv. 421 D ff. [39] Cp. Bk. 5, IX. [40] Cp. ll. 1–3.

Thus it is manifest that the best political community is formed by citizens of the middle class, and that those states are likely to be well-administered, in which the middle class is large, and stronger if possible than both the other classes, or at any rate than either singly; for the addition of the middle class turns the scale, and prevents either of the extremes from being dominant. Great then is the good fortune of a state in which the citizens have a moderate and sufficient property; for where some possess much, and the others nothing, there may arise an extreme democracy, or a pure oligarchy; or a tyranny may grow out of either extreme—either out of the most rampant democracy, or out of an oligarchy; but it is not so likely to arise out of the middle constitutions and those akin to them. I will explain the reason of this hereafter, when I speak of the revolutions of states.[41] The mean condition of states is clearly best, for no other is free from faction; and where the middle class is large, there are least likely to be factions and dissensions. For a similar reason large states are less liable to faction than small ones, because in them the middle class is large; whereas in small states it is easy to divide all the citizens into two classes who are either rich or poor, and to leave nothing in the middle. And democracies are safer[42] and more permanent than oligarchies, because they have a middle class which is more numerous and has a greater share in the government; for when there is no middle class, and the poor greatly exceed in number, troubles arise, and the state soon comes to an end. A proof of the superiority of the middle class is that the best legislators have been of a middle condition; for example, Solon, as his own verses testify; and Lycurgus, for he was not a king; and Charondas, and almost all legislators.

These considerations will help us to understand why most governments are either democratical or oligarchical. The reason is that the middle class is seldom numerous in them, and whichever party, whether the rich or the common people, transgresses the mean and predominates, draws the constitution its own way, and thus arises either oligarchy or democracy. There is another reason—the poor and the rich quarrel with one another, and whichever side gets the better, instead of establishing a just or popular

[41] Bk. 5, VIII.
[42] Cp. Bk. 5, I, VII.

government, regards political supremacy as the prize of victory, and the one party sets up a democracy and the other an oligarchy. Further, both the parties which had the supremacy in Hellas looked only to the interest of their own form of government, and established in states, the one, democracies, and the other, oligarchies; they thought of their own advantage, of the public not at all. For these reasons the middle form of government has rarely, if ever, existed, and among a very few only. One man alone of all who ever ruled in Hellas was induced to give this middle constitution to states. But it has now become a habit among the citizens of states, not even to care about equality; all men are seeking for dominion, or, if conquered, are willing to submit.

What then is the best form of government, and what makes it the best, is evident; and of other constitutions, since we say[43] that there are many kinds of democracy and many of oligarchy, it is not difficult to see which has the first and which the second or any other place in the order of excellence, now that we have determined which is the best. For that which is nearest to the best must of necessity be better, and that which is furthest from it worse, if we are judging absolutely and not relatively to given conditions: I say 'relatively to given conditions', since a particular government may be preferable, but another form may be better for some people.

XII We have now to consider what and what kind of government is suitable to what and what kind of men. I may begin by assuming, as a general principle common to all governments, that the portion of the state which desires the permanence of the constitution ought to be stronger than that which desires the reverse. Now every city is composed of quality and quantity. By quality I mean freedom, wealth, education, good birth, and by quantity, superiority of numbers. Quality may exist in one of the classes which make up the state, and quantity in the other. For example, the meanly-born may be more in number than the well-born, or the poor than the rich, yet they may not so much exceed in quantity as they fall short in quality; and therefore there must be a comparison of quantity and quality. Where the number of the

[43] Bk. 4, I, IV, V, VI.

poor is more than proportioned to the wealth of the rich, there will naturally be a democracy, varying in form with the sort of people who compose it in each case. If, for example, the husbandmen exceed in number, the first form of democracy will then arise; if the artisans and labouring class, the last; and so with the intermediate forms. But where the rich and the notables exceed in quality more than they fall short in quantity, there oligarchy arises, similarly assuming various forms according to the kind of superiority possessed by the oligarchs.

The legislator should always include the middle class in his government; if he makes his laws oligarchical, to the middle class let him look; if he makes them democratical, he should equally by his laws try to attach this class to the state. There only can the government ever be stable where the middle class exceeds one or both of the others, and in that case there will be no fear that the rich will unite with the poor against the rulers. For neither of them will ever be willing to serve the other, and if they look for some form of government more suitable to both, they will find none better than this, for the rich and the poor will never consent to rule in turn, because they mistrust one another. The arbiter is always the one trusted, and he who is in the middle is an arbiter. The more perfect the admixture of the political elements, the more lasting will be the constitution. Many even of those who desire to form aristocratical governments make a mistake, not only in giving too much power to the rich, but in attempting to overreach the people. There comes a time when out of a false good there arises a true evil, since the encroachments of the rich are more destructive to the constitution than those of the people.

XIII The devices by which oligarchies deceive the people are five in number; they relate to (1) the assembly; (2) the magistracies; (3) the courts of law; (4) the use of arms; (5) gymnastic exercises. (1) The assemblies are thrown open to all, but either the rich only are fined for non-attendance, or a much larger fine is inflicted upon them. (2) As to the magistracies, those who are qualified by property cannot decline office upon oath, but the poor may. (3) In the law-courts the rich, and the rich only, are fined if they do not serve, the poor are let off with impunity, or, as in the laws of Charondas, a larger fine is inflicted on the rich, and a smaller one on the poor. In some states all citizens who have registered themselves are allowed to attend the assembly and to try causes; but if after registration they do not attend either in the assembly or at the courts, heavy fines are imposed upon them. The intention is that through fear of the fines they may avoid registering themselves, and then they cannot sit in the law-courts or in the assembly. Concerning (4) the possession of arms, and (5) gymnastic exercises, they legislate in a similar spirit. For the poor are not obliged to have arms, but the rich are fined for not having them; and in like manner no penalty is inflicted on the poor for non-attendance at the gymnasium, and consequently, having nothing to fear, they do not attend, whereas the rich are liable to a fine, and therefore they take care to attend.

These are the devices of oligarchical legislators, and in democracies they have counter devices. They pay the poor for attending the assemblies and the law-courts, and they inflict no penalty on the rich for non-attendance. It is obvious that he who would duly mix the two principles should combine the practice of both, and provide that the poor should be paid to attend, and the rich fined if they do not attend, for then all will take part; if there is no such combination, power will be in the hands of one party only. The government should be confined to those who carry arms. As to the property qualification, no absolute rule can be laid down, but we must see what is the highest qualification sufficiently comprehensive to secure that the number of those who have the rights of citizens exceeds the number of those excluded. Even if they have no share in office, the poor, provided only that they are not outraged or deprived of their property, will be quiet enough.

But to secure gentle treatment for the poor is not an easy thing, since a ruling class is not always humane. And in time of war the poor are apt to hesitate unless they are fed; when fed, they are willing enough to fight. In some states the government is vested, not only in those who are actually serving, but also in those who have served; among the Malians, for example, the governing body consisted of the latter, while the magistrates were chosen from those actually on service. And the earliest government which existed among the Hellenes, after the overthrow of the kingly power, grew up out of the warrior class, and was originally taken from the knights (for strength and superiority in war at that time depended on cavalry[44]; indeed, without discipline, infantry are useless, and in ancient times there was no military knowledge or tactics, and therefore the strength of armies lay in their cavalry). But when cities increased and the heavy-armed grew in strength, more had a share in the government; and this is the reason why the states which we call constitutional governments have been hitherto called democracies. Ancient constitutions, as might be expected, were oligarchical and royal; their population being small they had no considerable middle class; the people were weak in numbers and organization, and were therefore more contented to be governed.

I have explained why there are various forms of government, and why there are more than is generally supposed; for democracy, as well as other constitutions, has more than one form: also what their differences are, and whence they arise, and what is the best form of government, speaking generally, and to whom the various forms of government are best suited; all this has now been explained.

XIV Having thus gained an appropriate basis of discussion, we will proceed to speak of the points which follow next in order. We will consider the subject not only in general but with reference to particular constitutions. All constitutions have three elements, concerning which the good lawgiver has to regard what is expedient for each constitution. When they are well-ordered, the constitution is well-ordered, and as they differ from one another, constitutions differ. There is (1) one element which deliberates about public affairs; secondly (2) that concerned with the magistracies—the question being, what they should be, over what they should exercise authority, and what should be the mode of electing to them; and thirdly (3) that which has judicial power.

The deliberative element has authority in matters of war and peace, in making and unmaking alliances; it passes laws, inflicts death, exile, confiscation, elects magistrates and audits their accounts. These powers must be assigned either all to all the citizens or all to some of them (for example, to one or more magistracies, or different causes to different magistracies), or some of

[44] Cp. Bk. 4, II; Bk. 6, VI.

them to all, and others of them only to some. That all things should be decided by all is characteristic of democracy; this is the sort of equality which the people desire. But there are various ways in which all may share in the government; they may deliberate, not all in one body, but by turns, as in the constitution of Telecles the Milesian. There are other constitutions in which the boards of magistrates meet and deliberate, but come into office by turns, and are elected out of the tribes and the very smallest divisions of the state, until every one has obtained office in his turn. The citizens, on the other hand, are assembled only for the purposes of legislation, and to consult about the constitution, and to hear the edicts of the magistrates. In another variety of democracy the citizens form one assembly, but meet only to elect magistrates, to pass laws, to advise about war and peace, and to make scrutinies. Other matters are referred severally to special magistrates, who are elected by vote or by lot out of all the citizens. Or again, the citizens meet about election to offices and about scrutinies, and deliberate concerning war or alliances while other matters are administered by the magistrates, who, as far as is possible,[45] are elected by vote. I am speaking of those magistracies in which special knowledge is required. A fourth form of democracy is when all the citizens meet to deliberate about everything, and the magistrates decide nothing, but only make the preliminary inquiries; and that is the way in which the last and worst form of democracy, corresponding, as we maintain,[46] to the close family oligarchy and to tyranny, is at present administered. All these modes are democratical.

On the other hand, that some should deliberate about all is oligarchical. This again is a mode which, like the democratical, has many forms. When the deliberative class being elected out of those who have a moderate qualification are numerous and they respect and obey the prohibitions of the law without altering it, and any one who has the required qualification shares in the government, then, just because of this moderation, the oligarchy inclines towards polity. But when only selected individuals and not the whole people share in the deliberations of the state, then, although, as in the former case, they observe the law, the government is a pure oligarchy. Or, again, when those who have the

[45] *sc.* in an advanced democracy. Cp. Bk. 6, II.
[46] Bk. 4, IV, VI.

power of deliberation are self-elected, and son succeeds father, and they and not the laws are supreme—the government is of necessity oligarchical. Where, again, particular persons have authority in particular matters;—for example, when the whole people decide about peace and war and hold scrutinies, but the magistrates regulate everything else, and they are elected by vote—there the government is an aristocracy. And if some questions are decided by magistrates elected by vote, and others by magistrates elected by lot, either absolutely or out of select candidates, or elected partly by vote, partly by lot—these practices are partly characteristic of an aristocratical government, and partly of a pure constitutional government.

These are the various forms of the deliberative body; they correspond to the various forms of government. And the government of each state is administered according to one or other of the principles which have been laid down. Now it is for the interest of democracy, according to the most prevalent notion of it (I am speaking of that extreme form of democracy in which the people are supreme even over the laws), with a view to better deliberation to adopt the custom of oligarchies respecting courts of law. For in oligarchies the rich who are wanted to be judges are compelled to attend under pain of a fine, whereas in democracies the poor are paid to attend. And this practice of oligarchies should be adopted by democracies in their public assemblies, for they will advise better if they all deliberate together—the people with the notables and the notables with the people. It is also a good plan that those who deliberate should be elected by vote or by lot in equal numbers out of the different classes; and that if the people greatly exceed in number those who have political training, pay should not be given to all, but only to as many as would balance the number of the notables, or that the number in excess should be eliminated by lot. But in oligarchies either certain persons should be co-opted from the mass, or a class of officers should be appointed such as exist in some states, who are termed probuli and guardians of the law; and the citizens should occupy themselves exclusively with matters on which these have previously deliberated; for so the people will have a share in the deliberations of the state, but will not be able to disturb the principles of the constitution. Again, in oligarchies either the people ought to accept the measures of the government, or not to pass anything contrary to them; or, if all are allowed to share in counsel, the decision should rest with the magistrates. The opposite of what is done in constitutional governments should be the rule in oligarchies; the veto of the majority should be final, their assent not final, but the proposal should be referred back to the magistrates. Whereas in constitutional governments they take the contrary course; the few have the negative, not the affirmative power; the affirmation of everything rests with the multitude.

These, then, are our conclusions respecting the deliberative, that is, the supreme element in states.

XV Next we will proceed to consider the distribution of offices; this too, being a part of politics concerning which many questions arise:—What shall their number be? Over what shall they preside, and what shall be their duration? Sometimes they last for six months, sometimes for less; sometimes they are annual, whilst in other cases offices are held for still longer periods. Shall they be for life or for a long term of years; or, if for a short term only, shall the same persons hold them over and over again, or once only? Also about the appointment to them—from whom are they to be chosen, by whom, and how? We should first be in a position to say what are the possible varieties of them, and then we may proceed to determine which are suited to different forms of government. But what are to be included under the term 'offices'? That is a question not quite so easily answered. For a political community requires many officers; and not every one who is chosen by vote or by lot is to be regarded as a ruler. In the first place there are the priests, who must be distinguished from political officers; masters of choruses and heralds, even ambassadors, are elected by vote. Some duties of superintendence again are political, extending either to all the citizens in a single sphere of action, like the office of the general who superintends them when they are in the field, or to a section of them only, like the inspectorships of women or of youth. Other offices are concerned with household management, like that of the corn measurers who exist in many states and are elected officers. There are also menial offices which the rich have executed by their slaves. Speaking generally, those are to be called offices to which the duties are assigned of deliberating about certain measures and of judging and commanding, especially the last; for to command is the especial duty of a magistrate. But the question is not of any importance in practice; no one has ever brought into court the meaning of the word, although such problems have a speculative interest.

What kinds of offices, and how many, are necessary to the existence of a state, and which, if not necessary, yet conduce to its well-being, are much more important considerations, affecting all constitutions, but more especially small states. For in great states it is possible, and indeed necessary, that every office should have a special function; where the citizens are numerous, many may hold office. And so it happens that some offices a man holds a second time only after a long interval, and others he holds once only; and certainly every work is better done which receives the sole, and not the divided attention of the worker. But in small states it is necessary to combine many offices in a few hands, since the small number of citizens does not admit of many holding office:—for who will there be to succeed them? And yet small states at times require the same offices and laws as large ones; the difference is that the one want them often, the others only after long intervals. Hence there is no reason why the care of many offices should not be imposed on the same person, for they will not interfere with each other. When the population is small, offices should be like the spits which also serve to hold a lamp.[47] We must first ascertain how many magistrates are necessary in every state, and also how many are not exactly necessary, but are nevertheless useful, and then there will be no difficulty in seeing what offices can be combined in one. We should also know over which matters several local tribunals are to have jurisdiction, and in which authority should be centralized: for example, should one person keep order in the market and another in some other place, or should the same person be responsible everywhere? Again, should offices be divided according to the subjects with which they deal, or according to the persons with whom they deal: I mean to say, should one person see to good order in general, or one look after the boys, another after the women, and so on? Further, under different constitutions, should the magistrates be the same or different? For example, in democracy, oligarchy, aristocracy, monarchy, should there be the same magistrates, al-

[47] Cp. Bk. 1, II.

though they are elected, not out of equal or similar classes of citizens, but differently under different constitutions—in aristocracies, for example, they are chosen from the educated, in oligarchies from the wealthy, and in democracies from the free—or are there certain differences in the offices answering to them as well, and may the same be suitable to some, but different offices to others? For in some states it may be convenient that the same office should have a more extensive, in other states a narrower sphere. Special offices are peculiar to certain forms of government:—for example that of probuli, which is not a democratic office, although a bule or council is. There must be some body of men whose duty is to prepare measures for the people in order that they may not be diverted from their business; when these are few in number, the state inclines to an oligarchy: or rather the probuli must always be few, and are therefore an oligarchical element. But when both institutions exist in a state, the probuli are a check on the council; for the counsellor is a democratic element, but the probuli are oligarchical. Even the power of the council disappears when democracy has taken that extreme form in which the people themselves are always meeting and deliberating about everything. This is the case when the members of the assembly receive abundant pay; for they have nothing to do and are always holding assemblies and deciding everything for themselves. A magistracy which controls the boys or the women, or any similar office, is suited to an aristocracy rather than to a democracy; for how can the magistrates prevent the wives of the poor from going out of doors? Neither is it an oligarchical office; for the wives of the oligarchs are too fine to be controlled.

Enough of these matters. I will now inquire into appointments to offices. The varieties depend on three terms, and the combinations of these give all possible modes: first, who appoints? secondly, from whom? and thirdly, how? Each of these three admits of three varieties: (A) All the citizens, or (B) only some, appoint. Either (1) the magistrates are chosen out of all or (2) out of some who are distinguished either by a property qualification, or by birth, or merit, or for some special reason, as at Megara only those were eligible who had returned from exile and fought together against the democracy. They may be appointed either (a) by vote or (b) by lot. Again, these several varieties may be coupled, I mean that (C) some officers may be elected by some, others by all, and (3) some again out of some, and others out of all, and (c) some by vote and others by lot. Each variety of these terms admits of four modes.

For either (A 1 a) all may appoint from all by vote, or (A 1 b) all from all by lot, or (A 2 a) all from some by vote, or (A 2 b) all from some by lot (and if from all, either by sections, as, for example, by tribes, and wards, and phratries, until all the citizens have been gone through; or the citizens may be in all cases eligible indiscriminately); or again (A 1 c, A 2 c) to some offices in the one way, to some in the other. Again, if it is only some that appoint, they may do so either (B 1 a) from all by vote, or (B 1 b) from all by lot, or (B 2 a) from some by vote, or (B 2 b) from some by lot, or to some offices in the one way, to others in the other, i.e. (B 1 c) from all, to some offices by vote, to some by lot, and (B 2 c) from some, to some offices by vote, to some by lot. Thus the modes that arise, apart from two (C, 3) out of the three couplings, number twelve. Of these systems two are popular, that all should appoint from all (A 1 a) by vote or (A 1 b) by lot—or (A 1 c) by both. That all should not appoint at once, but should appoint from all or from some either by lot or by vote or by both, or appoint to some offices from all and to others from some ('by both' meaning to some offices by lot, to others by vote), is characteristic of a polity. And (B 1 c) that some should appoint from all, to some offices by vote, to others by lot, is also characteristic of a polity, but more oligarchical than the former method. And (A 3 a, b, c, B 3 a, b, c) to appoint from both, to some offices from all, to others from some, is characteristic of a polity with a leaning towards aristocracy. That (B 2) some should appoint from some is oligarchical—even (B 2 b) that some should appoint from some by lot (and if this does not actually occur, it is none the less oligarchical in character), or (B 2 c) that some should appoint from some by both. (B 1 a) that some should appoint from all, and (A 2 a) that all should appoint from some, by vote, is aristocratic.

These are the different modes of constituting magistrates, and these correspond to different forms of government:—which are proper to which, or how they ought to be established, will be evident when we determine the nature of their powers.[48] By powers I mean such powers as a magistrate exercises over the revenue or in defence of the country; for there are various kinds of power:

[48] The promise is not fulfilled in the *Politics*.

the power of the general, for example, is not the same with that which regulates contracts in the market.

XVI Of the three parts of government, the judicial remains to be considered, and this we shall divide on the same principle. There are three points on which the varieties of law-courts depend: The persons from whom they are appointed, the matters with which they are concerned, and the manner of their appointment. I mean, (1) are the judges taken from all, or from some only? (2) how many kinds of law-courts are there? (3) are the judges chosen by vote or by lot?

First, let me determine how many kinds of law-courts there are. There are eight in number: One is the court of audits or scrutinies; a second takes cognizance of ordinary offences against the state; a third is concerned with treason against the constitution; the fourth determines disputes respecting penalties, whether raised by magistrates or by private persons; the fifth decides the more important civil cases; the sixth tries cases of homicide, which are of various kinds, (*a*) premeditated, (*b*) involuntary, (*c*) cases in which the guilt is confessed but the justice is disputed; and there may be a fourth court (*d*) in which murderers who have fled from justice are tried after their return; such as the Court of Phreatto is said to be at Athens. But cases of this sort rarely happen at all even in large cities. The different kinds of homicide may be tried either by the same or by different courts. (7) There are courts for strangers:—of these there are two subdivisions, (*a*) for the settlement of their disputes with one another, (*b*) for the settlement of disputes between them and the citizens. And besides all these there must be (8) courts for small suits about sums of a drachma up to five drachmas, or a little more, which have to be determined, but they do not require many judges.

Nothing more need be said of these small suits, nor of the courts for homicide and for strangers:—I would rather speak of political cases, which, when mismanaged, create division and disturbances in constitutions.

Now if all the citizens judge, in all the different cases which I have distinguished, they may be appointed by vote or by lot, or sometimes by lot and sometimes by vote. Or when a single class of causes are tried, the judges who decide them may be appointed, some by vote, and some by lot. These then are the four modes of appointing judges from the whole people, and there will be likewise four modes, if they are elected from a part only; for they may be appointed from some by vote and judge in all causes; or they may be appointed from some by lot and judge in all causes; or they may be elected in some cases by vote, and in some cases taken by lot, or some courts, even when judging the same causes, may be composed of members some appointed by vote and some by lot. These modes, then, as was said, answer to those previously mentioned.

Once more, the modes of appointment may be combined; I mean, that some may be chosen out of the whole people, others out of some, some out of both; for example, the same tribunal may be composed of some who were elected out of all, and of others who were elected out of some, either by vote or by lot or by both.

In how many forms law-courts can be established has now been considered. The first form, viz. that in which the judges are taken from all the citizens, and in which all causes are tried, is democratical; the second, which is composed of a few only who try all causes, oligarchical; the third, in which some courts are taken from all classes, and some from certain classes only, aristocratical and constitutional.

BOOK FIFTH

I The design which we proposed to ourselves is now nearly completed.[1] Next in order follow the causes of revolution in states, how many, and of what nature they are; what modes of destruction apply to particular states, and out of what, and into what they mostly change; also what are the modes of preservation in states generally, or in a particular state, and by what means each state may be best preserved: these questions remain to be considered.

In the first place we must assume as our starting-point that in the many forms of government which have sprung up there has always been an acknowledgement of justice and proportionate equality, although mankind fail in attaining them, as indeed I have already explained.[2] Democracy, for example, arises out of the notion that those who are equal in any respect are equal in all respects; because men are equally free, they claim to be absolutely equal. Oligarchy is based on the notion that those who are unequal in one respect are in all respects unequal; being unequal, that is, in property, they suppose themselves to be unequal absolutely. The democrats think that as they are equal they ought to be equal in all things; while the oligarchs, under the idea that they are unequal, claim too much, which is one form of inequality. All these forms of government have a kind of justice, but, tried by an absolute standard, they are faulty; and, therefore, both parties, whenever their share in the government does not accord with their preconceived ideas, stir up revolution. Those who excel in virtue have the best right of all to rebel (for they alone can with reason be deemed absolutely unequal),[3] but then they are of all men the least inclined to do so.[4] There is also a superiority which is claimed by men of rank; for they are thought noble because they spring from wealthy and virtuous ancestors.[5] Here then, so to speak, are opened the very springs and fountains of revolution; and hence arise two sorts of changes in governments; the one affecting the constitution, when men seek to change from an existing form into some other, for example, from democracy into oligarchy, and from oligarchy into democracy, or from either of

[1] Cp. Bk. 4, II.
[2] Bk. 3, XII, Cp. IX.
[3] Cp. Bk. 3, XIII.
[4] Cp. Bk. 5, IV.
[5] Cp. Bk. 4, VIII.

them into constitutional government or aristocracy, and conversely; the other not affecting the constitution, when, without disturbing the form of government, whether oligarchy, or monarchy, or any other, they try to get the administration into their own hands.[6] Further, there is a question of degree; an oligarchy, for example, may become more or less oligarchical, and a democracy more or less democratical; and in like manner the characteristics of the other forms of government may be more or less strictly maintained. Or the revolution may be directed against a portion of the constitution only, e. g. the establishment or overthrow of a particular office: as at Sparta it is said that Lysander attempted to overthrow the monarchy, and King Pausanias,[7] the Ephoralty. At Epidamnus, too, the change was partial. For instead of phylarchs or heads of tribes, a council was appointed; but to this day the magistrates are the only members of the ruling class who are compelled to go to the Heliaea when an election takes place, and the office of the single archon[8] was another oligarchical feature. Everywhere inequality is a cause of revolution, but an inequality in which there is no proportion—for instance, a perpetual monarchy among equals; and always it is the desire of equality which rises in rebellion.

Now equality is of two kinds, numerical and proportional; by the first I mean sameness or equality in number or size; by the second, equality of ratios. For example, the excess of three over two is numerically equal to the excess of two over one; whereas four exceeds two in the same ratio in which two exceeds one, for two is the same part of four that one is of two, namely, the half. As I was saying before,[9] men agree that justice in the abstract is proportion, but they differ in that some think that if they are equal in any respect they are equal absolutely, others that if they are unequal in any respect they should be unequal in all. Hence there are two principal forms of government, democracy and oligarchy; for good birth and virtue are rare, but wealth and numbers are more common. In what city shall we find a hundred persons of good birth and of virtue? whereas the rich everywhere abound. That a state should be ordered, simply and wholly, according to either kind of equality, is not a good thing; the proof is the fact that such forms of government never last. They are

[6] Cp. Bk. 4, VIII.
[7] Cp. Bk. 7, XVI.
[8] Cp. Bk. 3.
[9] Cp. l. 9.

originally based on a mistake, and, as they begin badly, cannot fail to end badly. The inference is that both kinds of equality should be employed; numerical in some cases, and proportionate in others.

Still democracy appears to be safer and less liable to revolution than oligarchy.[10] For in oligarchies[11] there is the double danger of the oligarchs falling out among themselves and also with the people; but in democracies[12] there is only the danger of a quarrel with the oligarchs. No dissension worth mentioning arises among the people themselves. And we may further remark that a government which is composed of the middle class more nearly approximates to democracy than to oligarchy, and is the safest of the imperfect forms of government.

II In considering how dissensions and political revolutions arise, we must first of all ascertain the beginnings and causes of them which affect constitutions generally. They may be said to be three in number; and we have now to give an outline of each. We want to know (1) what is the feeling? (2) what are the motives of those who make them? (3) whence arise political disturbances and quarrels? The universal and chief cause of this revolutionary feeling has been already mentioned[13]; viz. the desire of equality, when men think that they are equal to others who have more than themselves; or, again, the desire of inequality and superiority, when conceiving themselves to be superior they think that they have not more but the same or less than their inferiors; pretensions which may and may not be just. Inferiors revolt in order that they may be equal, and equals that they may be superior. Such is the state of mind which creates revolutions. The motives for making them are the desire of gain and honour, or the fear of dishonour and loss; the authors of them want to divert punishment or dishonour from themselves or their friends. The causes and reasons of revolutions, whereby men are themselves affected in the way described, and about the things which I have mentioned, viewed in one way may be regarded as seven, and in another as more than seven. Two of them have been already noticed[14]; but they act in a different manner, for men are excited

[10] Cp. Bk. 4, XI.
[11] Cp. VI.
[12] Cp. V.
[13] Bk. 4, XVI.
[14] l. 15.

against one another by the love of gain and honour—not, as in the case which I have just supposed, in order to obtain them for themselves, but at seeing others, justly or unjustly, engrossing them. Other causes are insolence, fear, excessive predominance, contempt, disproportionate increase in some part of the state; causes of another sort are election intrigues, carelessness, neglect about trifles, dissimilarity of elements.

III What share insolence and avarice have in creating revolutions, and how they work, is plain enough. When the magistrates are insolent and grasping they conspire against one another and also against the constitution from which they derive their power, making their gains either at the expense of individuals or of the public. It is evident, again, what an influence honour exerts and how it is a cause of revolution. Men who are themselves dishonoured and who see others obtaining honours rise in rebellion; the honour or dishonour when undeserved is unjust; and just when awarded according to merit. Again, superiority is a cause of revolution when one or more persons have a power which is too much for the state and the power of the government; this is a condition of affairs out of which there arises a monarchy, or a family oligarchy. And therefore, in some places, as at Athens and Argos, they have recourse to ostracism.[15] But how much better to provide from the first that there should be no such pre-eminent individuals instead of letting them come into existence and then finding a remedy.

Another cause of revolution is fear. Either men have committed wrong, and are afraid of punishment, or they are expecting to suffer wrong and are desirous of anticipating their enemy. Thus at Rhodes the notables conspired against the people through fear of the suits that were brought against them.[16] Contempt is also a cause of insurrection and revolution; for example, in oligarchies—when those who have no share in the state are the majority, they revolt, because they think that they are the stronger. Or, again, in democracies, the rich despise the disorder and anarchy of the state; at Thebes, for example, where, after the battle of

[15] Cp. Bk. 3, XIII.
[16] Cp. Bk. 5, IV.

Oenophyta, the bad administration of the democracy led to its ruin. At Megara the fall of the democracy was due to a defeat occasioned by disorder and anarchy. And at Syracuse the democracy aroused contempt before the tyranny of Gelo arose; at Rhodes, before the insurrection.

Political revolutions also spring from a disproportionate increase in any part of the state. For as a body is made up of many members, and every member ought to grow in proportion,[17] that symmetry may be preserved; but loses its nature if the foot be four cubits long and the rest of the body two spans; and, should the abnormal increase be one of quality as well as of quantity, may even take the form of another animal: even so a state has many parts, of which some one may often grow imperceptibly; for example, the number of poor in democracies and in constitutional states. And this disproportion may sometimes happen by an accident, as at Tarentum, from a defeat in which many of the notables were slain in a battle with the Iapygians just after the Persian War, the constitutional government in consequence becoming a democracy; or as was the case at Argos, where the Argives, after their army had been cut to pieces on the seventh day of the month by Cleomenes the Lacedaemonian, were compelled to admit to citizenship some of their perioeci; and at Athens, when, after frequent defeats of their infantry at the time of the Peloponnesian War, the notables were reduced in number, because the soldiers had to be taken from the roll of citizens. Revolutions arise from this cause as well, in democracies as in other forms of government, but not to so great an extent. When the rich grow numerous or properties increase, the form of government changes into an oligarchy or a government of families. Forms of government also change—sometimes even without revolution, owing to election contests, as at Heraea (where, instead of electing their magistrates, they took them by lot, because the electors were in the habit of choosing their own partisans); or owing to carelessness, when disloyal persons are allowed to find their way into the highest offices, as at Oreum, where, upon the accession of Heracleodorus to office, the oligarchy was overthrown, and changed by him into a constitutional and democratical government.

[17] Cp. Bk. 3, XIII.

Again, the revolution may be facilitated by the slightness of the change; I mean that a great change may sometimes slip into the constitution through neglect of a small matter; at Ambracia, for instance, the qualification for office, small at first, was eventually reduced to nothing. For the Ambraciots thought that a small qualification was much the same as none at all.

Another cause of revolution is difference of races which do not at once acquire a common spirit; for a state is not the growth of a day, any more than it grows out of a multitude brought together by accident. Hence the reception of strangers in colonies, either at the time of their foundation or afterwards, has generally produced revolution; for example, the Achaeans who joined the Troezenians in the foundation of Sybaris, becoming later the more numerous, expelled them; hence the curse fell upon Sybaris. At Thurii the Sybarites quarrelled with their fellow-colonists; thinking that the land belonged to them, they wanted too much of it and were driven out. At Byzantium the new colonists were detected in a conspiracy, and were expelled by force of arms; the people of Antissa, who had received the Chian exiles, fought with them, and drove them out; and the Zancleans, after having received the Samians, were driven by them out of their own city. The citizens of Apollonia on the Euxine, after the introduction of a fresh body of colonists, had a revolution; the Syracusans, after the expulsion of their tyrants, having admitted strangers and mercenaries to the rights of citizenship, quarrelled and came to blows; the people Amphipolis, having received Chalcidian colonists, were nearly all expelled by them.

Now, in oligarchies the masses make revolution under the idea that they are unjustly treated, because, as I said before,[18] they are equals, and have not an equal share, and in democracies the notables revolt, because they are not equals, and yet have only an equal share.

Again, the situation of cities is a cause of revolution when the country is not naturally adapted to preserve the unity of the state. For example, the Chytians at Clazomenae did not agree with the people of the island; and the people of Colophon quarrelled with the Notians; at Athens too, the inhabitants of the Piraeus are more democratic than those who live in the city. For just as in war the impediment of a ditch, though ever so small, may break a regi-

[18] Bk. 4, XVI.

ment, so every cause of difference, however slight, makes a breach in a city. The greatest opposition is confessedly that of virtue and vice; next comes that of wealth and poverty; and there are other antagonistic elements, greater or less, of which one is this difference of place.

IV In revolutions the occasions may be trifling, but great interests are at stake. Even trifles are most important when they concern the rulers, as was the case of old at Syracuse; for the Syracusan constitution was once changed by a love-quarrel of two young men, who were in the government. The story is that while one of them was away from home his beloved was gained over by his companion, and he to revenge himself seduced the other's wife. They then drew the members of the ruling class into their quarrel and so split all the people into portions. We learn from this story that we should be on our guard against the beginnings of such evils, and should put an end to the quarrels of chiefs and mighty men. The mistake lies in the beginning—as the proverb says—'Well begun is half done'; so an error at the beginning, though quite small, bears the same ratio to the errors in the other parts. In general, when the notables quarrel, the whole city is involved, as happened in Hestiaea after the Persian War. The occasion was the division of an inheritance; one of two brothers refused to give an account of their father's property and the treasure which he had found: so the poorer of the two quarrelled with him and enlisted in his cause the popular party, the other, who was very rich, the wealthy classes.

At Delphi, again, a quarrel about a marriage was the beginning of all the troubles which followed. In this case the bridegroom, fancying some occurrence to be of evil omen, came to the bride, and went away without taking her. Whereupon her relations, thinking that they were insulted by him, put some of the sacred treasure among his offerings while he was sacrificing, and then slew him, pretending that he had been robbing the temple. At Mytilene, too, a dispute about heiresses was the beginning of many misfortunes, and led to the war with the Athenians in which Paches took their city. A wealthy citizen, named Timophanes, left two daughters; Dexander, another citizen, wanted to obtain them for his sons; but he was rejected in his suit, whereupon he stirred up a revolution, and instigated the Athenians (of whom he was proxenus) to interfere. A similar quarrel about an heiress arose at Phocis between Mnaseas the father of Mnason, and Euthycrates the father of Onomarchus; this was the beginning of the Sacred War. A marriage-quarrel was also the cause of a change in the government of Epidamnus. A certain man betrothed his daughter to a person whose father, having been made a magistrate, fined the father of the girl, and the latter, stung by the insult, conspired with the unenfranchised classes to overthrow the state.

Governments also change into oligarchy or into democracy or into a constitutional government because the magistrates, or some other section of the state, increase in power or renown. Thus at Athens the reputation gained by the court of the Areopagus, in the Persian War, seemed to tighten the reins of government. On the other hand, the victory of Salamis,[19] which was gained by the common people who served in the fleet, and won for the Athenians the empire due to command of the sea, strengthened the democracy. At Argos, the notables, having distinguished themselves against the Lacedaemonians in the battle of Mantinea, attempted to put down the democracy. At Syracuse, the people, having been the chief authors of the victory in the war with the Athenians, changed the constitutional government into democracy. At Chalcis, the people, uniting with the notables, killed Phoxus the tyrant, and then seized the government. At Ambracia,[20] the people, in like manner, having joined with the conspirators in expelling the tyrant Periander, transferred the government to themselves. And generally, it should be remembered that those who have secured power to the state, whether private citizens, or magistrates, or tribes, or any other part or section of the state, are apt to cause revolutions. For either envy of their greatness draws others into rebellion, or they themselves, in their pride of superiority, are unwilling to remain on a level with others.

Revolutions also break out when opposite parties, e. g. the rich and the people, are equally balanced, and there is little or no middle class; for, if either party were manifestly superior, the other would not risk an attack upon them. And, for this reason, those who are eminent in virtue usually do not stir up insurrec-

19 Cp. Bk. 2, XII; Bk. 8, VI.

20 Cp. Bk. 5, X.

tions, always a minority. Such are the beginnings and causes of the disturbances and revolutions to which every form of government is liable.

Revolutions are effected in two ways, by force and by fraud. Force may be applied either at the time of making the revolution or afterwards. Fraud, again, is of two kinds; for (1) sometimes the citizens are deceived into acquiescing in a change of government, and afterwards they are held in subjection against their will. This was what happened in the case of the Four Hundred, who deceived the people by telling them that the king would provide money for the war against the Lacedaemonians, and, having cheated the people, still endeavoured to retain the government. (2) In other cases the people are persuaded at first, and afterwards, by a repetition of the persuasion, their goodwill and allegiance are retained. The revolutions which effect constitutions generally spring from the above-mentioned causes.[21]

V And now, taking each constitution separately, we must see what follows from the principles already laid down.

Revolutions in democracies are generally caused by the intemperance of demagogues, who either in their private capacity lay information against rich men until they compel them to combine (for a common danger unites even the bitterest enemies), or coming forward in public stir up the people against them. The truth of this remark is proved by a variety of examples. At Cos the democracy was overthrown because wicked demagogues arose, and the notables combined. At Rhodes the demagogues not only provided pay for the multitude, but prevented them from making good to the trierarchs the sums which had been expended by them; and they, in consequence of the suits which were brought against them, were compelled to combine and put down the democracy.[22] The democracy at Heraclea was overthrown shortly after the foundation of the colony by the injustice of the demagogues, which drove out the notables, who came back in a body and put an end to the democracy. Much in the same manner the democracy at Megara[23] was overturned; there the demagogues drove out many of the notables in order that they might be able

[21] Cp. Bk. 5, I.
[22] Cp. Bk. 5, III.
[23] Cp. Bk. 5, III; Bk. 4, XV.

to confiscate their property. At length the exiles, becoming numerous, returned, and, engaging and defeating the people, established the oligarchy. The same thing happened with the democracy of Cyme, which was overthrown by Thrasymachus. And we may observe that in most states the changes have been of this character. For sometimes the demagogues, in order to curry favour with the people, wrong the notables and so force them to combine;—either they make a division of their property, or diminish their incomes by the imposition of public services, and sometimes they bring accusations against the rich that they may have their wealth to confiscate.[24]

Of old, the demagogue was also a general, and then democracies changed into tyrannies. Most of the ancient tyrants were originally demagogues.[25] They are not so now, but they were then; and the reason is that they were generals and not orators, for oratory had not yet come into fashion. Whereas in our day, when the art of rhetoric has made such progress, the orators lead the people, but their ignorance of military matters prevents them from usurping power; at any rate instances to the contrary are few and slight. Tyrannies were more common formerly than now, for this reason also, that great power was placed in the hands of individuals; thus a tyranny arose at Miletus out of the office of the Prytanis, who had supreme authority in many important matters.[26] Moreover, in those days, when cities were not large, the people dwelt in the fields, busy at their work; and their chiefs, if they possessed any military talent, seized the opportunity, and winning the confidence of the masses by professing their hatred of the wealthy, they succeeded in obtaining the tyranny. Thus at Athens Peisistratus led a faction against the men of the plain, and Theagenes at Megara slaughtered the cattle of the wealthy, which he found by the river side, where they had put them to graze in land not their own. Dionysius, again, was thought worthy of the tyranny because he denounced Daphnaeus and the rich; his enmity to the notables won for him the confidence of the people. Changes also take place from the ancient to the latest form of democracy; for where there is a popular election of the magistrates and no property qualification, the aspirants for office get

[24] Cp. Bk. 5, VIII.
[25] Cp. Bk. 5, X; Plato, *Rep.* viii. 565 D.
[26] Cp. Bk. 5, X.

hold of the people, and contrive at last even to set them above the laws. A more or less complete cure for this state of things is for the separate tribes, and not the whole people, to elect the magistrates.

These are the principal causes of revolutions in democracies.

VI There are two patent causes of revolutions in oligarchies: (1) First, when the oligarchs oppress the people, for then anybody is good enough to be their champion, especially if he be himself a member of the oligarchy, as Lygdamis at Naxos, who afterwards came to be tyrant. But revolutions which commence outside the governing class may be further subdivided. Sometimes, when the government is very exclusive, the revolution is brought about by persons of the wealthy class who are excluded, as happened at Massalia and Istros and Heraclea, and other cities. Those who had no share in the government created a disturbance, until first the elder brothers, and then the younger, were admitted; for in some places father and son, in others elder and younger brothers, do not hold office together. At Massalia the oligarchy became more like a constitutional government, but at Istros ended in a democracy, and at Heraclea was enlarged to 600. At Cnidos, again, the oligarchy underwent a considerable change. For the notables fell out among themselves, because only a few shared in the government; there existed among them the rule already mentioned, that father and son could not hold office together, and, if there were several brothers, only the eldest was admitted. The people took advantage of the quarrel, and choosing one of the notables to be their leader, attacked and conquered the oligarchs, who were divided, and division is always a source of weakness. The city of Erythrae, too, in old times was ruled, and ruled well, by the Basilidae, but the people took offence at the narrowness of the oligarchy and changed the constitution.

(2) Of internal causes of revolutions in oligarchies one is the personal rivalry of the oligarchs, which leads them to play the demagogue. Now, the oligarchical demagogue is of two sorts: either (*a*) he practises upon the oligarchs themselves (for, although the oligarchy are quite a small number, there may be a demagogue among them, as at Athens Charicles' party won power by

courting the Thirty, that of Phrynichus by courting the Four Hundred); or (*b*) the oligarchs may play the demagogue with the people. This was the case at Larissa, where the guardians of the citizens endeavoured to gain over the people because they were elected by them; and such is the fate of all oligarchies in which the magistrates are elected, as at Abydos, not by the class to which they belong, but by the heavy-armed or by the people, although they may be required to have a high qualification, or to be members of a political club; or, again, where the law-courts are composed of persons outside the government, the oligarchs flatter the people in order to obtain a decision in their own favour, and so they change the constitution; this happened at Heraclea in Pontus. Again, oligarchies change whenever any attempt is made to narrow them; for then those who desire equal rights are compelled to call in the people. Changes in the oligarchy also occur when the oligarchs waste their private property by extravagant living; for then they want to innovate, and either try to make themselves tyrants, or install some one else in the tyranny, as Hipparinus did Dionysius at Syracuse, and as at Amphipolis[27] a man named Cleotimus introduced Chalcidian colonists, and when they arrived, stirred them up against the rich. For a like reason in Aegina the person who carried on the negotiation with Chares endeavoured to revolutionize the state. Sometimes a party among the oligarchs try directly to create a political change; sometimes they rob the treasury, and then either the thieves or, as happened at Apollonia in Pontus, those who resist them in their thieving quarrel with the rulers. But an oligarchy which is at unity with itself is not easily destroyed from within; of this we may see an example at Pharsalus, for there, although the rulers are few in number, they govern a large city, because they have a good understanding among themselves.

Oligarchies, again, are overthrown when another oligarchy is created within the original one, that is to say, when the whole governing body is small and yet they do not all share in the highest offices. Thus at Elis the governing body was a small senate; and very few ever found their way into it, because the senators were only ninety in number, and were elected for life and out of certain families in a manner similar to the Lacedaemonian elders. Oligarchy is liable to revolutions alike in war and in peace; in

[27] Cp. Bk. 5, III.

war because, not being able to trust the people, the oligarchs are compelled to hire mercenaries, and the general who is in command of them often ends in becoming a tyrant, as Timophanes did at Corinth; or if there are more generals than one they make themselves into a company of tyrants. Sometimes the oligarchs, fearing this danger, give the people a share in the government because their services are necessary to them. And in time of peace, from mutual distrust, the two parties hand over the defence of the state to the army and to an arbiter between the two factions, who often ends the master of both. This happened at Larissa when Simos the Aleuad had the government, and at Abydos in the days of Iphiades and the political clubs. Revolutions also arise out of marriages or lawsuits which lead to the overthrow of one party among the oligarchs by another. Of quarrels about marriages I have already mentioned[28] some instances; another occurred at Eretria, where Diagoras overturned the oligarchy of the knights because he had been wronged about a marriage. A revolution at Heraclea, and another at Thebes, both arose out of decisions of law-courts upon a charge of adultery; in both cases the punishment was just, but executed in the spirit of party, at Heraclea upon Eurytion, and at Thebes upon Archias; for their enemies were jealous of them and so had them pilloried in the agora. Many oligarchies have been destroyed by some members of the ruling class taking offence at their excessive despotism; for example, the oligarchy at Cnidus and at Chios.

Changes of constitutional governments, and also of oligarchies which limit the office of counsellor, judge, or other magistrate to persons having a certain money qualification, often occur by accident. The qualification may have been originally fixed according to the circumstances of the time, in such a manner as to include in an oligarchy a few only, or in a constitutional government the middle class. But after a time of prosperity, whether arising from peace or some other good fortune, the same property becomes many times as valuable, and then everybody participates in every office; this happens sometimes gradually and insensibly, and sometimes quickly. These are the causes of changes and revolutions in oligarchies.

We must remark generally, both of democracies and oligarchies, that they sometimes change, not into the opposite forms of

[28] Bk. 5, III–IV.

government, but only into another variety of the same class; I mean to say, from those forms of democracy and oligarchy which are regulated by law into those which are arbitrary, and conversely.

VII In aristocracies revolutions are stirred up when a few only share in the honours of the state; a cause which has been already shown[29] to affect oligarchies; for an aristocracy is a sort of oligarchy, and, like an oligarchy, is the government of a few, although few not for the same reason; hence the two are often confounded. And revolutions will be most likely to happen, and must happen, when the mass of the people are of the high-spirited kind, and have a notion that they are as good as their rulers. Thus at Lacedaemon the so-called Partheniae, who were the sons[30] of the Spartan peers, attempted a revolution, and, being detected, were sent away to colonize Tarentum. Again, revolutions occur when great men who are at least of equal merit are dishonoured by those higher in office, as Lysander was by the kings of Sparta; or, when a brave man is excluded from the honours of the state, like Cinadon, who conspired against the Spartans in the reign of Agesilaus; or, again, when some are very poor and others very rich, a state of society which is most often the result of war, as at Lacedaemon in the days of the Messenian War; this is proved from the poem of Tyrtaeus, entitled 'Good Order'; for he speaks of certain citizens who were ruined by the war and wanted to have a redistribution of the land. Again, revolutions arise when an individual who is great, and might be greater, wants to rule alone, as, at Lacedaemon, Pausanias, who was general in the Persian War, or like Hanno at Carthage.

Constitutional governments and aristocracies are commonly overthrown owing to some deviation from justice in the constitution itself; the cause of the downfall is, in the former, the ill-mingling of the two elements, democracy and oligarchy; in the latter, of the three elements, democracy, oligarchy, and virtue, but especially democracy and oligarchy. For to combine these is the endeavour of constitutional governments; and most of the so-called aristocracies have a like aim,[31] but differ from polities in

[29] Bk. 5, VI.
[30] i. e. the illegitimate sons.
[31] Cp. Bk. 4, VII.

the mode of combination; hence some of them are more and some less permanent. Those which incline more to oligarchy are called aristocracies, and those which incline to democracy constitutional governments. And therefore the latter are the safer of the two; for the greater the number, the greater the strength, and when men are equal they are contented. But the rich, if the constitution gives them power, are apt to be insolent and avaricious; and, in general, whichever way the constitution inclines, in that direction it changes as either party gains strength, a constitutional government becoming a democracy, an aristocracy an oligarchy. But the process may be reversed, and aristocracy may change into democracy. This happens when the poor, under the idea that they are being wronged, force the constitution to take an opposite form. In like manner constitutional governments change into oligarchies. The only stable principle of government is equality according to proportion, and for every man to enjoy his own.

What I have just mentioned actually happened at Thurii,[32] where the qualification for office, at first high, was therefore reduced, and the magistrates increased in number. The notables had previously acquired the whole of the land contrary to law; for the government tended to oligarchy, and they were able to encroach. . . . But the people, who had been trained by war, soon got the better of the guards kept by the oligarchs, until those who had too much gave up their land.

Again, since all aristocratical governments incline to oligarchy, the notables are apt to be grasping; thus at Lacedaemon, where property tends to pass into few hands,[33] the notables can do too much as they like, and are allowed to marry whom they please. The city of Locri was ruined by a marriage connexion with Dionysius, but such a thing could never have happened in a democracy, or in a well-balanced aristocracy.

I have already remarked that in all states revolutions are occasioned by trifles.[34] In aristocracies, above all, they are of a gradual and imperceptible nature. The citizens begin by giving up some part of the constitution, and so with greater ease the government change something else which is a little more important, until they have undermined the whole fabric of the state. At Thurii there was a law that generals should only be re-elected after an

[32] Cp. Bk. 5, III.
[33] Cp. Bk. 2, IX.
[34] Bk. 5, III.

interval of five years, and some young men who were popular with the soldiers of the guard for their military prowess, despising the magistrates and thinking that they would easily gain their purpose, wanted to abolish this law and allow their generals to hold perpetual commands; for they well knew that the people would be glad enough to elect them. Whereupon the magistrates who had charge of these matters, and who are called councillors, at first determined to resist, but they afterwards consented, thinking that, if only this one law was changed, no further inroad would be made on the constitution. But other changes soon followed which they in vain attempted to oppose; and the state passed into the hands of the revolutionists, who established a dynastic oligarchy.

All constitutions are overthrown either from within or from without; the latter, when there is some government close at hand having an opposite interest, or at a distance, but powerful. This was exemplified in the old times of the Athenians and the Lacedaemonians; the Athenians everywhere put down the oligarchies, and the Lacedaemonians the democracies.[35]

I have now explained what are the chief causes of revolutions and dissensions in states.

VIII We have next to consider what means there are of preserving constitutions in general, and in particular cases. In the first place it is evident that if we know the causes which destroy constitutions, we also know the causes which preserve them; for opposites produce opposites, and destruction is the opposite of preservation.[36]

In all well-attempered governments there is nothing which should be more jealously maintained than the spirit of obedience to law, more especially in small matters; for transgression creeps in unperceived and at last ruins the state, just as the constant recurrence of small expenses in time eats up a fortune. The expense does not take place all at once, and therefore is not observed; the mind is deceived, as in the fallacy which says that 'if each part is little, then the whole is little'. And this is true in one way, but not in another, for the whole and the all are not little, although they are made up of littles.

[35] Cp. Bk. 4, XI.

[36] Cp. *Nic. Eth.* v. 1129ª 13.

In the first place, then, men should guard against the beginning of change, and in the second place they should not rely upon the political devices of which I have already spoken[37] invented only to deceive the people, for they are proved by experience to be useless. Further, we note that oligarchies as well as aristocracies may last, not from any inhcrent stability in such forms of government, but because the rulers are on good terms both with the unenfranchised and with the governing classes, not maltreating any who are excluded from the government, but introducing into it the leading spirits among them.[38] They should never wrong the ambitious in a matter of honour, or the common people in a matter of money; and they should treat one another and their fellow-citizens in a spirit of equality. The equality which the friends of democracy seek to establish for the multitude is not only just but likewise expedient among equals. Hence, if the governing class are numerous, many democratic institutions are useful; for example, the restriction of the tenure of offices to six months, that all those who are of equal rank may share in them. Indeed, equals or peers when they are numerous become a kind of democracy, and therefore demagogues are very likely to arise among them, as I have already remarked.[39] The short tenure of office prevents oligarchies and aristocracies from falling into the hands of families; it is not easy for a person to do any great harm when his tenure of office is short, whereas long possession begets tyranny in oligarchies and democracies. For the aspirants to tyranny are either the principal men of the state, who in democracies are demagogues and in oligarchies members of ruling houses, or those who hold great offices, and have a long tenure of them.[40]

Constitutions are preserved when their destroyers are at a distance, and sometimes also because they are near, for the fear of them makes the government keep in hand the constitution. Wherefore the ruler who has a care of the constitution should invent terrors, and bring distant dangers near, in order that the citizens may be on their guard, and, like sentinels in a night-watch, never relax their attention. He should endeavour too by help of the laws to control the contentions and quarrels of the notables, and to prevent those who have not hitherto taken part

[37] Cp. Bk. 4, XII.
[38] Cp. Bk. 6, VI.
[39] Bk. 5, VI.
[40] Cp. Bk. 5, V.

in them from catching the spirit of contention. No ordinary man can discern the beginning of evil,[41] but only the true statesman.

As to the change produced in oligarchies and constitutional governments[42] by the alteration of the qualification, when this arises, not out of any variation in the qualification but only out of the increase of money, it is well to compare the general valuation of property with that of past years, annually in those cities in which the census is taken annually, and in larger cities every third or fifth year. If the whole is many times greater or many times less than when the ratings recognized by the constitution were fixed, there should be power given by law to raise or lower the qualification as the amount is greater or less. Where this is not done a constitutional government passes into an oligarchy, and an oligarchy is narrowed to a rule of families; or in the opposite case constitutional government becomes democracy, and oligarchy either constitutional government or democracy.

It is a principle common to democracy, oligarchy, and every other form of government not to allow the disproportionate increase of any citizen, but to give moderate honour for a long time rather than great honour for a short time. For men are easily spoilt; not every one can bear prosperity. But if this rule is not observed, at any rate the honours which are given all at once should be taken away by degrees and not all at once. Especially should the laws provide against any one having too much power, whether derived from friends or money; if he has, he should be sent clean out of the country.[43] And since innovations creep in through the private life of individuals also, there ought to be a magistracy which will have an eye to those whose life is not in harmony with the government, whether oligarchy or democracy or any other. And for a like reason an increase of prosperity in any part of the state should be carefully watched. The proper remedy for this evil is always to give the management of affairs and offices of state to opposite elements; such opposites are the virtuous and the many, or the rich and the poor. Another way is to combine the poor and the rich in one body, or to increase the middle class: thus an end will be put to the revolutions which arise from inequality.

But above all every state should be so administered and so

[41] Cp. Bk. 5, III.

[42] Cp. Bk. 5, VI.

[43] Cp. Bk. 5, III; Bk. 3, XIII.

regulated by law that its magistrates cannot possibly make money.[44] In oligarchies special precautions should be used against this evil. For the people do not take any great offence at being kept out of the government—indeed they are rather pleased than otherwise at having leisure for their private business—but what irritates them is to think that their rulers are stealing the public money; then they are doubly annoyed; for they lose both honour and profit. If office brought no profit, then and then only could democracy and aristocracy be combined; for both notables and people might have their wishes gratified. All would be able to hold office, which is the aim of democracy, and the notables would be magistrates, which is the aim of aristocracy. And this result may be accomplished when there is no possibility of making money out of the offices; for the poor will not want to have them when there is nothing to be gained from them—they would rather be attending to their own concerns; and the rich, who do not want money from the public treasury, will be able to take them; and so the poor will keep to their work and grow rich, and the notables will not be governed by the lower class. In order to avoid peculation of the public money, the transfer of the revenue should be made at a general assembly of the citizens, and duplicates of the accounts deposited with the different brotherhoods, companies, and tribes. And honours should be given by law to magistrates who have the reputation of being incorruptible. In democracies the rich should be spared; not only should their property not be divided, but their incomes also, which in some states are taken from them imperceptibly, should be protected. It is a good thing to prevent the wealthy citizens, even if they are willing, from undertaking expensive and useless public services, such as the giving of choruses, torch-races, and the like. In an oligarchy, on the other hand, great care should be taken of the poor, and lucrative offices should go to them; if any of the wealthy classes insult them, the offender should be punished more severely than if he had wronged one of his own class. Provision should be made that estates pass by inheritance and not by gift, and no person should have more than one inheritance; for in this way properties will be equalized, and more of the poor rise to competency. It is also expedient both in a democracy and in an oligarchy to assign to those who have less share in the govern-

[44] Cp. Bk. 5, XII.

ment (i. e. to the rich in a democracy and to the poor in an oligarchy) an equality or preference in all but the principal offices of state. The latter should be entrusted chiefly or only to members of the governing class.

IX There are three qualifications required in those who have to fill the highest offices—(1) first of all, loyalty to the established constitution; (2) the greatest administrative capacity; (3) virtue and justice of the kind proper to each form of government; for, if what is just is not the same in all governments, the quality of justice must also differ. There may be a doubt, however, when all these qualities do not meet in the same person, how the selection is to be made; suppose, for example, a good general is a bad man and not a friend to the constitution, and another man is loyal and just, which should we choose? In making the election ought we not to consider two points? what qualities are common, and what are rare. Thus in the choice of a general, we should regard his skill rather than his virtue; for few have military skill, but many have virtue. In any office of trust or stewardship, on the other hand, the opposite rule should be observed; for more virtue than ordinary is required in the holder of such an office, but the necessary knowledge is of a sort which all men possess.

It may, however, be asked what a man wants with virtue if he have political ability and is loyal, since these two qualities alone will make him do what is for the public interest. But may not men have both of them and yet be deficient in self-control? If, knowing and loving their own interests, they do not always attend to them, may they not be equally negligent of the interests of the public?

Speaking generally, we may say that whatever legal enactments are held to be for the interest of various constitutions, all these preserve them. And the great preserving principle is the one which has been repeatedly mentioned[45]—to have a care that the loyal citizens should be stronger than the disloyal. Neither should we forget the mean, which at the present day is lost sight of in perverted forms of government; for many practices which appear to be democratical are the ruin of democracies, and many which appear to be oligarchical are the ruin of oligarchies. Those who

[45] Bk. 4, XI; Bk. 6, V, Cp. Bk. 2, IX; Bk. 4, IX.

think that all virtue is to be found in their own party principles push matters to extremes; they do not consider that disproportion destroys a state. A nose which varies from the ideal of straightness to a hook or snub may still be of good shape and agreeable to the eye; but if the excess be very great, all symmetry is lost, and the nose at last ceases to be a nose at all on account of some excess in one direction or defect in the other; and this is true of every other part of the human body. The same law of proportion equally holds in states. Oligarchy or democracy, although a departure from the most perfect form, may yet be a good enough government, but if any one attempts to push the principles of either to an extreme, he will begin by spoiling the government and end by having none at all. Wherefore the legislator and the statesman ought to know what democratical measures save and what destroy a democracy, and what oligarchical measures save or destroy an oligarchy. For neither the one nor the other can exist or continue to exist unless both rich and poor are included in it. If equality of property is introduced, the state must of necessity take another form; for when by laws carried to excess one or other element in the state is ruined, the constitution is ruined.

There is an error common both to oligarchies and to democracies:—in the latter the demagogues, when the multitude are above the law, are always cutting the city in two by quarrels with the rich, whereas they should always profess to be maintaining their cause; just as in oligarchies the oligarchs should profess to maintain the cause of the people, and should take oaths the opposite of those which they now take. For there are cities in which they swear—'I will be an enemy to the people, and will devise all the harm against them which I can'; but they ought to exhibit and to entertain the very opposite feeling; in the form of their oath there should be an express declaration—'I will do no wrong to the people'.

But of all the things which I have mentioned that which most contributes to the permanence of constitutions is the adaptation of education to the form of government,[46] and yet in our own day this principle is universally neglected. The best laws, though sanctioned by every citizen of the state, will be of no avail unless the young are trained by habit and education in the spirit of the constitution, if the laws are democratical, democratically, or oli-

[46] Cp. Bk. 8, I.

garchically, if the laws are oligarchical. For there may be a want of self-discipline in states as well as in individuals. Now, to have been educated in the spirit of the constitution is not to perform the actions in which oligarchs or democrats delight, but those by which the existence of an oligarchy or of a democracy is made possible. Whereas among ourselves the sons of the ruling class in an oligarchy live in luxury,[47] but the sons of the poor are hardened by exercise and toil, and hence they are both more inclined and better able to make a revolution.[48] And in democracies of the more extreme type there has arisen a false idea of freedom which is contradictory to the true interests of the state. For two principles are characteristic of democracy, the government of the majority and freedom. Men think that what is just is equal; and that equality is the supremacy of the popular will; and that freedom means the doing what a man likes. In such democracies every one lives as he pleases, or in the words of Euripides, 'according to his fancy'. But this is all wrong; men should not think it slavery to live according to the rule of the constitution; for it is their salvation.

I have now discussed generally the causes of the revolution and destruction of states, and the means of their preservation and continuance.

X I have still to speak of monarchy, and the causes of its destruction and preservation. What I have said already respecting forms of constitutional government applies almost equally to royal and to tyrannical rule. For royal rule is of the nature of an aristocracy, and a tyranny is a compound of oligarchy and democracy in their most extreme forms; it is therefore most injurious to its subjects, being made up of two evil forms of government, and having the perversions and errors of both. These two forms of monarchy are contrary in their very origin. The appointment of a king is the resource of the better classes against the people, and he is elected by them out of their own number, because either he himself or his family excel in virtue and virtuous actions; whereas a tyrant is chosen from the people to be their protector against the notables, and in order to prevent them from being injured.

[47] Cp. Bk. 4, XI.

[48] Cp. Pl. *Rep.* viii. 556 D.

History shows that almost all tyrants have been demagogues who gained the favour of the people by their accusation of the notables.[49] At any rate this was the manner in which the tyrannies arose in the days when cities had increased in power. Others which were older originated in the ambition of kings wanting to overstep the limits of their hereditary power and become despots. Others again grew out of the class which were chosen to be chief magistrates; for in ancient times the people who elected them gave the magistrates, whether civil or religious, a long tenure. Others arose out of the custom which oligarchies had of making some individual supreme over the highest offices. In any of these ways an ambitious man had no difficulty, if he desired, in creating a tyranny, since he had the power in his hands already, either as king or as one of the officers of state.[50] Thus Pheidon at Argos and several others were originally kings, and ended by becoming tyrants; Phalaris, on the other hand, and the Ionian tyrants, acquired the tyranny by holding great offices. Whereas Panaetius at Leontini, Cypselus at Corinth, Peisistratus at Athens, Dionysius at Syracuse, and several others who afterwards became tyrants, were at first demagogues.

And so, as I was saying,[51] royalty ranks with aristocracy, for it is based upon merit, whether of the individual or of his family, or on benefits conferred,[52] or on these claims with power added to them. For all who have obtained this honour have benefited, or had in their power to benefit, states and nations; some, like Codrus, have prevented the state from being enslaved in war; others, like Cyrus, have given their country freedom, or have settled or gained a territory, like the Lacedaemonian, Macedonian, and Molossian kings. The idea of a king is to be a protector of the rich against unjust treatment, of the people against insult and oppression. Whereas a tyrant, as has often been repeated,[53] has no regard to any public interest, except as conducive to his private ends; his aim is pleasure, the aim of a king, honour. Wherefore also in their desires they differ; the tyrant is desirous of riches, the king, of what brings honour. And the guards of a king are citizens, but of a tyrant mercenaries.[54]

[49] Cp. Bk. 5, V; Plato, *Rep.* viii. 565 D.
[50] Cp. Bk. 5, V.
[51] l. 2.
[52] Cp. Bk. 3, XIV.
[53] Bk. 3, VII; Bk. 4, X.
[54] Cp. Bk. 3, XIV.

That tyranny has all the vices both of democracy and oligarchy is evident. As of oligarchy so of tyranny, the end is wealth; (for by wealth only can the tyrant maintain either his guard or his luxury). Both mistrust the people, and therefore deprive them of their arms. Both agree too in injuring the people and driving them out of the city and dispersing them. From democracy tyrants have borrowed the art of making war upon the notables and destroying them secretly or openly, or of exiling them because they are rivals and stand in the way of their power; and also because plots against them are contrived by men of this class, who either want to rule or to escape subjection. Hence Periander advised Thrasybulus[55] by cutting off the tops of the tallest ears of corn, meaning that he must always put out of the way the citizens who overtop the rest. And so, as I have already intimated,[56] the beginnings of change are the same in monarchies as in forms of constitutional government; subjects attack their sovereigns out of fear or contempt, or because they have been unjustly treated by them. And of injustice, the most common form is insult, another is confiscation of property.

The ends sought by conspiracies against monarchies, whether tyrannies or royalties, are the same as the ends sought by conspiracies against other forms of government. Monarchs have great wealth and honour, which are objects of desire to all mankind. The attacks are made sometimes against their lives, sometimes against the office; where the sense of insult is the motive, against their lives. Any sort of insult (and there are many) may stir up anger, and when men are angry, they commonly act out of revenge, and not from ambition. For example, the attempt made upon the Peisistratidae arose out of the public dishonour offered to the sister of Harmodius and the insult to himself. He attacked the tyrant for his sister's sake, and Aristogeiton joined in the attack for the sake of Harmodius. A conspiracy was also formed against Periander, the tyrant of Ambracia, because, when drinking with a favourite youth, he asked him whether by this time he was not with child by him. Philip, too, was attacked by Pausanias because he permitted him to be insulted by Attalus and his friends, and Amyntas the little, by Derdas, because he boasted of

[55] Cp. Bk. 3, XIII.
[56] Bk. 5, IX.

having enjoyed his youth. Evagoras of Cyprus, again, was slain by the eunuch to revenge an insult; for his wife had been carried off by Evagoras's son. Many conspiracies have originated in shameful attempts made by sovereigns on the persons of their subjects. Such was the attack of Crataeas upon Archelaus; he had always hated the connexion with him, and so, when Archelaus, having promised him one of his two daughters in marriage, did not give him either of them, but broke his word and married the elder to the king of Elymeia, when he was hard pressed in a war against Sirrhas and Arrhabaeus, and the younger to his own son Amyntas, under the idea that Amyntas would then be less likely to quarrel with his son by Cleopatra—Crataeas made this slight a pretext for attacking Archelaus, though even a less reason would have sufficed, for the real cause of the estrangement was the disgust which he felt at his connexion with the king. And from a like motive Hellanocrates of Larissa conspired with him; for when Archelaus, who was his lover, did not fulfil his promise of restoring him to his country, he thought that the connexion between them had originated, not in affection, but in the wantonness of power. Pytho, too, and Heracleides of Aenos, slew Cotys in order to avenge their father, and Adamas revolted from Cotys in revenge for the wanton outrage which he had committed in mutilating him when a child.

Many, too, irritated at blows inflicted on the person which they deemed an insult, have either killed or attempted to kill officers of state and royal princes by whom they have been injured. Thus, at Mytilene, Megacles and his friends attacked and slew the Penthilidae, as they were going about and striking people with clubs. At a later date Smerdis, who had been beaten and torn away from his wife by Penthilus, slew him. In the conspiracy against Archelaus, Decamnichus stimulated the fury of the assassins and led the attack; he was enraged because Archelaus had delivered him to Euripides to be scourged; for the poet had been irritated at some remark made by Decamnichus on the foulness of his breath. Many other examples might be cited of murders and conspiracies which have arisen from similar causes.

Fear is another motive which, as we have said,[57] has caused conspiracies as well in monarchies as in more popular forms of

[57] Cp. Bk. 5, III, X.

government. Thus Artapanes conspired against Xerxes and slew him, fearing that he would be accused of hanging Darius against his orders—he having been under the impression that Xerxes would forget what he had said in the middle of a meal, and that the offence would be forgiven.

Another motive is contempt, as in the case of Sardanapalus, whom some one saw carding wool with his women, if the story-tellers say truly; and the tale may be true, if not of him, of some one else.[58] Dion attacked the younger Dionysius because he despised him, and saw that he was equally despised by his own subjects, and that he was always drunk. Even the friends of a tyrant will sometimes attack him out of contempt; for the confidence which he reposes in them breeds contempt, and they think that they will not be found out. The expectation of success is likewise a sort of contempt; the assailants are ready to strike, and think nothing of the danger, because they seem to have the power in their hands. Thus generals of armies attack monarchs; as, for example, Cyrus attacked Astyages, despising the effeminacy of his life, and believing that his power was worn out. Thus again, Seuthes the Thracian conspired against Amadocus, whose general he was.

And sometimes men are actuated by more than one motive, like Mithridates, who conspired against Ariobarzanes, partly out of contempt and partly from the love of gain.

Bold natures, placed by their sovereigns in a high military position, are most likely to make the attempt in the expectation of success; for courage is emboldened by power, and the union of the two inspires them with the hope of an easy victory.

Attempts of which the motive is ambition arise in a different way as well as in those already mentioned. There are men who will not risk their lives in the hope of gains and honours however great, but who nevertheless regard the killing of a tyrant simply as an extraordinary action which will make them famous and honourable in the world; they wish to acquire, not a kingdom, but a name. It is rare, however, to find such men; he who would kill a tyrant must be prepared to lose his life if he fail. He must have the resolution of Dion, who, when he made war upon Dionysius, took with him very few troops, saying 'that whatever measure of

[58] Cp. Bk. 1, XI.

success he might attain would be enough for him, even if he were to die the moment he landed; such a death would be welcome to him'. But this is a temper to which few can attain.

Once more, tyrannies, like all other governments, are destroyed from without by some opposite and more powerful form of government. That such a government will have the will to attack them is clear; for the two are opposed in principle; and all men, if they can, do what they will. Democracy is antagonistic to tyranny, on the principle of Hesiod, 'Potter hates Potter', because they are nearly akin, for the extreme form of democracy is tyranny; and royalty and aristocracy are both alike opposed to tyranny, because they are constitutions of a different type. And therefore the Lacedaemonians put down most of the tyrannies, and so did the Syracusans during the time when they were well governed.

Again, tyrannies are destroyed from within, when the reigning family are divided among themselves, as that of Gelo was, and more recently that of Dionysius; in the case of Gelo because Thrasybulus, the brother of Hiero, flattered the son of Gelo and led him into excesses in order that he might rule in his name. Whereupon the family got together a party to get rid of Thrasybulus and save the tyranny; but those of the people who conspired with them seized the opportunity and drove them all out. In the case of Dionysius, Dion, his own relative, attacked and expelled him with the assistance of the people; he afterwards perished himself.

There are two chief motives which induce men to attack tyrannies—hatred and contempt. Hatred of tyrants is inevitable, and contempt is also a frequent cause of their destruction. Thus we see that most of those who have acquired, have retained their power, but those who have inherited,[59] have lost it, almost at once; for, living in luxurious ease, they have become contemptible, and offer many opportunities to their assailants. Anger, too, must be included under hatred, and produces the same effects. It is oftentimes even more ready to strike—the angry are more impetuous in making an attack, for they do not follow rational principle. And men are very apt to give way to their passions when they are insulted. To this cause is to be attributed the fall of the

[59] Cp. Plato, *Laws*, iii. 695.

Peisistratidae and of many others. Hatred is more reasonable, for anger is accompanied by pain, which is an impediment to reason, whereas hatred is painless.[60]

In a word, all the causes which I have mentioned[61] as destroying the last and most unmixed form of oligarchy, and the extreme form of democracy, may be assumed to affect tyranny; indeed the extreme forms of both are only tyrannies distributed among several persons. Kingly rule is little affected by external causes, and is therefore lasting; it is generally destroyed from within. And there are two ways in which the destruction may come about; (1) when the members of the royal family quarrel among themselves, and (2) when the kings attempt to administer the state too much after the fashion of a tyranny, and to extend their authority contrary to the law. Royalties do not now come into existence; where such forms of government arise, they are rather monarchies or tyrannies. For the rule of a king is over voluntary subjects, and he is supreme in all important matters; but in our own day men are more upon an equality, and no one is so immeasurably superior to others as to represent adequately the greatness and dignity of the office. Hence mankind will not, if they can help, endure it, and any one who obtains power by force or fraud is at once thought to be a tyrant. In hereditary monarchies a further cause of destruction is the fact that kings often fall into contempt, and, although possessing not tyrannical power, but only royal dignity, are apt to outrage others. Their overthrow is then readily effected; for there is an end to the king when his subjects do not want to have him, but the tyrant lasts, whether they like him or not.

The destruction of monarchies is to be attributed to these and the like causes.

XI And they are preserved, to speak generally, by the opposite causes; or, if we consider them separately, (1) royalty is preserved by the limitation of its powers. The more restricted the functions of kings, the longer their power will last unimpaired; for then they are more moderate and not so despotic in their ways; and they are less envied by their subjects. This is the reason why the kingly office has lasted so long among the Molossians. And for a

[60] Cp. *Rhetoric*, ii. 1382a 12.

[61] Bk. 5, III, IV, VI.

similar reason it has continued among the Lacedaemonians, because there it was always divided between two, and afterwards further limited by Theopompus in various respects, more particularly by the establishment of the Ephoralty. He diminished the power of the kings, but established on a more lasting basis the kingly office, which was thus made in a certain sense not less, but greater. There is a story that when his wife once asked him whether he was not ashamed to leave to his sons a royal power which was less than he had inherited from his father, 'No indeed', he replied, 'for the power which I leave to them will be more lasting'.

As to (2) tyrannies, they are preserved in two most opposite ways. One of them is the old traditional method in which most tyrants administer their government. Of such arts Periander of Corinth is said to have been the great master, and many similar devices may be gathered from the Persians in the administration of their government. There are firstly the prescriptions mentioned some distance back,[62] for the preservation of a tyranny, in so far as this is possible; viz. that the tyrant should lop off those who are too high; he must put to death men of spirit; he must not allow common meals, clubs, education, and the like; he must be upon his guard against anything which is likely to inspire either courage or confidence among his subjects; he must prohibit literary assemblies or other meetings for discussion, and he must take every means to prevent people from knowing one another (for acquaintance begets mutual confidence). Further, he must compel all persons staying in the city to appear in public and live at his gates; then he will know what they are doing: if they are always kept under, they will learn to be humble. In short, he should practise these and the like Persian and barbaric arts, which all have the same object. A tyrant should also endeavour to know what each of his subjects says or does, and should employ spies, like the 'female detectives' at Syracuse, and the eavesdroppers whom Hiero was in the habit of sending to any place of resort or meeting; for the fear of informers prevents people from speaking their minds, and if they do, they are more easily found out. Another art of the tyrant is to sow quarrels among the citizens; friends should be embroiled with friends, the people with the

[62] Bk. 5, X.

notables, and the rich with one another. Also he should impoverish his subjects; he thus provides against the maintenance of a guard by the citizens, and the people, having to keep hard at work, are prevented from conspiring. The Pyramids of Egypt afford an example of this policy; also the offerings of the family of Cypselus, and the building of the temple of Olympian Zeus by the Peisistratidae, and the great Polycratean monuments at Samos; all these works were alike intended to occupy the people and keep them poor. Another practice of tyrants is to multiply taxes, after the manner of Dionysius at Syracuse, who contrived that within five years his subjects should bring into the treasury their whole property. The tyrant is also fond of making war in order that his subjects may have something to do and be always in want of a leader. And whereas the power of a king is preserved by his friends, the characteristic of a tyrant is to distrust his friends, because he knows that all men want to overthrow him, and they above all have the power.

Again, the evil practices of the last and worst form of democracy[63] are all found in tyrannies. Such are the power given to women in their families in the hope that they will inform against their husbands, and the licence which is allowed to slaves in order that they may betray their masters; for slaves and women do not conspire against tyrants; and they are of course friendly to tyrannies and also to democracies, since under them they have a good time. For the people too would fain be a monarch, and therefore by them, as well as by the tyrant, the flatterer is held in honour; in democracies he is the demagogue; and the tyrant also has those who associate with him in a humble spirit, which is a work of flattery.

Hence tyrants are always fond of bad men, because they love to be flattered, but no man who has the spirit of a freeman in him will lower himself by flattery; good men love others, or at any rate do not flatter them. Moreover, the bad are useful for bad purposes; 'nail knocks out nail,' as the proverb says. It is characteristic of a tyrant to dislike every one who has dignity or independence; he wants to be alone in his glory, but any one who claims a like dignity or asserts his independence encroaches upon his prerogative, and is hated by him as an enemy to his power.

[63] Cp. Bk. 6, IV.

Another mark of a tyrant is that he likes foreigners better than citizens, and lives with them and invites them to his table; for the one are enemies, but the others enter into no rivalry with him.

Such are the notes of the tyrant and the arts by which he preserves his power; there is no wickedness too great for him. All that we have said may be summed up under three heads, which answer to the three aims of the tyrant. These are, (1) the humiliation of his subjects; he knows that a mean-spirited man will not conspire against anybody: (2) the creation of mistrust among them; for a tyrant is not overthrown until men begin to have confidence in one another; and this is the reason why tyrants are at war with the good; they are under the idea that their power is endangered by them, not only because they will not be ruled despotically, but also because they are loyal to one another, and to other men, and do not inform against one another or against other men: (3) the tyrant desires that his subjects shall be incapable of action, for no one attempts what is impossible, and they will not attempt to overthrow a tyranny, if they are powerless. Under these three heads the whole policy of a tyrant may be summed up, and to one or other of them all his ideas may be referred: (1) he sows distrust among his subjects; (2) he takes away their power; (3) he humbles them.

This then is one of the two methods by which tyrannies are preserved; and there is another which proceeds upon an almost opposite principle of action. The nature of this latter method may be gathered from a comparison of the causes which destroy kingdoms, for as one mode of destroying kingly power is to make the office of king more tyrannical, so the salvation of a tyranny is to make it more like the rule of a king. But of one thing the tyrant must be careful; he must keep power enough to rule over his subjects, whether they like him or not, for if he once gives this up he gives up his tyranny. But though power must be retained as the foundation, in all else the tyrant should act or appear to act in the character of a king. In the first place he should pretend a care of the public revenues, and not waste money in making presents of a sort at which the common people get excited when they see their hard-won earnings snatched from them and lavished on courtesans and strangers and artists. He should give an account of what he receives and of what he spends (a practice which has been adopted by some tyrants); for then he will seem to be a steward of the public rather than a tyrant; nor need he fear that, while he is the lord of the city, he will ever be in want of money. Such a policy is at all events much more advantageous for the tyrant when he goes from home, than to leave behind him a hoard, for then the garrison who remain in the city will be less likely to attack his power; and a tyrant, when he is absent from home, has more reason to fear the guardians of his treasure than the citizens, for the one accompany him, but the others remain behind. In the second place, he should be seen to collect taxes and to require public services only for state purposes, and that he may form a fund in case of war, and generally he ought to make himself the guardian and treasurer of them, as if they belonged, not to him, but to the public. He should appear, not harsh, but dignified, and when men meet him they should look upon him with reverence, and not with fear. Yet it is hard for him to be respected if he inspires no respect, and therefore whatever virtues he may neglect, at least he should maintain the character of a great soldier, and produce the impression that he is one. Neither he nor any of his associates should ever be guilty of the least offence against modesty towards the young of either sex who are his subjects, and the women of his family should observe a like self-control towards other women; the insolence of women has ruined many tyrannies. In the indulgence of pleasures he should be the opposite of our modern tyrants, who not only begin at dawn and pass whole days in sensuality, but want other men to see them, that they may admire their happy and blessed lot. In these things a tyrant should if possible be moderate, or at any rate should not parade his vices to the world; for a drunken and drowsy tyrant is soon despised and attacked; not so he who is temperate and wide awake. His conduct should be the very reverse of nearly everything which has been said before[64] about tyrants. He ought to adorn and improve his city, as though he were not a tyrant, but the guardian of the state. Also he should appear to be particularly earnest in the service of the Gods; for if men think that a ruler is religious and has a reverence for the Gods, they are less afraid of suffering injustice at his hands, and they are less disposed to conspire against him, because they be-

[64] Bk. 5, X, XI.

lieve him to have the very Gods fighting on his side. At the same time his religion must not be thought foolish. And he should honour men of merit, and make them think that they would not be held in more honour by the citizens if they had a free government. The honour he should distribute himself, but the punishment should be inflicted by officers and courts of law. It is a precaution which is taken by all monarchs not to make one person great; but if one, then two or more should be raised, that they may look sharply after one another. If after all some one has to be made great, he should not be a man of bold spirit; for such dispositions are ever most inclined to strike. And if any one is to be deprived of his power, let it be diminished gradually, not taken from him all at once.[65] The tyrant should abstain from all outrage; in particular from personal violence and from wanton conduct towards the young. He should be especially careful of his behaviour to men who are lovers of honour; for as the lovers of money are offended when their property is touched, so are the lovers of honour and the virtuous when their honour is affected. Therefore a tyrant ought either not to commit such acts at all; or he should be thought only to employ fatherly correction, and not to trample upon others—and his acquaintance with youth should be supposed to arise from affection, and not from the insolence of power, and in general he should compensate the appearance of dishonour by the increase of honour.

Of those who attempt assassination they are the most dangerous, and require to be most carefully watched, who do not care to survive, if they effect their purpose. Therefore special precaution should be taken about any who think that either they or those for whom they care have been insulted; for when men are led away by passion to assault others they are regardless of themselves. As Heracleitus says, 'It is difficult to fight against anger; for a man will buy revenge with his soul'.

And whereas states consist of two classes, of poor men and of rich, the tyrant should lead both to imagine that they are preserved and prevented from harming one another by his rule, and whichever of the two is stronger he should attach to his government; for, having this advantage, he has no need either to emancipate slaves or to disarm the citizens; either party added to the

[65] Cp. Bk. 5, VIII.

force which he already has, will make him stronger than his assailants.

But enough of these details;—what should be the general policy of the tyrant is obvious. He ought to show himself to his subjects in the light, not of a tyrant, but of a steward and a king. He should not appropriate what is theirs, but should be their guardian; he should be moderate, not extravagant in his way of life; he should win the notables by companionship, and the multitude by flattery. For then his rule will of necessity be nobler and happier, because he will rule over better men[66] whose spirits are not crushed, over men to whom he himself is not an object of hatred, and of whom he is not afraid. His power too will be more lasting. His disposition will be virtuous, or at least half virtuous; and he will not be wicked, but half wicked only.

XII Yet no forms of government are so short-lived as oligarchy and tyranny. The tyranny which lasted longest was that of Orthagoras and his sons at Sicyon; this continued for a hundred years. The reason was that they treated their subjects with moderation, and to a great extent observed the laws; and in various ways gained the favour of the people by the care which they took of them. Cleisthenes, in particular, was respected for his military ability. If report may be believed, he crowned the judge who decided against him in the games; and, as some say, the sitting statue in the Agora of Sicyon is the likeness of this person. (A similar story is told of Peisistratus, who is said on one occasion to have allowed himself to be summoned and tried before the Areopagus.)

Next in duration to the tyranny of Orthagoras was that of the Cypselidae at Corinth, which lasted seventy-three years and six months: Cypselus reigned thirty years, Periander forty and a half, and Psammetichus the son of Gorgus three. Their continuance was due to similar causes: Cypselus was a popular man, who during the whole time of his rule never had a body-guard; and Periander, although he was a tyrant, was a great soldier. Third in duration was the rule of the Peisistratidae at Athens, but it was interrupted; for Peisistratus was twice driven out, so that during three and

[66] Cp. Bk. 1, IV.

thirty years he reigned only seventeen; and his sons reigned eighteen—altogether thirty-five years. Of other tyrannies, that of Hiero and Gelo at Syracuse was the most lasting. Even this, however, was short, not more than eighteen years in all; for Gelo continued tyrant for seven years, and died in the eighth; Hiero reigned for ten years, and Thrasybulus was driven out in the eleventh month. In fact, tyrannies generally have been of quite short duration.

I have now gone through almost all the causes by which constitutional governments and monarchies are either destroyed or preserved.

In the *Republic* of Plato,[67] Socrates treats of revolutions, but not well, for he mentions no cause of change which peculiarly affects the first, or perfect state. He only says that the cause is that nothing is abiding, but all things change in a certain cycle; and that the origin of the change consists in those numbers 'of which 4 and 3, married with 5, furnish two harmonies'—(he means when the number of this figure becomes solid); he conceives that nature at certain times produces bad men who will not submit to education; in which latter particular he may very likely be not far wrong, for there may well be some men who cannot be educated and made virtuous. But why is such a cause of change peculiar to his ideal state, and not rather common to all states, nay, to everything which comes into being at all? And is it by the agency of time, which, as he declares, makes all things change, that things which did not begin together, change together? For example, if something has come into being the day before the completion of the cycle, will it change with things that came into being before? Further, why should the perfect state change into the Spartan?[68] For governments more often take an opposite form than one akin to them. The same remark is applicable to the other changes; he says that the Spartan constitution changes into an oligarchy, and this into a democracy, and this again into a tyranny. And yet the contrary happens quite as often; for a democracy is even more likely to change into an oligarchy than into a monarchy. Further, he never says whether tyranny is, or is not, liable to revolutions, and if it is, what is the cause of them, or into what form it changes.

[67] This is an extract from the much fuller account in *Rep.* viii. 546 B.C.

[68] *Rep.* viii. 544 C.

And the reason is, that he could not very well have told: for there is no rule; according to him it should revert to the first and best, and then there would be a complete cycle. But in point of fact a tyranny often changes into a tyranny, as that at Sicyon changed from the tyranny of Myron into that of Cleisthenes; into oligarchy, as the tyranny of Antileon did at Chalcis; into democracy, as that of Gelo's family did at Syracuse; into aristocracy, as at Carthage, and the tyranny of Charilaus at Lacedaemon. Often an oligarchy changes into a tyranny, like most of the ancient oligarchies in Sicily; for example, the oligarchy at Leontini changed into the tyranny of Panaetius; that at Gela into the tyranny of Cleander; that at Rhegium into the tyranny of Anaxilaus; the same thing has happened in many other states. And it is absurd to suppose that the state changes into oligarchy merely because the ruling class are lovers and makers of money,[69] and not because the very rich think it unfair that the very poor should have an equal share in the government with themselves. Moreover, in many oligarchies there are laws against making money in trade. But at Carthage, which is a democracy, there is no such prohibition; and yet to this day the Carthaginians have never had a revolution. It is absurd too for him to say that an oligarchy is two cities, one of the rich, and the other of the poor.[70] Is not this just as much the case in the Spartan constitution, or in any other in which either all do not possess equal property, or all are not equally good men? Nobody need be any poorer than he was before, and yet the oligarchy may change all the same into a democracy, if the poor form the majority; and a democracy may change into an oligarchy, if the wealthy class are stronger than the people, and the one are energetic, the other indifferent. Once more, although the causes of the change[71] are very numerous, he mentions only one,[72] which is, that the citizens become poor through dissipation and debt, as though he thought that all, or the majority of them, were originally rich. This is not true: though it is true that when any of the leaders lose their property they are ripe for revolution; but, when anybody else, it is no great matter, and an oligarchy does not even then more often pass into a democracy than into any other form of government. Again, if men are deprived of the honours of state, and are wronged, and insulted, they make revolutions, and change

[69] *Rep.* viii. 550 E.
[70] *Rep.* viii. 551 D.
[71] *sc.* from oligarchy to democracy.
[72] *Rep.* viii. 555 D.

forms of government, even although they have not wasted their substance because they might do what they liked—of which extravagance he declares excessive freedom to be the cause.[73]

Finally, although there are many forms of oligarchies and democracies, Socrates speaks of their revolutions as though there were only one form of either of them.

[73] *Rep.* viii. 557 c, 564.

BOOK SIXTH

I We have now considered the varieties of the deliberative or supreme power in states, and the various arrangements of law-courts and state offices, and which of them are adapted to different forms of government.[1] We have also spoken of the destruction and preservation of constitutions, how and from what causes they arise.[2]

Of democracy and all other forms of government there are many kinds; and it will be well to assign to them severally the modes of organization which are proper and advantageous to each, adding what remains to be said about them.[3] Moreover, we ought to consider the various combinations of these modes themselves; for such combinations make constitutions overlap one another, so that aristocracies have an oligarchical character, and constitutional governments incline to democracies.[4]

When I speak of the combinations which remain to be considered, and thus far have not been considered by us, I mean such as these:—when the deliberative part of the government and the election of officers is constituted oligarchically, and the law-courts aristocratically, or when the courts and the deliberative part of the state are oligarchical, and the election to office aristocratical, or when in any other way there is a want of harmony in the composition of a state.[5]

I have shown already[6] what forms of democracy are suited to particular cities, and what of oligarchy to particular peoples, and to whom each of the other forms of government is suited. Further, we must not only show which of these governments is the best for each state, but also briefly proceed to consider[7] how these and other forms of government are to be established.

First of all let us speak of democracy, which will also bring to light the opposite form of government commonly called oligarchy. For the purposes of this inquiry we need to ascertain all the elements and characteristics of democracy, since from the combinations of these the varieties of democratic government arise. There are several of these differing from each other, and the difference is

[1] Bk. 4, XIV–XVI.
[2] Bk. 5.
[3] Bk. 6, IV.
[4] Cp. Bk. 4, VIII.
[5] These questions are not actually discussed by A.
[6] Bk. 4 XII.
[7] Cp. Bk. 4, II.

due to two causes. One (1) has been already mentioned[8]—differences of population; for the popular element may consist of husbandmen, or of mechanics, or of labourers, and if the first of these be added to the second, or the third to the two others, not only does the democracy become better or worse, but its very nature is changed. A second cause (2) remains to be mentioned: the various properties and characteristics of democracy, when variously combined, make a difference. For one democracy will have less and another will have more, and another will have all of these characteristics. There is an advantage in knowing them all, whether a man wishes to establish some new form of democracy, or only to remodel an existing one.[9] Founders of states try to bring together all the elements which accord with the ideas of the several constitutions; but this is a mistake of theirs, as I have already remarked[10] when speaking of the destruction and preservation of states. We will now set forth the principles, characteristics, and aims of such states.

II The basis of a democratic state is liberty; which, according to the common opinion of men, can only be enjoyed in such a state;—this they affirm to be the great end of every democracy.[11] One principle of liberty is for all to rule and be ruled in turn, and indeed democratic justice is the application of numerical not proportionate equality; whence it follows that the majority must be supreme, and that whatever the majority approve must be the end and the just. Every citizen, it is said, must have equality, and therefore in a democracy the poor have more power than the rich, because there are more of them, and the will of the majority is supreme. This, then, is one note of liberty which all democrats affirm to be the principle of their state. Another is that a man should live as he likes.[12] This, they say, is the privilege of a freeman, since, on the other hand, not to live as a man likes is the mark of a slave. This is the second characteristic of democracy, whence has arisen the claim of men to be ruled by none, if possible, or, if this is impossible, to rule and be ruled in turns; and so it contributes to the freedom based upon equality.

[8] Bk. 4, IV, V, XI.
[9] Cp. Bk. 4, I.
[10] Bk. 5, IX.
[11] Cp. Plato, *Rep.* viii. 557 sqq.
[12] Cp. Bk. 5, IX.

Such being our foundation and such the principle from which we start, the characteristics of democracy are as follows:—the election of officers by all out of all; and that all should rule over each, and each in his turn over all; that the appointment to all offices, or to all but those which require experience and skill,[13] should be made by lot; that no property qualification should be required for offices, or only a very low one; that a man should not hold the same office twice, or not often, or in the case of few except military offices: that the tenure of all offices, or of as many as possible, should be brief; that all men should sit in judgement, or that judges selected out of all should judge, in all matters, or in most and in the greatest and most important—such as the scrutiny of accounts, the constitution, and private contracts; that the assembly should be supreme over all causes, or at any rate over the most important, and the magistrates over none or only over a very few. Of all magistracies, a council is the most democratic[14] when there is not the means of paying all the citizens, but when they are paid even this is robbed of its power; for the people then draw all cases to themselves, as I said in the previous discussion.[15] The next characteristic of democracy is payment for services; assembly, law-courts, magistrates, everybody receives pay, when it is to be had; or when it is not to be had for all, then it is given to the law-courts and to the stated assemblies, to the council and to the magistrates, or at least to any of them who are compelled to have their meals together. And whereas oligarchy is characterized by birth, wealth, and education, the notes of democracy appear to be the opposite of these—low birth, poverty, mean employment. Another note is that no magistracy is perpetual, but if any such have survived some ancient change in the constitution it should be stripped of its power, and the holders should be elected by lot and no longer by vote. These are the points common to all democracies; but democracy and demos in their truest form are based upon the recognized principle of democratic justice, that all should count equally; for equality implies that the poor should have no more share in the government than the rich, and should not be the only rulers, but that all should rule equally according to their numbers.[16] And in this way men think that they will secure equality and freedom in their state.

[13] Cp. Bk. 4, XIV.

[14] Cp. Bk. 4, XV.

[15] Cp. Bk. 4, XV.

[16] Cp. Bk. 4, IV.

III Next comes the question, how is this equality to be obtained? Are we to assign to a thousand poor men the property qualifications of five hundred rich men? and shall we give the thousand a power equal to that of the five hundred? or, if this is not to be the mode, ought we, still retaining the same ratio, to take equal numbers from each and give them the control of the elections and of the courts?—Which, according to the democratical notion, is the juster form of the constitution—this or one based on numbers only? Democrats say that justice is that to which the majority agree, oligarchs that to which the wealthier class; in their opinion the decision should be given according to the amount of property. In both principles there is some inequality and injustice. For if justice is the will of the few, any one person who has more wealth than all the rest of the rich put together, ought, upon the oligarchical principle, to have the sole power—but this would be tyranny; or if justice is the will of the majority, as I was before saying,[17] they will unjustly confiscate the property of the wealthy minority. To find a principle of equality in which they both agree we must inquire into their respective ideas of justice.

Now they agree in saying that whatever is decided by the majority of the citizens is to be deemed law. Granted:—but not without some reserve; since there are two classes out of which a state is composed—the poor and the rich—that is to be deemed law, on which both or the greater part of both agree; and if they disagree, that which is approved by the greater number, and by those who have the higher qualification. For example, suppose that there are ten rich and twenty poor, and some measure is approved by six of the rich and is disapproved by fifteen of the poor, and the remaining four of the rich join with the party of the poor, and the remaining five of the poor with that of the rich; in such a case the will of those whose qualifications, when both sides are added up, are the greatest, should prevail. If they turn out to be equal, there is no greater difficulty than at present, when, if the assembly or the courts are divided, recourse is had to the lot, or to some similar expedient. But, although it may be difficult in theory to know what is just and equal, the practical difficulty of inducing those to forbear who can, if they like, encroach, is far greater, for the weaker are always asking for equality and justice, but the stronger care for none of these things.

[17] Cp. Bk. 3, X.

IV Of the four kinds of democracy, as was said in the previous discussion,[18] the best is that which comes first in order; it is also the oldest of them all. I am speaking of them according to the natural classification of their inhabitants. For the best material of democracy is an agricultural population[19]; there is no difficulty in forming a democracy where the mass of the people live by agriculture or tending of cattle. Being poor, they have no leisure, and therefore do not often attend the assembly, and not having the necessaries of life they are always at work, and do not covet the property of others. Indeed, they find their employment pleasanter than the cares of government or office where no great gains can be made out of them, for the many are more desirous of gain than of honour.[20] A proof is that even the ancient tyrannies were patiently endured by them, as they still endure oligarchies, if they are allowed to work and are not deprived of their property; for some of them grow quickly rich and the others are well enough off. Moreover, they have the power of electing the magistrates and calling them to account[21]; their ambition, if they have any, is thus satisfied; and in some democracies, although they do not all share in the appointment of offices, except through representatives elected in turn out of the whole people, as at Mantinea;—yet, if they have the power of deliberating, the many are contented. Even this form of government may be regarded as a democracy, and was such at Mantinea. Hence it is both expedient and customary in the afore-mentioned[22] type of democracy that all should elect to offices, and conduct scrutinies, and sit in the law-courts, but that the great offices should be filled up by election and from persons having a qualification; the greater requiring a greater qualification, or, if there be no offices for which a qualification is required, then those who are marked out by special ability should be appointed. Under such a form of government the citizens are sure to be governed well (for the offices will always be held by the best persons; the people are willing enough to elect them and are not jealous of the good). The good and the notables will then be satisfied, for they will not be governed by men who are their inferiors, and the persons elected will rule justly, because others will call them to account. Every man should be responsible to others, nor should any one be allowed to do just

[18] Bk. 4, V, VI.
[19] Cp. Bk. 4, VIII.
[20] Cp. Bk. 4, XIII.
[21] Cp. Bk. 2, XII.
[22] l. 5.

as he pleases; for where absolute freedom is allowed there is nothing to restrain the evil which is inherent in every man. But the principle of responsibility secures that which is the greatest good in states; the right persons rule and are prevented from doing wrong, and the people have their due. It is evident that this is the best kind of democracy, and why? Because the people are drawn from a certain class. Some of the ancient laws of most states were, all of them, useful with a view to making the people husbandmen. They provided either that no one should possess more than a certain quantity of land, or that, if he did, the land should not be within a certain distance from the town or the acropolis. Formerly in many states there was a law forbidding any one to sell his original allotment of land.[23] There is a similar law attributed to Oxylus, which is to the effect that there should be a certain portion of every man's land on which he could not borrow money. A useful corrective to the evil of which I am speaking would be the law of the Aphytaeans, who, although they are numerous, and do not possess much land, are all of them husbandmen. For their properties are reckoned in the census; not entire, but only in such small portions that even the poor may have more than the amount required.

Next best to an agricultural, and in many respects similar, are a pastoral people, who live by their flocks; they are the best trained of any for war, robust in body and able to camp out. The people of whom other democracies consist are far inferior to them, for their life is inferior; there is no room for moral excellence in any of their employments, whether they be mechanics or traders or labourers. Besides, people of this class can readily come to the assembly, because they are continually moving about in the city and in the agora; whereas husbandmen are scattered over the country and do not meet, or equally feel the want of assembling together. Where the territory also happens to extend to a distance from the city, there is no difficulty in making an excellent democracy or constitutional government; for the people are compelled to settle in the country, and even if there is a town population the assembly ought not to meet, in democracies, when the country people cannot come. We have thus explained how the first and best form of democracy should be constituted; it is clear that the other or inferior sorts will deviate in a regular order, and

[23] Cp. Bk. 2, VII.

the population which is excluded will at each stage be of a lower kind.

The last form of democracy, that in which all share alike, is one which cannot be borne by all states, and will not last long unless well regulated by laws and customs. The more general causes which tend to destroy this or other kinds of government have been pretty fully considered.[24] In order to constitute such a democracy and strengthen the people, the leaders have been in the habit of including as many as they can, and making citizens not only of those who are legitimate, but even of the illegitimate, and of those who have only one parent a citizen, whether father or mother[25]; for nothing of this sort comes amiss to such a democracy. This is the way in which demagogues proceed. Whereas the right thing would be to make no more additions when the number of the commonalty exceeds that of the notables and of the middle class—beyond this not to go. When in excess of this point, the constitution becomes disorderly, and the notables grow excited and impatient of the democracy, as in the insurrection at Cyrene; for no notice is taken of a little evil, but when it increases it strikes the eye. Measures like those which Cleisthenes[26] passed when he wanted to increase the power of the democracy at Athens, or such as were taken by the founders of popular government at Cyrene, are useful in the extreme form of democracy. Fresh tribes and brotherhoods should be established; the private rites of families should be restricted and converted into public ones; in short, every contrivance should be adopted which will mingle the citizens with one another and get rid of old connections. Again, the measures which are taken by tyrants appear all of them to be democratic; such, for instance, as the licence permitted to slaves (which may be to a certain extent advantageous) and also that of women and children, and the allowing everybody to live as he likes.[27] Such a government will have many supporters, for most persons would rather live in a disorderly than in a sober manner.

V The mere establishment of a democracy is not the only or principal business of the legislator, or of those who wish to create

[24] Bk. 5, X.
[25] Cp. Bk. 3, V.
[26] Cp. Bk. 3, II.
[27] Cp. Bk. 5, XI.

such a state, for any state, however badly constituted, may last one, two, or three days; a far greater difficulty is the preservation of it. The legislator should therefore endeavour to have a firm foundation according to the principles already laid down concerning the preservation and destruction of states[28]; he should guard against the destructive elements, and should make laws, whether written or unwritten, which will contain all the preservatives of states. He must not think the truly democratical or oligarchical measure to be that which will give the greatest amount of democracy or oligarchy, but that which will make them last longest.[29] The demagogues of our own day often get property confiscated[30] in the law-courts in order to please the people. But those who have the welfare of the state at heart should counteract them, and make a law that the property of the condemned should not be public and go into the treasury but be sacred. Thus offenders will be as much afraid, for they will be punished all the same, and the people, having nothing to gain, will not be so ready to condemn the accused. Care should also be taken that state trials are as few as possible, and heavy penalties should be inflicted on those who bring groundless accusations; for it is the practice to indict, not members of the popular party, but the notables, although the citizens ought to be all attached to the constitution as well, or at any rate should not regard their rulers as enemies.

Now, since in the last and worst form of democracy the citizens are very numerous, and can hardly be made to assemble unless they are paid, and to pay them when there are no revenues presses hardly upon the notables (for the money must be obtained by a property-tax and confiscations and corrupt practices of the courts, things which have before now overthrown many democracies); where, I say, there are no revenues, the government should hold few assemblies, and the law-courts should consist of many persons, but sit for a few days only. This system has two advantages: first, the rich do not fear the expense, even although they are unpaid themselves when the poor are paid; and secondly, causes are better tried, for wealthy persons, although they do not like to be long absent from their own affairs, do not mind going for a few days to the law-courts. Where there are revenues the demagogues should not be allowed after their manner to distribute the surplus;

[28] Cp. Bk. 5. [29] Cp. Bk. 5, X. [30] Cp. Bk. 5, V.

the poor are always receiving and always wanting more and more, for such help is like water poured into a leaky cask. Yet the true friend of the people should see that they be not too poor, for extreme poverty lowers the character of the democracy; measures therefore should be taken which will give them lasting prosperity; and as this is equally the interest of all classes, the proceeds of the public revenues should be accumulated and distributed among its poor, if possible, in such quantities as may enable them to purchase a little farm, or, at any rate, make a beginning in trade or husbandry. And if this benevolence cannot be extended to all, money should be distributed in turn according to tribes or other divisions, and in the meantime the rich should pay the fee for the attendance of the poor at the necessary assemblies; and should in return be excused from useless public services. By administering the state in this spirit the Carthaginians retain the affections of the people; their policy is from time to time to send some of them into their dependent towns, where they grow rich.[31] It is also worthy of a generous and sensible nobility to divide the poor amongst them, and give them the means of going to work. The example of the people of Tarentum is also well deserving of imitation, for, by sharing the use of their own property with the poor, they gain their good will.[32] Moreover, they divide all their offices into two classes, some of them being elected by vote, the others by lot; the latter, that the people may participate in them, and the former, that the state may be better administered. A like result may be gained by dividing the same offices, so as to have two classes of magistrates, one chosen by vote, the other by lot.

Enough has been said of the manner in which democracies ought to be constituted.

VI From these considerations there will be no difficulty in seeing what should be the constitution of oligarchies. We have only to reason from opposites and compare each form of oligarchy with the corresponding form of democracy.

The first and best attempered of oligarchies is akin to a constitutional government. In this there ought to be two standards of qualification; the one high, the other low—the lower qualifying for the humbler yet indispensable offices and the higher for the

[31] Cp. Bk. 2, XI.

[32] Cp. Bk. 2, V.

superior ones. He who acquires the prescribed qualification should have the rights of citizenship. The number of those admitted should be such as will make the entire governing body stronger than those who are excluded, and the new citizen should be always taken out of the better class of the people. The principle, narrowed a little, gives another form of oligarchy; until at length we reach the most cliquish and tyrannical of them all, answering to the extreme democracy, which, being the worst, requires vigilance in proportion to its badness. For as healthy bodies and ships well provided with sailors may undergo many mishaps and survive them, whereas sickly constitutions and rotten ill-manned ships are ruined by the very least mistake, so do the worst forms of government require the greatest care. The populousness of democracies generally preserves them (for number is to democracy in the place of justice based on proportion); whereas the preservation of an oligarchy clearly depends on an opposite principle, viz. good order.

VII As there are four chief divisions of the common people—husbandmen, mechanics, retail traders, labourers; so also there are four kinds of military forces—the cavalry, the heavy infantry, the light-armed troops, the navy.[33] When the country is adapted for cavalry, then a strong oligarchy is likely to be established. For the security of the inhabitants depends upon a force of this sort, and only rich men can afford to keep horses. The second form of oligarchy prevails when the country is adapted to heavy infantry; for this service is better suited to the rich than to the poor. But the light-armed and the naval element are wholly democratic; and nowadays, where they are numerous, if the two parties quarrel, the oligarchy are often worsted by them in the struggle. A remedy for this state of things may be found in the practice of generals who combine a proper contingent of light-armed troops with cavalry and heavy-armed. And this is the way in which the poor get the better of the rich in civil contests; being lightly armed, they fight with advantage against cavalry and heavy infantry. An oligarchy which raises such a force out of the lower classes raises a power against itself. And therefore, since the ages of the citizens vary and some are older and some younger, the fathers should

[33] Cp. Bk. 4. II

have their own sons, while they are still young, taught the agile movements of light-armed troops; and these, when they have been taken out of the ranks of the youth, should become light-armed warriors in reality. The oligarchy should also yield a share in the government to the people, either, as I said before, to those who have a property qualification,[34] or, as in the case of Thebes,[35] to those who have abstained for a certain number of years from mean employments, or, as at Massalia, to men of merit who are selected for their worthiness, whether previously citizens or not. The magistracies of the highest rank, which ought to be in the hands of the governing body, should have expensive duties attached to them, and then the people will not desire them and will take no offence at the privileges of their rulers when they see that they pay a heavy fine for their dignity. It is fitting also that the magistrates on entering office should offer magnificent sacrifices or erect some public edifice, and then the people who participate in the entertainments, and see the city decorated with votive offerings and buildings, will not desire an alteration in the government, and the notables will have memorials of their munificence. This, however, is anything but the fashion of our modern oligarchs, who are as covetous of gain as they are of honour; oligarchies like theirs may be well described as petty democracies. Enough of the manner in which democracies and oligarchies should be organized.

VIII Next in order follows the right distribution of offices, their number, their nature, their duties, of which indeed we have already spoken.[36] No state can exist not having the necessary offices, and no state can be well administered not having the offices which tend to preserve harmony and good order. In small states, as we have already remarked,[37] there must not be many of them, but in larger there must be a larger number, and we should carefully consider which offices may properly be united and which separated.

First among necessary offices is that which has the care of the market; a magistrate should be appointed to inspect contracts and

[34] Bk. 6, V.
[35] Cp. Bk. 3, V.
[36] Bk. 4, XV.
[37] Bk. 4, XV.

to maintain order. For in every state there must inevitably be buyers and sellers who will supply one another's wants; this is the readiest way to make a state self-sufficing and so fulfil the purpose for which men come together into one state.[38] A second office of a similar kind undertakes the supervision and embellishment of public and private buildings, the maintaining and repairing of houses and roads, the prevention of disputes about boundaries, and other concerns of a like nature. This is commonly called the office of City-warden, and has various departments, which, in more populous towns, are shared among different persons, one, for example, taking charge of the walls, another of the fountains, a third of harbours. There is another equally necessary office, and of a similar kind, having to do with the same matters without the walls and in the country—the magistrates who hold this office are called Wardens of the country, or Inspectors of the woods. Besides these three there is a fourth office of receivers of taxes, who have under their charge the revenue which is distributed among the various departments; these are called Receivers or Treasurers. Another officer registers all private contracts, and decisions of the courts, all public indictments, and also all preliminary proceedings. This office again is sometimes subdivided, in which case one officer is appointed over all the rest. These officers are called Recorders or Sacred Recorders, Presidents, and the like.

Next to these comes an office of which the duties are the most necessary and also the most difficult, viz. that to which is committed the execution of punishments, or the exaction of fines from those who are posted up according to the registers; and also the custody of prisoners. The difficulty of this office arises out of the odium which is attached to it; no one will undertake it unless great profits are to be made, and any one who does is loath to execute the law. Still the office is necessary; for judicial decisions are useless if they take no effect; and if society cannot exist without them, neither can it exist without the execution of them. It is an office which, being so unpopular, should not be entrusted to one person, but divided among several taken from different courts. In like manner an effort should be made to distribute among different persons the writing up of those who are on the register of public debtors. Some sentences should be executed by the magis-

[38] Cp. Bk. 1, II; *Nic. Eth.* v. 1134[a] 26; Pl. *Rep.* ii. 369.

trates also, and in particular penalties due to the outgoing magistrates should be exacted by the incoming ones; and as regards those due to magistrates already in office, when one court has given judgement, another should exact the penalty; for example, the wardens of the city should exact the fines imposed by the wardens of the agora, and others again should exact the fines imposed by *them*. For penalties are more likely to be exacted when less odium attaches to the exaction of them; but a double odium is incurred when the judges who have passed also execute the sentence, and if they are always the executioners, they will be the enemies of all.

In many places, while one magistracy executes the sentence, another has the custody of the prisoners, as, for example, 'the Eleven' at Athens. It is well to separate off the jailorship also, and try by some device to render the office less unpopular. For it is quite as necessary as that of the executioners; but good men do all they can to avoid it, and worthless persons cannot safely be trusted with it; for they themselves require a guard, and are not fit to guard others. There ought not therefore to be a single or permanent officer set apart for this duty; but it should be entrusted to the young, wherever they are organized into a band or guard, and different magistrates acting in turn should take charge of it.

These are the indispensable officers, and should be ranked first; —next in order follow others, equally necessary, but of higher rank, and requiring great experience and fidelity. Such are the officers to which are committed the guard of the city, and other military functions. Not only in time of war but of peace their duty will be to defend the walls and gates, and to muster and marshal the citizens. In some states there are many such offices; in others there are a few only, while small states are content with one; these officers are called generals or commanders. Again, if a state has cavalry or light-armed troops or archers or a naval force, it will sometimes happen that each of these departments has separate officers, who are called admirals, or generals of cavalry or of light-armed troops. And there are subordinate officers called naval captains, and captains of light-armed troops and of horse; having others under them:—all these are included in the department of war. Thus much of military command.

But since many, not to say all, of these offices handle the public money, there must of necessity be another office which examines and audits them, and has no other functions. Such officers are called by various names—Scrutineers, Auditors, Accountants, Controllers. Besides all these offices there is another which is supreme over them, and to this is often entrusted both the introduction and the ratification of measures, or at all events it presides, in a democracy, over the assembly. For there must be a body which convenes the supreme authority in the state. In some places they are called 'probuli', because they hold previous deliberations, but in a democracy more commonly 'councillors'.[39] These are the chief political offices.

Another set of officers is concerned with the maintenance of religion; priests and guardians see to the preservation and repair of the temples of the Gods and to other matters of religion. One office of this sort may be enough in small places, but in larger ones there are a great many besides the priesthood; for example superintendents of public worship, guardians of shrines, treasurers of the sacred revenues. Nearly connected with these there are also the officers appointed for the performance of the public sacrifices, except any which the law assigns to the priests; such sacrifices derive their dignity from the public hearth of the city. They are sometimes called archons, sometimes kings,[40] and sometimes prytanes.

These, then, are the necessary offices, which may be summed up as follows: offices concerned with matters of religion, with war, with the revenue and expenditure, with the market, with the city, with the harbours, with the country; also with the courts of law, with the records of contracts, with execution of sentences, with custody of prisoners, with audits and scrutinies and accounts of magistrates; lastly, there are those which preside over the public deliberations of the state. There are likewise magistracies characteristic of states which are peaceful and prosperous, and at the same time have a regard to good order: such as the offices of guardians of women, guardians of the law, guardians of children, and directors of gymnastics; also superintendents of gymnastic and Dionysiac contests, and of other similar spectacles. Some of these are clearly not democratic offices; for example, the guardianships of women and children[41]—the poor, not having any slaves, must employ both their women and children as servants.

[39] Cp. Bk. 4, XV.
[40] Cp. Bk. 3, XIV.
[41] Cp. Bk. 4, XV.

Once more: there are three offices according to whose directions the highest magistrates are chosen in certain states—guardians of the law, probuli, councillors—of these, the guardians of the law are an aristocratical, the probuli an oligarchical, the council a democratical institution. Enough of the different kinds of offices.

BOOK SEVENTH

I He who would duly inquire about the best form of a state ought first to determine which is the most eligible life; while this remains uncertain the best form of the state must also be uncertain; for, in the natural order of things, those may be expected to lead the best life who are governed in the best manner of which their circumstances admit. We ought therefore to ascertain, first of all, which is the most generally eligible life, and then whether the same life is or is not best for the state and for individuals.

Assuming that enough has been already said in discussions outside the school concerning the best life, we will now only repeat what is contained in them. Certainly no one will dispute the propriety of that partition of goods which separates them into three classes,[1] viz. external goods, goods of the body, and goods of the soul, or deny that the happy man must have all three. For no one would maintain that he is happy who has not in him a particle of courage or temperance or justice or prudence, who is afraid of every insect which flutters past him, and will commit any crime, however great, in order to gratify his lust of meat or drink, who will sacrifice his dearest friend for the sake of half-a-farthing, and is as feeble and false in mind as a child or a madman. These propositions are almost universally acknowledged as soon as they are uttered, but men differ about the degree or relative superiority of this or that good. Some think that a very moderate amount of virtue is enough, but set no limit to their desires of wealth, property, power, reputation, and the like. To whom we reply by an appeal to facts, which easily prove that mankind do not acquire or preserve virtue by the help of external goods, but external goods by the help of virtue, and that happiness, whether consisting in pleasure or virtue, or both, is more often found with those who are most highly cultivated in their mind and in their character, and have only a moderate share of external goods, than among those who possess external goods to a useless extent but are deficient in higher qualities; and this is not only matter of experience, but, if reflected upon, will easily appear to be in accordance with reason. For, whereas external goods have a limit, like any other instrument,[2] and all things useful are of such a nature

[1] Cp. *Laws*, iii. 697 B, v. 743 E; *N. Eth.* i. 1098b 12.
[2] Cp. Bk. 1, VIII.

that where there is too much of them they must either do harm, or at any rate be of no use, to their possessors, every good of the soul, the greater it is, is also of greater use, if the epithet useful as well as noble is appropriate to such subjects. No proof is required to show that the best state of one thing in relation to another corresponds in degree of excellence to the interval between the natures of which we say that these very states are states: so that, if the soul is more noble than our possessions or our bodies, both absolutely and in relation to us, it must be admitted that the best state of either has a similar ratio to the other. Again, it is for the sake of the soul that goods external and goods of the body are eligible at all, and all wise men ought to choose them for the sake of the soul, and not the soul for the sake of them.

Let us acknowledge then that each one has just so much of happiness as he has of virtue and wisdom, and of virtuous and wise action. God is a witness to us of this truth, for he is happy and blessed, not by reason of any external good, but in himself and by reason of his own nature. And herein of necessity lies the difference between good fortune and happiness; for external goods come of themselves, and chance is the author of them, but no one is just or temperate by or through chance.[3] In like manner, and by a similar train of argument, the happy state may be shown to be that which is best and which acts rightly; and rightly it cannot act without doing right actions, and neither individual nor state can do right actions without virtue and wisdom. Thus the courage, justice, and wisdom of a state have the same form and nature as the qualities which give the individual who possesses them the name of just, wise, or temperate.

Thus much may suffice by way of preface: for I could not avoid touching upon these questions, neither could I go through all the arguments affecting them; these are the business of another science.

Let us assume then that the best life, both for individuals and states, is the life of virtue, when virtue has external goods enough for the performance of good actions. If there are any who controvert our assertion, we will in this treatise pass them over, and consider their objections hereafter.

[3] *Nic. Eth.* i. 1099b 20.

II There remains to be discussed the question, Whether the happiness of the individual is the same as that of the state, or different? Here again there can be no doubt—no one denies that they are the same. For those who hold that the well-being of the individual consists in his wealth, also think that riches make the happiness of the whole state, and those who value most highly the life of a tyrant deem that city the happiest which rules over the greatest number; while they who approve an individual for his virtue say that the more virtuous a city is, the happier it is. Two points here present themselves for consideration: first (1), which is the more eligible life, that of a citizen who is a member of a state, or that of an alien who has no political ties; and again (2), which is the best form of constitution or the best condition of a state, either on the supposition that political privileges are desirable for all, or for a majority only? Since the good of the state and not of the individual is the proper subject of political thought and speculation, and we are engaged in a political discussion, while the first of these two points has a secondary interest for us, the latter will be the main subject of our inquiry.

Now it is evident that the form of government is best in which every man, whoever he is, can act best and live happily. But even those who agree in thinking that the life of virtue is the most eligible raise a question, whether the life of business and politics is or is not more eligible than one which is wholly independent of external goods, I mean than a contemplative life, which by some is maintained to be the only one worthy of a philosopher. For these two lives—the life of the philosopher and the life of the statesman—appear to have been preferred by those who have been most keen in the pursuit of virtue, both in our own and in other ages. Which is the better is a question of no small moment; for the wise man, like the wise state, will necessarily regulate his life according to the best end. There are some who think that while a despotic rule over others is the greatest injustice, to exercise a constitutional rule over them, even though not unjust, is a great impediment to a man's individual well-being. Others take an opposite view; they maintain that the true life of man is the practical and political, and that every virtue admits of being practised, quite as much by statesmen and rulers as by private individuals. Others, again, are of opinion that arbitrary and tyrannical rule alone consists with happiness; indeed, in some states the entire aim both of the laws and of the constitution is to give men despotic power over their neighbours. And, therefore, although in most cities the laws may be said generally to be in a chaotic state, still, if they aim at anything, they aim at the maintenance of power: thus in Lacedaemon and Crete the system of education and the greater part of the laws are framed with a view to war.[4] And in all nations which are able to gratify their ambition military power is held in esteem, for example among the Scythians and Persians and Thracians and Celts. In some nations there are even laws tending to stimulate the warlike virtues, as at Carthage, where we are told that men obtain the honour of wearing as many armlets as they have served campaigns. There was once a law in Macedonia that he who had not killed an enemy should wear a halter, and among the Scythians no one who had not slain his man was allowed to drink out of the cup which was handed round at a certain feast. Among the Iberians, a warlike nation, the number of enemies whom a man has slain is indicated by the number of obelisks which are fixed in the earth round his tomb; and there are numerous practices among other nations of a like kind, some of them established by law and others by custom. Yet to a reflecting mind it must appear very strange that the statesman should be always considering how he can dominate and tyrannize over others, whether they will or not. How can that which is not even lawful be the business of the statesman or the legislator? Unlawful it certainly is to rule without regard to justice, for there may be might where there is no right. The other arts and sciences offer no parallel; a physician is not expected to persuade or coerce his patients, nor a pilot the passengers in his ship. Yet most men appear to think that the art of despotic government is statesmanship, and what men affirm to be unjust and inexpedient in their own case they are not ashamed of practising towards others; they demand just rule for themselves, but where other men are concerned they care nothing about it. Such behaviour is irrational; unless the one party is, and the other is not, born to serve, in which case men have a right to command, not indeed all their fellows, but only those who are intended to be subjects; just as we ought not to hunt mankind, whether for food or sacrifice, but only the animals which may be hunted for food or sacrifice, this is to say, such wild animals as are eatable. And surely there may be a city happy

[4] Cp. Plato, *Laws*, i. 633 ff.

in isolation, which we will assume to be well-governed (for it is quite possible that a city thus isolated might be well-administered and have good laws); but such a city would not be constituted with any view to war or the conquest of enemies—all that sort of thing must be excluded. Hence we see very plainly that warlike pursuits, although generally to be deemed honourable, are not the supreme end of all things, but only means. And the good lawgiver should inquire how states and races of men and communities may participate in a good life, and in the happiness which is attainable by them. His enactments will not be always the same; and where there are neighbours[5] he will have to see what sort of studies should be practised in relation to their several characters, or how the measures appropriate in relation to each are to be adopted. The end at which the best form of government should aim may be properly made a matter of future consideration.[6]

III Let us now address those who, while they agree that the life of virtue is the most eligible, differ about the manner of practising it. For some renounce political power, and think that the life of the freeman is different from the life of the statesman and the best of all; but others think the life of the statesman best. The argument of the latter is that he who does nothing cannot do well, and that virtuous activity is identical with happiness. To both we say: 'you are partly right and partly wrong'. The first class are right in affirming that the life of the freeman is better than the life of the despot; for there is nothing grand or noble in having the use of a slave, in so far as he is a slave; or in issuing commands about necessary things. But it is an error to suppose that every sort of rule is despotic like that of a master over slaves, for there is as great a difference between the rule over freemen and the rule over slaves as there is between slavery by nature and freedom by nature, about which I have said enough at the commencement of this treatise.[7] And it is equally a mistake to place inactivity above action, for happiness is activity, and the actions of the just and wise are the realization of much that is noble.

But perhaps some one, accepting these premises, may still maintain that supreme power is the best of all things, because the pos-

[5] Cp. Bk. 2, VI, VII.
[6] Bk. 7, VII.
[7] Bk. 1, IV–VII.

sessors of it are able to perform the greatest number of noble actions. If so, the man who is able to rule, instead of giving up anything to his neighbour, ought rather to take away his power; and the father should make no account of his son, nor the son of his father, nor friend of friend; they should not bestow a thought on one another in comparison with this higher object, for the best is the most eligible and 'doing well' is the best. There might be some truth in such a view if we assume that robbers and plunderers attain the chief good. But this can never be; their hypothesis is false. For the actions of a ruler cannot really be honourable, unless he is as much superior to other men as a husband is to a wife, or a father to his children, or a master to his slaves. And therefore he who violates the law can never recover by any success, however great, what he has already lost in departing from virtue. For equals the honourable and the just consist in sharing alike, as is just and equal. But that the unequal should be given to equals, and the unlike to those who are like, is contrary to nature, and nothing which is contrary to nature is good. If therefore, there is any one[8] superior in virtue and in the power of performing the best actions, him we ought to follow and obey, but he must have the capacity for action as well as virtue.

If we are right in our view, and happiness is assumed to be virtuous activity, the active life will be the best, both for every city collectively, and for individuals. Not that a life of action must necessarily have relation to others, as some persons think, nor are those ideas only to be regarded as practical which are pursued for the sake of practical results, but much more the thoughts and contemplations which are independent and complete in themselves; since virtuous activity, and therefore a certain kind of action, is an end, and even in the case of external actions the directing mind is most truly said to act. Neither, again, is it necessary that states which are cut off from others and choose to live alone should be inactive; for activity, as well as other things, may take place by sections; there are many ways in which the sections of a state act upon one another. The same thing is equally true of every individual. If this were otherwise, God and the universe, who have no external actions over and above their own energies, would be far enough from perfection. Hence it is evident that the same

[8] Cp. Bk. 3, XIII and XVII.

life is best for each individual, and for states and for mankind collectively.

IV Thus far by way of introduction. In what has preceded[9] I have discussed other forms of government; in what remains the first point to be considered is what should be the conditions of the ideal or perfect state; for the perfect state cannot exist without a due supply of the means of life. And therefore we must presuppose many purely imaginary conditions,[10] but nothing impossible. There will be a certain number of citizens, a country in which to place them, and the like. As the weaver or shipbuilder or any other artisan must have the material proper for his work (and in proportion as this is better prepared, so will the result of his art be nobler), so the statesman or legislator must also have the materials suited to him.

First among the materials required by the statesman is population: he will consider what should be the number and character of the citizens, and then what should be the size and character of the country. Most persons think that a state in order to be happy ought to be large; but even if they are right, they have no idea what is a large and what a small state. For they judge of the size of the city by the number of the inhabitants; whereas they ought to regard, not their number, but their power. A city too, like an individual, has a work to do; and that city which is best adapted to the fulfilment of its work is to be deemed greatest, in the same sense of the word great in which Hippocrates might be called greater, not as a man, but as a physician, than some one else who was taller. And even if we reckon greatness by numbers, we ought not to include everybody, for there must always be in cities a multitude of slaves and sojourners and foreigners; but we should include those only who are members of the state, and who form an essential part of it. The number of the latter is a proof of the greatness of a city; but a city which produces numerous artisans and comparatively few soldiers cannot be great, for a great city is not to be confounded with a populous one. Moreover, experience shows that a very populous city can rarely, if ever, be well governed; since all cities which have a reputation for good govern-

[9] Bk. 2.

[10] Cp. Bk. 2, VI.

ment have a limit of population. We may argue on grounds of reason, and the same result will follow. For law is order, and good law is good order; but a very great multitude cannot be orderly: to introduce order into the unlimited is the work of a divine power —of such a power as holds together the universe. Beauty is realized in number and magnitude,[11] and the state which combines magnitude with good order must necessarily be the most beautiful. To the size of states there is a limit, as there is to other things, plants, animals, implements; for none of these retain their natural power when they are too large or too small, but they either wholly lose their nature, or are spoiled. For example,[12] a ship which is only a span long will not be a ship at all, nor a ship a quarter of a mile long; yet there may be a ship of a certain size, either too large or too small, which will still be a ship, but bad for sailing. In like manner a state when composed of too few is not, as a state ought to be, self-sufficing; when of too many, though self-sufficing in all mere necessaries, as a nation may be, it is not a state, being almost incapable of constitutional government. For who can be the general of such a vast multitude, or who the herald, unless he have the voice of a Stentor?

A state, then, only begins to exist when it has attained a population sufficient for a good life in the political community: it may indeed, if it somewhat exceed this number, be a greater state. But, as I was saying, there must be a limit. What should be the limit will be easily ascertained by experience. For both governors and governed have duties to perform; the special functions of a governor are to command and to judge. But if the citizens of a state are to judge and to distribute offices according to merit, then they must know each other's characters; where they do not possess this knowledge, both the election to offices and the decision of lawsuits will go wrong. When the population is very large they are manifestly settled at haphazard, which clearly ought not to be. Besides, in an over-populous state foreigners and metics will readily acquire the rights of citizens, for who will find them out? Clearly then the best limit of the population of a state is the largest number which suffices for the purposes of life, and can be taken in at a single view. Enough concerning the size of a state.

[11] Cp. *Poet.* 1450^{b} 36.

[12] Cp. Bk. 5, IX.

V Much the same principle will apply to the territory of the state: every one would agree in praising the territory which is most entirely self-sufficing; and that must be the territory which is all-producing, for to have all things and to want nothing is sufficiency. In size and extent it should be such as may enable the inhabitants to live at once temperately and liberally in the enjoyment of leisure.[13] Whether we are right or wrong in laying down this limit we will inquire more precisely hereafter,[14] when we have occasion to consider what is the right use of property and wealth: a matter which is much disputed, because men are inclined to rush into one of two extremes, some into meanness, others into luxury.

It is not difficult to determine the general character of the territory which is required (there are, however, some points on which military authorities should be heard); it should be difficult of access to the enemy, and easy of egress to the inhabitants. Further, we require that the land as well as the inhabitants of whom we were just now speaking[15] should be taken in at a single view, for a country which is easily seen can be easily protected. As to the position of the city, if we could have what we wish, it should be well situated in regard both to sea and land. This then is one principle, that it should be a convenient centre for the protection of the whole country: the other is, that it should be suitable for receiving the fruits of the soil, and also for the bringing in of timber and any other products that are easily transported.

VI Whether a communication with the sea is beneficial to a well-ordered state or not is a question which has often been asked. It is argued that the introduction of strangers brought up under other laws, and the increase of population, will be adverse to good order; the increase arises from their using the sea and having a crowd of merchants coming and going, and is inimical to good government.[16] Apart from these considerations, it would be undoubtedly better, both with a view to safety and to the provision of necessaries, that the city and territory should be connected with the sea; the defenders of a country, if they are to maintain themselves against an enemy, should be easily relieved both by land

[13] Cp. Bk. 2, VI.

[14] This promise is not fulfilled.

[15] Bk. 7, V.

[16] Cp. Plato, *Laws*, iv. 704 D–705 B.

and by sea; and even if they are not able to attack by sea and land at once, they will have less difficulty in doing mischief to their assailants on one element, if they themselves can use both. Moreover, it is necessary that they should import from abroad what is not found in their own country, and that they should export what they have in excess; for a city ought to be a market, not indeed for others, but for herself.

Those who make themselves a market for the world only do so for the sake of revenue, and if a state ought not to desire profit of this kind it ought not to have such an emporium. Nowadays we often see in countries and cities dockyards and harbours very conveniently placed outside the city, but not too far off; and they are kept in dependence by walls and similar fortifications. Cities thus situated manifestly reap the benefit of intercourse with their ports; and any harm which is likely to accrue may be easily guarded against by the laws, which will pronounce and determine who may hold communication with one another, and who may not.

There can be no doubt that the possession of a moderate naval force is advantageous to a city; the city should be formidable not only to its own citizens but to some of its neighbours,[17] or, if necessary, able to assist them by sea as well as by land. The proper number or magnitude of this naval force is relative to the character of the state; for if her function is to take a leading part in politics, her naval power should be commensurate with the scale of her enterprises. The population of the state need not be much increased, since there is no necessity that the sailors should be citizens: the marines who have the control and command will be freemen, and belong also to the infantry; and wherever there is a dense population of Perioeci and husbandmen, there will always be sailors more than enough. Of this we see instances at the present day. The city of Heraclea, for example, although small in comparison with many others, can man a considerable fleet. Such are our conclusions respecting the territory of the state, its harbours, its towns, its relations to the sea, and its maritime power.

VII Having spoken of the number of the citizens,[18] we will proceed to speak of what should be their character. This is a subject

[17] Cp. Bk. 2, VI.

[18] Bk. 7, IV.

which can be easily understood by any one who casts his eye on the more celebrated states of Hellas, and generally on the distribution of races in the habitable world. Those who live in a cold climate and in Europe are full of spirit, but wanting in intelligence and skill; and therefore they retain comparative freedom, but have no political organization, and are incapable of ruling over others. Whereas the natives of Asia are intelligent and inventive, but they are wanting in spirit, and therefore they are always in a state of subjection and slavery. But the Hellenic race, which is situated between them, is likewise intermediate in character, being high-spirited and also intelligent.[19] Hence it continues free, and is the best governed of any nation, and, if it could be formed into one state, would be able to rule the world. There are also similar differences in the different tribes of Hellas; for some of them are of a one-sided nature, and are intelligent or courageous only, while in others there is a happy combination of both qualities. And clearly those whom the legislator will most easily lead to virtue may be expected to be both intelligent and courageous. Some[20] say that the guardians should be friendly towards those whom they know, fierce towards those whom they do not know. Now, passion is the quality of the soul which begets friendship and enables us to love; notably the spirit within us is more stirred against our friends and acquaintances than against those who are unknown to us, when we think that we are despised by them; for which reason Archilochus, complaining of his friends, very naturally addresses his soul in these words:

'For surely thou are plagued on account of friends'.

The power of command and the love of freedom are in all men based upon this quality, for passion is commanding and invincible. Nor is it right to say that the guardians should be fierce towards those whom they do not know, for we ought not to be out of temper with any one; and a lofty spirit is not fierce by nature, but only when excited against evil-doers. And this, as I was saying before, is a feeling which men show most strongly towards their friends if they think they have received a wrong at their hands: as indeed is reasonable; for, besides the actual injury, they seem to be deprived of a benefit by those who owe them one. Hence the saying:

[19] Cp. Plato, *Rep.* iv. 435 E, 436 A.

[20] *Rep.* ii. 375 C.

'Cruel is the strife of brethren',

and again:

'They who love in excess also hate in excess'.

Thus we have nearly determined the number and character of the citizens of our state, and also the size and nature of their territory. I say 'nearly', for we ought not to require the same minuteness in theory as in the facts given by perception.[21]

VIII As in other natural compounds the conditions of a composite whole are not necessarily organic parts of it, so in a state or in any other combination forming a unity not everything is a part, which is a necessary condition.[22] The members of an association have necessarily some one thing the same and common to all, in which they share equally or unequally; for example, food or land or any other thing. But where there are two things of which one is a means and the other an end, they have nothing in common except that the one receives what the other produces. Such, for example, is the relation in which workmen and tools stand to their work; the house and the builder have nothing in common, but the art of the builder is for the sake of the house. And so states require property, but property, even though living beings are included in it,[23] is no part of a state; for a state is not a community of living beings only, but a community of equals, aiming at the best life possible. Now, whereas happiness is the highest good, being a realization and perfect practice of virtue, which some can attain, while others have little or none of it, the various qualities of men are clearly the reason why there are various kinds of states and many forms of government; for different men seek after happiness in different ways and by different means, and so make for themselves different modes of life and forms of government. We must see also how many things are indispensable to the existence of a state, for what we call the parts of a state will be found among the indispensables. Let us then enumerate the functions of a state, and we shall easily elicit what we want:

[21] Cp. Bk. 7, XIII.
[22] Cp. Bk. 3, V.
[23] Cp. Bk. 1, IV.

First, there must be food; secondly, arts, for life requires many instruments; thirdly, there must be arms, for the members of a community have need of them, and in their own hands, too, in order to maintain authority both against disobedient subjects and against external assailants; fourthly, there must be a certain amount of revenue, both for internal needs, and for the purposes of war; fifthly, or rather first, there must be a care of religion, which is commonly called worship; sixthly, and most necessary of all, there must be a power of deciding what is for the public interest, and what is just in men's dealings with one another.

These are the services which every state may be said to need. For a state is not a mere aggregate of persons, but a union of them sufficing for the purposes of life; and if any of these things be wanting, it is as we maintain[24] impossible that the community can be absolutely self-sufficing. A state then should be framed with a view to the fulfilment of these functions. There must be husbandmen to procure food, and artisans, and a warlike and a wealthy class, and priests, and judges to decide what is necessary and expedient.

IX Having determined these points, we have in the next place to consider whether all ought to share in every sort of occupation. Shall every man be at once husbandman, artisan, councillor, judge, or shall we suppose the several occupations just mentioned assigned to different persons? or, thirdly, shall some employments be assigned to individuals and others common to all? The same arrangement, however, does not occur in every constitution; as we were saying, all may be shared by all, or not all by all, but only by some; and hence arise the differences of constitutions, for in democracies all share in all, in oligarchies the opposite practice prevails. Now, since we are here speaking of the best form of government, i.e. that under which the state will be most happy (and happiness, as has been already said, cannot exist without virtue[25]), it clearly follows that in the state which is best governed and possesses men who are just absolutely, and not merely relatively to the principle of the constitution, the citizens must not lead the

[24] Cp. Bk. 2, II; Bk. 3, II; Bk. 5, III.
[25] Cp. Bk. 6, VIII–Bk. 7, II, VII.

life of mechanics or tradesmen, for such a life is ignoble, and inimical to virtue.[26] Neither must they be husbandmen, since leisure is necessary both for the development of virtue and the performance of political duties.

Again, there is in a state a class of warriors, and another of councillors, who advise about the expedient and determine matters of law, and these seem in an especial manner parts of a state. Now, should these two classes be distinguished, or are both functions to be assigned to the same persons? Here again there is no difficulty in seeing that both functions will in one way belong to the same, in another, to different persons. To different persons in so far as these employments are suited to different primes of life,[27] for the one requires wisdom and the other strength. But on the other hand, since it is an impossible thing that those who are able to use or to resist force should be willing to remain always in subjection, from this point of view the persons are the same; for those who carry arms can always determine the fate of the constitution. It remains therefore that both functions should be entrusted by the ideal constitution to the same persons, not, however, at the same time, but in the order prescribed by nature, who has given to young men strength and to older men wisdom. Such a distribution of duties will be expedient and also just, and is founded upon a principle of conformity to merit. Besides, the ruling class should be the owners of property, for they are citizens, and the citizens of a state should be in good circumstances; whereas mechanics or any other class which is not a producer of virtue have no share in the state. This follows from our first principle,[28] for happiness cannot exist without virtue, and a city is not to be termed happy in regard to a portion of the citizens, but in regard to them all.[29] And clearly property should be in their hands, since the husbandmen will of necessity be slaves or barbarian Perioeci.[30]

Of the classes enumerated there remain only the priests, and the manner in which their office is to be regulated is obvious. No husbandman or mechanic should be appointed to it; for the Gods

[26] Cp. Plato, *Laws*, xi. 919 C–E.
[27] i. e. the physical and the mental.
[28] Cp. Bk. 7, VIII.
[29] Cp. Bk. 2, V.
[30] Cp. *infra*, Bk. 7, X.

should receive honour from the citizens only. Now since the body of the citizens is divided into two classes, the warriors and the councillors, and it is beseeming that the worship of the Gods should be duly performed, and also a rest provided in their service for those who from age have given up active life, to the old men of these two classes should be assigned the duties of the priesthood.

We have shown what are the necessary conditions, and what the parts of a state: husbandmen, craftsmen, and labourers of all kinds are necessary to the existence of states, but the parts of the state are the warriors and councillors. And these are distinguished severally from one another, the distinction being in some cases permanent, in others not.

X It is not a new or recent discovery of political philosophers that the state ought to be divided into classes, and that the warriors should be separated from the husbandmen. The system has continued in Egypt and in Crete to this day, and was established, as tradition says, by a law of Sesostris in Egypt and of Minos in Crete. The institution of common tables also appears to be of ancient date, being in Crete as old as the reign of Minos, and in Italy far older. The Italian historians say that there was a certain Italus king of Oenotria, from whom the Oenotrians were called Italians, and who gave the name of Italy to the promontory of Europe lying within the Scylletic and Lametic Gulfs,[31] which are distant from one another only half a day's journey. They say that this Italus converted the Oenotrians from shepherds into husbandmen, and besides other laws which he gave them, was the founder of their common meals; even in our day some who are derived from him retain this institution and certain other laws of his. On the side of Italy towards Tyrrhenia dwelt the Opici, who are now, as of old, called Ausones; and on the side towards Iapygia and the Ionian Gulf, in the district called Siritis, the Chones, who are likewise of Oenotrian race. From this part of the world originally came the institution of common tables; the separation into castes from Egypt, for the reign of Sesostris is of far greater antiquity than that of Minos. It is true indeed that these and

[31] i. e. between these gulfs and the Strait of Messina.

many other things have been invented several times over[32] in the course of ages, or rather times without number; for necessity may be supposed to have taught men the inventions which were absolutely required, and when these were provided, it was natural that other things which would adorn and enrich life should grow up by degrees. And we may infer that in political institutions the same rule holds. Egypt[33] witnesses to the antiquity of all these things, for the Egyptians appear to be of all people the most ancient; and they have laws and a regular constitution existing from time immemorial. We should therefore make the best use of what has been already discovered, and try to supply defects.

I have already remarked that the land ought to belong to those who possess arms and have a share in the government,[34] and that the husbandmen ought to be a class distinct from them; and I have determined what should be the extent and nature of the territory. Let me proceed to discuss the distribution of the land, and the character of the agricultural class; for I do not think that property ought to be common, as some maintain,[35] but only that by friendly consent there should be a common use of it; and that no citizen should be in want of subsistence.

As to common meals, there is a general agreement that a well-ordered city should have them; and we will hereafter explain what are our own reasons for taking this view.[36] They ought, however, to be open to all the citizens.[37] And yet it is not easy for the poor to contribute the requisite sum out of their private means, and to provide also for their household. The expense of religious worship should likewise be a public charge. The land must therefore be divided into two parts, one public and the other private, and each part should be subdivided, part of the public land being appropriated to the service of the Gods, and the other part used to defray the cost of the common meals; while of the private land, part should be near the border, and the other near the city, so that, each citizen having two lots, they may all of them have land

[32] Cp. Plato, *Laws*, iii. 676; Aristotle, *Metaph.* xii. 1074b 10; and *Pol.* Bk. 2, V.

[33] Cp. *Metaph.* i. 981b 23; *Meteor.* i. 14. 352b 19; Plato, *Timaeus*, 22 B; *Laws*, ii. 656, 657.

[34] Bk. 7, VIII–IX, V.

[35] Cp. Bk. 2, V, *Rep.* iii. 416 D.

[36] Aristotle does not give any explanation in the *Politics*.

[37] Cp. Bk. 2, IX.

in both places; there is justice and fairness in such a division, and it tends to inspire unanimity among the people in their border wars. Where there is not this arrangement, some of them are too ready to come to blows with their neighbours, while others are so cautious that they quite lose the sense of honour. Wherefore there is a law in some places which forbids those who dwell near the border to take part in public deliberations about wars with neighbours, on the ground that their interests will pervert their judgement. For the reasons already mentioned, then, the land should be divided in the manner described. The very best thing of all would be that the husbandmen should be slaves taken from among men who are not all of the same race[38] and not spirited, for if they have no spirit they will be better suited for their work, and there will be no danger of their making a revolution. The next best thing would be that they should be Perioeci of foreign race,[39] and of a like inferior nature; some of them should be the slaves of individuals, and employed in the private estates of men of property, the remainder should be the property of the state and employed on the common land.[40] I will hereafter explain[41] what is the proper treatment of slaves, and why it is expedient that liberty should be always held out to them as the reward of their services.

XI We have already said that the city should be open to the land and to the sea,[42] and to the whole country as far as possible. In respect of the place itself our wish would be that its situation should be fortunate in four things. The first, health—this is a necessity: cities which lie towards the east, and are blown upon by winds coming from the east, are the healthiest; next in healthfulness are those which are sheltered from the north wind, for they have a milder winter. The site of the city should likewise be convenient both for political administration and for war. With a view to the latter it should afford easy egress to the citizens, and at the same time be inaccessible and difficult of capture to enemies.[43] There should be a natural abundance of springs and foun-

[38] Cp. Plato, *Laws*, vi. 777 C, D.
[39] Cp. Bk. 7, IX.
[40] Cp. Bk. 2, VII.
[41] A. does not do so in the *Politics*, but Cp. *Oec.* 1344^b 15.
[42] Bk. 7, VI.
[43] Repetition of Bk. 7, V.

tains in the town, or, if there is a deficiency of them, great reservoirs may be established for the collection of rainwater, such as will not fail when the inhabitants are cut off from the country by war. Special care should be taken of the health of the inhabitants, which will depend chiefly on the healthiness of the locality and of the quarter to which they are exposed, and secondly, on the use of pure water; this latter point is by no means a secondary consideration. For the elements which we use most and oftenest for the support of the body contribute most to health, and among these are water and air. Wherefore, in all wise states, if there is a want of pure water, and the supply is not all equally good, the drinking water ought to be separated from that which is used for other purposes.

As to strongholds, what is suitable to different forms of government varies: thus an acropolis is suited to an oligarchy or a monarchy, but a plain to a democracy; neither to an aristocracy, but rather a number of strong places. The arrangement of private houses is considered to be more agreeable and generally more convenient, if the streets are regularly laid out after the modern fashion which Hippodamus[44] introduced, but for security in war the antiquated mode of building, which made it difficult for strangers to get out of a town and for assailants to find their way in, is preferable. A city should therefore adopt both plans of building: it is possible to arrange the houses irregularly, as husbandmen plant their vines in what are called 'clumps'. The whole town should not be laid out in straight lines, but only certain quarters and regions; thus security and beauty will be combined.

As to walls, those who say[45] that cities making any pretension to military virtue should not have them, are quite out of date in their notions; and they may see the cities which prided themselves on this fancy confuted by facts. True, there is little courage shown in seeking for safety behind a rampart when an enemy is similar in character and not much superior in number; but the superiority of the besiegers may be and often is too much both for ordinary human valour and for that which is found only in a few; and if they are to be saved and to escape defeat and outrage, the strongest wall will be the truest soldierly precaution, more especially now that missiles and siege engines have been brought

[44] Cp. Bk. 2, VII.
[45] Cp. Plato, *Laws*, vi. 778 D.

to such perfection. To have no walls would be as foolish as to choose a site for a town in an exposed country, and to level the heights; or as if an individual were to leave his house unwalled, lest the inmates should become cowards. Nor must we forget that those who have their cities surrounded by walls may either take advantage of them or not, but cities which are unwalled have no choice.

If our conclusions are just, not only should cities have walls, but care should be taken to make them ornamental, as well as useful for warlike purposes, and adapted to resist modern inventions. For as the assailants of a city do all they can to gain an advantage, so the defenders should make use of any means of defence which have been already discovered, and should devise and invent others, for when men are well prepared no enemy even thinks of attacking them.

XII As the walls are to be divided by guard-houses and towers built at suitable intervals, and the body of citizens must be distributed at common tables,[46] the idea will naturally occur that we should establish some of the common tables in the guard-houses. These might be arranged as has been suggested; while the principal common tables of the magistrates will occupy a suitable place, and there also will be the buildings appropriated to religious worship except in the case of those rites which the law or the Pythian oracle has restricted to a special locality.[47] The site should be a spot seen far and wide, which gives due elevation to virtue and towers over the neighbourhood. Below this spot should be established an agora, such as that which the Thessalians call the 'freemen's agora'; from this all trade should be excluded, and no mechanic, husbandman, or any such person allowed to enter, unless he be summoned by the magistrates. It would be a charming use of the place, if the gymnastic exercises of the elder men were performed there. For in this noble practice different ages should be separated, and some of the magistrates should stay with the boys, while the grown-up men remain with the magistrates; for the presence of the magistrates is the best mode of inspiring true modesty and ingenuous fear. There should also be

[46] Cp. Bk. 7, X.

[47] Cp. Plato, *Laws*, v. 738 B–D, vi. 759 C, 778 C, viii. 848 D–E.

a traders' agora, distinct and apart from the other, in a situation which is convenient for the reception of goods both by sea and land.

But in speaking of the magistrates we must not forget another section of the citizens, viz. the priests, for whom public tables should likewise be provided in their proper place near the temples. The magistrates who deal with contracts, indictments, summonses, and the like, and those who have the care of the agora and of the city respectively, ought to be established near an agora and some public place of meeting; the neighbourhood of the traders' agora will be a suitable spot; the upper agora we devote to the life of leisure, the other is intended for the necessities of trade.

The same order should prevail in the country, for there too the magistrates, called by some 'Inspectors of Forests' and by others 'Wardens of the Country', must have guard-houses and common tables while they are on duty; temples should also be scattered throughout the country, dedicated, some to Gods, and some to heroes.

But it would be a waste of time for us to linger over details like these. The difficulty is not in imagining but in carrying them out. We may talk about them as much as we like, but the execution of them will depend upon fortune. Wherefore let us say no more about these matters for the present.

XIII Returning to the constitution itself, let us seek to determine out of what and what sort of elements the state which is to be happy and well-governed should be composed. There are two things in which all well-being consists: one of them is the choice of a right end and aim of action, and the other the discovery of the actions which are means towards it; for the means and the end may agree or disagree. Sometimes the right end is set before men, but in practice they fail to attain it; in other cases they are successful in all the means, but they propose to themselves a bad end; and sometimes they fail in both. Take, for example, the art of medicine; physicians do not always understand the nature of health, and also the means which they use may not effect the desired end. In all arts and sciences both the end and the means should be equally within our control.

The happiness and well-being which all men manifestly desire, some have the power of attaining, but to others, from some accident or defect of nature, the attainment of them is not granted; for a good life requires a supply of external goods, in a less degree when men are in a good state, in a greater degree when they are in a lower state. Others again, who possess the conditions of happiness, go utterly wrong from the first in the pursuit of it. But since our object is to discover the best form of government, that, namely, under which a city will be best governed, and since the city is best governed which has the greatest opportunity of obtaining happiness, it is evident that we must clearly ascertain the nature of happiness.

We maintain, and have said in the *Ethics*,[48] if the arguments there adduced are of any value, that happiness is the realization and perfect exercise of virtue, and this not conditional, but absolute. And I used the term 'conditional' to express that which is indispensable, and 'absolute' to express that which is good in itself. Take the case of just actions; just punishments and chastisements do indeed spring from a good principle, but they are good only because we cannot do without them—it would be better that neither individuals nor states should need anything of the sort—but actions which aim at honour and advantage are absolutely the best. The conditional action is only the choice of a lesser evil; whereas these are the foundation and creation of good. A good man may make the best even of poverty and disease, and the other ills of life; but he can only attain happiness under the opposite conditions[49] (for this also has been determined in accordance with ethical arguments,[50] that the good man is he for whom, because he is virtuous, the things that are absolutely good are good; it is also plain that his use of these goods must be virtuous and in the absolute sense good). This makes men fancy that external goods are the cause of happiness, yet we might as well say that a brilliant performance on the lyre was to be attributed to the instrument and not to the skill of the performer.

It follows then from what has been said that some things the legislator must find ready to his hand in a state, others he must provide. And therefore we can only say: May our state be con-

[48] *Nic. Eth.* i. 1098ᵃ 16, x. 1176ᵇ 4; and Cp. Bk. 7, VII.
[49] *Nic. Eth.* i. 1100ᵇ 22, 1101ᵃ 13.
[50] *Nic. Eth.* iii. 1113ᵃ 22–ᵇ1; *E. E.* vii. 1248ᵇ 26; *M. M.* ii. 1207ᵇ 31.

stituted in such a manner as to be blessed with the goods of which fortune disposes (for we acknowledge her power): whereas virtue and goodness in the state are not a matter of chance but the result of knowledge and purpose. A city can be virtuous only when the citizens who have a share in the government are virtuous, and in our state all the citizens share in the government; let us then inquire how a man becomes virtuous. For even if we could suppose the citizen body to be virtuous, without each of them being so, yet the latter would be better, for in the virtue of each the virtue of all is involved.

There are three things which make men good and virtuous; these are nature, habit, rational principle.[51] In the first place, every one must be born a man and not some other animal; so, too, he must have a certain character, both of body and soul. But some qualities there is no use in having at birth, for they are altered by habit, and there are some gifts which by nature are made to be turned by habit to good or bad. Animals lead for the most part a life of nature, although in lesser particulars some are influenced by habit as well. Man has rational principle, in addition, and man only. Wherefore nature, habit, rational principle must be in harmony with one another; for they do not always agree; men do many things against habit and nature, if rational principle persuades them that they ought. We have already determined what natures are likely to be most easily moulded by the hands of the legislator.[52] All else is the work of education; we learn some things by habit and some by instruction.

XIV Since every political society is composed of rulers and subjects let us consider whether the relations of one to the other should interchange or be permanent.[53] For the education of the citizens will necessarily vary with the answer given to this question. Now, if some men excelled others in the same degree in which gods and heroes are supposed to excel mankind in general (having in the first place a great advantage even in their bodies, and secondly in their minds), so that the superiority of the governors was undisputed and patent to their subjects, it would clearly be better that once for all the one class should rule and

[51] Cp. *Nic. Eth.* x. 1179^b 20.

[52] Bk. 7, VI.

[53] Cp. Bk. 3, VII.

the other serve.[54] But since this is unattainable, and kings have no marked superiority over their subjects, such as Scylax affirms to be found among the Indians, it is obviously necessary on many grounds that all the citizens alike should take their turn of governing and being governed. Equality consists in the same treatment of similar persons, and no government can stand which is not founded upon justice. For if the government be unjust every one in the country unites with the governed in the desire to have a revolution, and it is an impossibility that the members of the government can be so numerous as to be stronger than all their enemies put together. Yet that governors should excel their subjects is undeniable. How all this is to be effected, and in what way they will respectively share in the government, the legislator has to consider. The subject has been already mentioned.[55] Nature herself has provided the distinction when she made a difference between old and young within the same species, of whom she fitted the one to govern and the other to be governed. No one takes offence at being governed when he is young, nor does he think himself better than his governors, especially if he will enjoy the same privilege when he reaches the required age.

We conclude that from one point of view governors and governed are identical, and from another different. And therefore their education must be the same and also different. For he who would learn to command well must, as men say, first of all learn to obey.[56] As I observed in the first part of this treatise, there is one rule which is for the sake of the rulers and another rule which is for the sake of the ruled;[57] the former is a despotic, the latter a free government. Some commands differ not in the thing commanded, but in the intention with which they are imposed. Wherefore, many apparently menial offices are an honour to the free youth by whom they are performed; for actions do not differ as honourable or dishonourable in themselves so much as in the end and intention of them. But since we say[58] that the virtue of the citizen and ruler is the same as that of the good man, and that the same person must first be a subject and then a ruler, the legislator has to see that they become good men, and by what means this may be accomplished, and what is the end of the perfect life.

[54] Cp. Bk. 1, V, XIII.
[55] Bk. 7, IX.
[56] Cp. Bk. 3, IV.
[57] Bk. 3, VI–VII, Cp. IV.
[58] Cp. Bk. 3, IV, V.

Now the soul of man is divided into two parts, one of which has a rational principle in itself, and the other, not having a rational principle in itself, is able to obey such a principle.[59] And we call a man in any way good because he has the virtues of these two parts. In which of them the end is more likely to be found is no matter of doubt to those who adopt our division; for in the world both of nature and of art the inferior always exists for the sake of the better or superior, and the better or superior is that which has a rational principle. This principle, too, in our ordinary way of speaking, is divided into two kinds, for there is a practical and a speculative principle.[60] This part, then, must evidently be similarly divided. And there must be a corresponding division of actions; the actions of the naturally better part are to be preferred by those who have it in their power to attain to two out of the three or to all, for that is always to every one the most eligible which is the highest attainable by him. The whole of life is further divided into two parts, business and leisure,[61] war and peace, and of actions some aim at what is necessary and useful, and some at what is honourable. And the preference given to one or the other class of actions must necessarily be like the preference given to one or other part of the soul and its actions over the other; there must be war for the sake of peace, business for the sake of leisure, things useful and necessary for the sake of things honourable. All these points the statesman should keep in view when he frames his laws; he should consider the parts of the soul and their functions, and above all the better and the end; he should also remember the diversities of human lives and actions. For men must be able to engage in business and go to war, but leisure and peace are better; they must do what is necessary and indeed what is useful, but what is honourable is better. On such principles children and persons of every age which requires education should be trained. Whereas even the Hellenes of the present day who are reputed to be best governed, and the legislators who gave them their constitutions, do not appear to have framed their governments with a regard to the best end, or to have given them laws and education with a view to all the virtues, but in a vulgar spirit have fallen back on those which promised to be more useful and profitable. Many modern writers have taken a

[59] Cp. *Nic. Eth.* i. 1102ᵇ 28.
[60] Cp. *Nic. Eth.* vi. 1139ᵃ 6.
[61] *Nic. Eth.* x. 1177ᵇ 4.

similar view: they commend the Lacedaemonian constitution, and praise the legislator for making conquest and war his sole aim,[62] a doctrine which may be refuted by argument and has long ago been refuted by facts. For most men desire empire in the hope of accumulating the goods of fortune; and on this ground Thibron and all those who have written about the Lacedaemonian constitution have praised their legislator, because the Lacedaemonians, by being trained to meet dangers, gained great power. But surely they are not a happy people now that their empire has passed away, nor was their legislator right. How ridiculous is the result, if, while they are continuing in the observance of his laws and no one interferes with them, they have lost the better part of life! These writers further err about the sort of government which the legislator should approve, for the government of freemen is nobler and implies more virtue than despotic government.[63] Neither is a city to be deemed happy or a legislator to be praised because he trains his citizens to conquer and obtain dominion over their neighbours, for there is great evil in this. On a similar principle any citizen who could, should obviously try to obtain the power in his own state—the crime which the Lacedaemonians accuse king Pausanias of attempting,[64] although he had so great honour already. No such principle and no law having this object is either statesmanlike or useful or right. For the same things are best both for individuals and for states, and these are the things which the legislator ought to implant in the minds of his citizens. Neither should men study war with a view to the enslavement of those who do not deserve to be enslaved; but first of all they should provide against their own enslavement, and in the second place obtain empire for the good of the governed, and not for the sake of exercising a general despotism, and in the third place they should seek to be masters only over those who deserve to be slaves. Facts, as well as arguments, prove that the legislator should direct all his military and other measures to the provision of leisure and the establishment of peace. For most of these military states are safe only while they are at war,[65] but fall when they have acquired their empire; like unused iron they lose their temper in time of peace. And for this the legislator is to blame, he never having taught them how to lead the life of peace.

[62] Cp. Plato, *Laws*, i. 628, 638.
[63] Cp. Bk. 1, IV.
[64] Cp. Bk. 5, I, VII.
[65] Cp. Bk. 2, IX.

XV Since the end of individuals and of states is the same, the end of the best man and of the best constitution must also be the same; it is therefore evident that there ought to exist in both of them the virtues of leisure; for peace, as has been often repeated,[66] is the end of war, and leisure of toil. But leisure and cultivation may be promoted, not only by those virtues which are practised in leisure, but also by some of those which are useful to business.[67] For many necessaries of life have to be supplied before we can have leisure. Therefore a city must be temperate and brave, and able to endure: for truly, as the proverb says, 'There is no leisure for slaves', and those who cannot face danger like men are the slaves of any invader. Courage and endurance are required for business and philosophy for leisure, temperance and justice for both, and more especially in times of peace and leisure, for war compels men to be just and temperate, whereas the enjoyment of good fortune and the leisure which comes with peace tend to make them insolent. Those then who seem to be the best-off and to be in the possession of every good, have special need of justice and temperance—for example, those (if such there be, as the poets say) who dwell in the Islands of the Blest; they above all will need philosophy and temperance and justice, and all the more the more leisure they have, living in the midst of abundance. There is no difficulty in seeing why the state that would be happy and good ought to have these virtues. If it be disgraceful in men not to be able to use the goods of life, it is peculiarly disgraceful not to be able to use them in time of leisure—to show excellent qualities in action and war, and when they have peace and leisure to be no better than slaves. Wherefore we should not practise virtue after the manner of the Lacedaemonians.[68] For they, while agreeing with other men in their conception of the highest goods, differ from the rest of mankind in thinking that they are to be obtained by the practice of a single virtue. And since [they think] these goods and the enjoyment of them greater than the enjoyment derived from the virtues . . . and that [it should be practised] for its own sake, is evident from what

[66] Bk. 7, XIV.

[67] i. e. 'not only by some of the speculative but also by some of the practical virtues'.

[68] Cp. Bk. 2, IX.

has been said; we must now consider how and by what means it is to be attained.

We have already determined that nature and habit and rational principle are required,[69] and, of these, the proper *nature* of the citizens has also been defined by us.[70] But we have still to consider whether the training of early life is to be that of rational principle or habit, for these two must accord, and when in accord they will then form the best of harmonies. The rational principle may be mistaken and fail in attaining the highest ideal of life, and there may be a like evil influence of habit. Thus much is clear in the first place, that, as in all other things, birth implies an antecedent beginning,[71] and that there are beginnings whose end is relative to a further end. Now, in men rational principle and mind are the end towards which nature strives,[72] so that the birth and moral discipline of the citizens ought to be ordered with a view to them. In the second place, as the soul and body are two, we see also that there are two parts of the soul, the rational and the irrational, and two corresponding states—reason and appetite. And as the body is prior in order of generation to the soul, so the irrational is prior to the rational. The proof is that anger and wishing and desire are implanted in children from their very birth, but reason and understanding are developed as they grow older. Wherefore, the care of the body ought to precede that of the soul, and the training of the appetitive part should follow: none the less our care of it must be for the sake of the reason, and our care of the body for the sake of the soul.

XVI Since the legislator should begin by considering how the frames of the children whom he is rearing may be as good as possible, his first care will be about marriage—at what age should his citizens marry, and who are fit to marry? In legislating on this subject he ought to consider the persons and the length of their life, that their procreative life may terminate at the same period, and that they may not differ in their bodily powers, as will be the

[69] Bk. 7, XIII. [70] VII.

[71] i. e. the union of the parents.

[72] i. e. the birth of the offspring, which is the end of the union of the parents, points to a further end, the development of mind.

case if the man is still able to beget children while the woman is unable to bear them, or the woman able to bear while the man is unable to beget, for from these causes arise quarrels and differences between married persons. Secondly, he must consider the time at which the children will succeed to their parents; there ought not to be too great an interval of age, for then the parents will be too old to derive any pleasure from their affection, or to be of any use to them. Nor ought they to be too nearly of an age; to youthful marriages there are many objections—the children will be wanting in respect to the parents, who will seem to be their contemporaries, and disputes will arise in the management of the household. Thirdly, and this is the point from which we digressed,[73] the legislator must mould to his will the frames of newly-born children. Almost all these objects may be secured by attention to one point. Since the time of generation is commonly limited within the age of seventy years in the case of a man, and of fifty in the case of a woman, the commencement of the union should conform to these periods. The union of male and female when too young is bad for the procreation of children; in all other animals the offspring of the young are small and ill-developed, and with a tendency to produce female children, and therefore also in man, as is proved by the fact that in those cities in which men and women are accustomed to marry young, the people are small and weak; in childbirth also younger women suffer more, and more of them die; some persons say that this was the meaning of the response once given to the Troezenians[74]—the oracle really meant that many died because they married too young; it had nothing to do with the ingathering of the harvest. It also conduces to temperance not to marry too soon; for women who marry early are apt to be wanton; and in men too the bodily frame is stunted if they marry while the seed is growing (for there is a time when the growth of the seed, also, ceases, or continues to but a slight extent). Women should marry when they are about eighteen years of age, and men at seven and thirty; then they are in the prime of life, and the decline in the powers of both will coincide. Further, the children, if their birth takes place soon, as may reasonably be expected, will succeed in the beginning of their prime, when the fathers are already in the decline of life, and have nearly reached their term of three-score years and ten.

[73] Bk. 7, XV.

[74] 'Plough not the young field'.

Thus much of the age proper for marriage: the season of the year should also be considered; according to our present custom, people generally limit marriage to the season of winter, and they are right. The precepts of physicians and natural philosophers about generation should also be studied by the parents themselves; the physicians give good advice about the favourable conditions of the body, and the natural philosophers about the winds; of which they prefer the north to the south.

What constitution in the parent is most advantageous to the offspring is a subject which we will consider more carefully[75] when we speak of the education of children, and we will only make a few general remarks at present. The constitution of an athlete is not suited to the life of a citizen, or to health, or to the procreation of children, any more than the valetudinarian or exhausted constitution, but one which is in a mean between them. A man's constitution should be inured to labour, but not to labour which is excessive or of one sort only, such as is practised by athletes; he should be capable of all the actions of a freeman. These remarks apply equally to both parents.

Women who are with child should be careful of themselves; they should take exercise and have a nourishing diet. The first of these prescriptions the legislator will easily carry into effect by requiring that they shall take a walk daily to some temple, where they can worship the gods who preside over birth.[76] Their minds, however, unlike their bodies, they ought to keep quiet, for the offspring derive their natures from their mothers as plants do from the earth.

As to the exposure and rearing of children, let there be a law that no *deformed* child shall live, but that on the ground of an *excess* in the number of children, if the established customs of the state forbid this (for in our state population has a limit), no child is to be exposed, but when couples have children in excess, let abortion be procured before sense and life have begun; what may or may not be lawfully done in these cases depends on the question of life and sensation.

And now, having determined at what ages men and women are to begin their union, let us also determine how long they shall continue to beget and bear offspring for the state; men who are too old, like men who are too young, produce children who are

[75] A. does not actually do so.

[76] Cp. Plato, *Laws*, vii. 789 E.

defective in body and mind; the children of very old men are weakly. The limit, then, should be the age which is the prime of their intelligence, and this in most persons, according to the notion of some poets who measure life by periods of seven years, is about fifty; at four or five years later, they should cease from having families; and from that time forward only cohabit with one another for the sake of health; or for some similar reason.

As to adultery, let it be held disgraceful, in general, for any man or woman to be found in any way unfaithful when they are married, and called husband and wife. If during the time of bearing children anything of the sort occur, let the guilty person be punished with a loss of privileges in proportion to the offence.[77]

XVII After the children have been born, the manner of rearing them may be supposed to have a great effect on their bodily strength. It would appear from the example of animals, and of those nations who desire to create the military habit, that the food which has most milk in it is best suited to human beings; but the less wine the better, if they would escape diseases. Also all the motions to which children can be subjected at their early age are very useful. But in order to preserve their tender limbs from distortion, some nations have had recourse to mechanical appliances which straighten their bodies. To accustom children to the cold from their earliest years is also an excellent practice, which greatly conduces to health, and hardens them for military service. Hence many barbarians have a custom of plunging their children at birth into a cold stream; others, like the Celts, clothe them in a light wrapper only. For human nature should be early habituated to endure all which by habit it can be made to endure; but the process must be gradual. And children, from their natural warmth, may be easily trained to bear cold. Such care should attend them in the first stage of life.

The next period lasts to the age of five; during this no demand should be made upon the child for study or labour, lest its growth be impeded; and there should be sufficient motion to prevent the limbs from being inactive. This can be secured, among other ways, by amusement, but the amusement should not be vulgar or tiring or effeminate. The Directors of Education, as they are

[77] Cp. *Laws*, viii. 841 D, E.

termed, should be careful what tales or stories the children hear,[78] for all such things are designed to prepare the way for the business of later life, and should be for the most part imitations of the occupations which they will hereafter pursue in earnest.[79] Those are wrong who in their laws attempt to check the loud crying and screaming of children, for these contribute towards their growth, and, in a manner, exercise their bodies.[80] Straining the voice has a strengthening effect similar to that produced by the retention of the breath in violent exertions. The Directors of Education should have an eye to their bringing up, and in particular should take care that they are left as little as possible with slaves. For until they are seven years old they must live at home; and therefore, even at this early age, it is to be expected that they should acquire a taint of meanness from what they hear and see. Indeed, there is nothing which the legislator should be more careful to drive away than indecency of speech; for the light utterance of shameful words leads soon to shameful actions. The young especially should never be allowed to repeat or hear anything of the sort. A freeman who is found saying or doing what is forbidden, if he be too young as yet to have the privilege of reclining at the public tables, should be disgraced and beaten, and an elder person degraded as his slavish conduct deserves. And since we do not allow improper language, clearly we should also banish pictures or speeches from the stage which are indecent. Let the rulers take care that there be no image or picture representing unseemly actions, except in the temples of those Gods at whose festivals the law permits even ribaldry, and whom the law also permits to be worshipped by persons of mature age on behalf of themselves, their children, and their wives. But the legislator should not allow youth to be spectators of iambi or of comedy until they are of an age to sit at the public tables and to drink strong wine; by that time education will have armed them against the evil influences of such representations.

We have made these remarks in a cursory manner—they are enough for the present occasion; but hereafter[81] we will return to the subject and after a fuller discussion determine whether such liberty should or should not be granted, and in what way granted, if at all. Theodorus, the tragic actor, was quite right in saying that

[78] Plato, *Rep.* ii. 377 ff.
[79] Plato, *Laws*, i. 643.
[80] Plato, *Laws*, vii. 792 A.
[81] An unfulfilled promise.

he would not allow any other actor, not even if he were quite second-rate, to enter before himself, because the spectators grew fond of the voices which they first heard. And the same principle applies universally to association with things as well as with persons, for we always like best whatever comes first. And therefore youth should be kept strangers to all that is bad, and especially to things which suggest vice or hate. When the five years have passed away, during the two following years they must look on at the pursuits which they are hereafter to learn. There are two periods of life with reference to which education has to be divided, from seven to the age of puberty, and onwards to the age of one and twenty. The poets who divide ages by sevens[82] are in the main right: but we should observe the divisions actually made by nature; for the deficiencies of nature are what art and education seek to fill up.

Let us then first inquire if any regulations are to be laid down about children, and secondly, whether the care of them should be the concern of the state or of private individuals, which latter is in our own day the common custom, and in the third place, what these regulations should be.

[82] Cp. Bk. 7, XVI.

BOOK EIGHTH

I No one will doubt that the legislator should direct his attention above all to the education of youth; for the neglect of education does harm to the constitution. The citizen should be moulded to suit the form of government under which he lives.[1] For each government has a peculiar character which originally formed and which continues to preserve it. The character of democracy creates democracy, and the character of oligarchy creates oligarchy; and always the better the character, the better the government.

Again, for the exercise of any faculty or art a previous training and habituation are required; clearly therefore for the practice of virtue. And since the whole city has one end, it is manifest that education should be one and the same for all, and that it should be public, and not private—not as at present, when every one looks after his own children separately, and gives them separate instruction of the sort which he thinks best; the training in things which are of common interest should be the same for all. Neither must we suppose that any one of the citizens belongs to himself, for they all belong to the state, and are each of them a part of the state, and the care of each part is inseparable from the care of the whole. In this particular as in some others the Lacedaemonians are to be praised, for they take the greatest pains about their children, and make education the business of the state.[2]

II That education should be regulated by law and should be an affair of state is not to be denied, but what should be the character of this public education, and how young persons should be educated, are questions which remain to be considered. As things are, there is disagreement about the subjects. For mankind are by no means agreed about the things to be taught, whether we look to virtue or the best life. Neither is it clear whether education is more concerned with intellectual or with moral virtue. The existing practice is perplexing; no one knows on what principle we should proceed—should the useful in life, or should virtue, or should the higher knowledge, be the aim of our training; all three opinions have been entertained. Again, about the means there is

[1] Cp. Bk. 5, IX.

[2] Cp. *Nic. Eth.* x. 1180ᵃ 24.

no agreement; for different persons, starting with different ideas about the nature of virtue, naturally disagree about the practice of it. There can be no doubt that children should be taught those useful things which are really necessary, but not all useful things; for occupations are divided into liberal and illiberal; and to young children should be imparted only such kinds of knowledge as will be useful to them without vulgarizing them. And any occupation, art, or science, which makes the body or soul or mind of the freeman less fit for the practice or exercise of virtue, is vulgar; wherefore we call those arts vulgar which tend to deform the body, and likewise all paid employments, for they absorb and degrade the mind. There are also some liberal arts quite proper for a freeman to acquire, but only in a certain degree, and if he attend to them too closely, in order to attain perfection in them, the same evil effects will follow. The object also which a man sets before him makes a great difference; if he does or learns anything for his own sake[3] or for the sake of his friends, or with a view to excellence, the action will not appear illiberal; but if done for the sake of others, the very same action will be thought menial and servile. The received subjects of instruction, as I have already remarked,[4] are partly of a liberal and partly of an illiberal character.

III The customary branches of education are in number four; they are—(1) reading and writing, (2) gymnastic exercises, (3) music, to which is sometimes added (4) drawing. Of these, reading and writing and drawing are regarded as useful for the purposes of life in a variety of ways, and gymnastic exercises are thought to infuse courage. Concerning music a doubt may be raised—in our own day most men cultivate it for the sake of pleasure, but originally it was included in education, because nature herself, as has been often said,[5] requires that we should be able, not only to work well, but to use leisure well; for, as I must repeat once again, the first principle of all action is leisure. Both are required, but leisure is better than occupation and is its end; and therefore the question must be asked, what ought we to do when at leisure? Clearly we ought not to be amusing ourselves, for

[3] Cp. Bk. 3, IV. [4] II, l. 8–15.
[5] Bk. 2, IX; Bk. 7, XIV–XV; *Nic. Eth.* x. 6.

then amusement would be the end of life. But if this is inconceivable, and amusement is needed more amid serious occupations than at other times (for he who is hard at work has need of relaxation, and amusement gives relaxation, whereas occupation is always accompanied with exertion and effort), we should introduce amusements only at suitable times, and they should be our medicines, for the emotion which they create in the soul is a relaxation, and from the pleasure we obtain rest. But leisure of itself gives pleasure and happiness and enjoyment of life, which are experienced, not by the busy man, but by those who have leisure. For he who is occupied has in view some end which he has not attained; but happiness is an end, since all men deem it to be accompanied with pleasure and not with pain. This pleasure, however, is regarded differently by different persons, and varies according to the habit of individuals; the pleasure of the best man is the best, and springs from the noblest sources. It is clear then that there are branches of learning and education which we must study merely with a view to leisure spent in intellectual activity, and these are to be valued for their own sake; whereas those kinds of knowledge which are useful in business are to be deemed necessary, and exist for the sake of other things. And therefore our fathers admitted music into education, not on the ground either of its necessity or utility, for it is not necessary, nor indeed useful in the same manner as reading and writing, which are useful in money-making, in the management of a household, in the acquisition of knowledge and in political life, nor like drawing, useful for a more correct judgement of the works of artists, nor again like gymnastic, which gives health and strength; for neither of these is to be gained from music. There remains, then, the use of music for intellectual enjoyment in leisure; which is in fact evidently the reason of its introduction, this being one of the ways in which it is thought that a freeman should pass his leisure; as Homer says—

'But he who alone should be called[6] *to the pleasant feast'*,

and afterwards he speaks of others whom he describes as inviting

'The bard who would delight them all'.[7]

[6] The line does not occur in the text of Homer, but in Aristotle's text it probably came instead of, or after, *Od.* xvii. 383.

[7] *Od.* xvii. 385.

And in another place Odysseus says there is no better way of passing life than when men's hearts are merry and

'The banqueters in the hall, sitting in order, hear the voice of the minstrel'.[8]

It is evident, then, that there is a sort of education in which parents should train their sons, not as being useful or necessary, but because it is liberal or noble. Whether this is of one kind only, or of more than one, and if so, what they are, and how they are to be imparted, must hereafter be determined.[9] Thus much we are now in a position to say, that the ancients witness to us; for their opinion may be gathered from the fact that music is one of the received and traditional branches of education. Further, it is clear that children should be instructed in some useful things—for example, in reading and writing—not only for their usefulness, but also because many other sorts of knowledge are acquired through them. With a like view they may be taught drawing, not to prevent their making mistakes in their own purchases, or in order that they may not be imposed upon in the buying or selling of articles, but perhaps rather because it makes them judges of the beauty of the human form. To be always seeking after the useful does not become free and exalted souls.[10] Now it is clear that in education practice must be used before theory, and the body be trained before the mind; and therefore boys should be handed over to the trainer, who creates in them the proper habit of body, and to the wrestling-master, who teaches them their exercises.

IV Of those states which in our own day seem to take the greatest care of children, some aim at producing in them an athletic habit, but they only injure their forms and stunt their growth. Although the Lacedaemonians have not fallen into this mistake, yet they brutalize their children by laborious exercises which they think will make them courageous. But in truth, as we have often repeated,[11] education should not be exclusively, or principally,

[8] *Od.* ix. 7.
[9] An unfulfilled promise.
[10] Cp. Plato, *Rep.* vii. 525 ff.
[11] Bk. 2, IX; Bk. 7, XIV.

directed to this end. And even if we suppose the Lacedaemonians to be right in their end, they do not attain it. For among barbarians and among animals courage is found associated, not with the greatest ferocity, but with a gentle and lionlike temper. There are many races who are ready enough to kill and eat men, such as the Achaeans and Heniochi, who both live about the Black Sea[12]; and there are other mainland tribes, as bad or worse, who all live by plunder, but have no courage. It is notorious that the Lacedaemonians themselves, while they alone were assiduous in their laborious drill, were superior to others, but now they are beaten both in war and gymnastic exercises. For their ancient superiority did not depend on their mode of training their youth, but only on the circumstance that they trained them when their only rivals did not. Hence we may infer that what is noble, not what is brutal, should have the first place; no wolf or other wild animal will face a really noble danger; such dangers are for the brave man.[13] And parents who devote their children to gymnastics while they neglect their necessary education, in reality vulgarize them; for they make them useful to the art of statesmanship in one quality only, and even in this the argument proves them to be inferior to others. We should judge the Lacedaemonians not from what they have been, but from what they are; for now they have rivals who compete with their education; formerly they had none.

It is an admitted principle, that gymnastic exercises should be employed in education, and that for children they should be of a lighter kind, avoiding severe diet or painful toil, lest the growth of the body be impaired. The evil of excessive training in early years is strikingly proved by the example of the Olympic victors; for not more than two or three of them have gained a prize both as boys and as men; their early training and severe gymnastic exercises exhausted their constitutions. When boyhood is over, three years should be spent in other studies; the period of life which follows may then be devoted to hard exercise and strict diet. Men ought not to labour at the same time with their minds and with their bodies[14]; for the two kinds of labour are opposed to one another; the labour of the body impedes the mind, and the labour of the mind the body.

[12] Cp. *Nic. Eth.* vii, 1148^b 21.

[13] Cp. *Nic. Eth.* iii. 1115^a 29.

[14] Cp. Plato, *Rep.* vii. 537 B.

V Concerning music there are some questions which we have already raised[15]; these we may now resume and carry further; and our remarks will serve as a prelude to this or any other discussion of the subject. It is not easy to determine the nature of music, or why any one should have a knowledge of it. Shall we say, for the sake of amusement and relaxation, like sleep or drinking, which are not good in themselves, but are pleasant, and at the same time 'make care to cease', as Euripides says? And for this end men also appoint music, and make use of all three alike —sleep, drinking, music—to which some add dancing. Or shall we argue that music conduces to virtue, on the ground that it can form our minds and habituate us to true pleasures as our bodies are made by gymnastic to be of a certain character? Or shall we say that it contributes to the enjoyment of leisure and mental cultivation, which is a third alternative? Now obviously youths are not to be instructed with a view to their amusement, for learning is no amusement, but is accompanied with pain. Neither is intellectual enjoyment suitable to boys of that age, for it is the end, and that which is imperfect cannot attain the perfect or end. But perhaps it may be said that boys learn music for the sake of the amusement which they will have when they are grown up. If so, why should they learn themselves, and not, like the Persian and Median kings, enjoy the pleasure and instruction which is derived from hearing others? (for surely persons who have made music the business and profession of their lives will be better performers than those who practise only long enough to learn). If they must learn music, on the same principle they should learn cookery, which is absurd. And even granting that music may form the character, the objection still holds: why should we learn ourselves? Why cannot we attain true pleasure and form a correct judgement from hearing others, like the Lacedaemonians?— for they, without learning music, nevertheless can correctly judge, as they say, of good and bad melodies. Or again, if music should be used to promote cheerfulness and refined intellectual enjoyment, the objection still remains—why should we learn ourselves instead of enjoying the performances of others? We may illustrate what we are saying by our conception of the Gods; for in the poets Zeus does not himself sing or play on the lyre. Nay, we call professional performers vulgar; no freeman would play or

[15] Bk. 8, II–III.

sing unless he were intoxicated or in jest. But these matters may be left for the present.[16]

The first question is whether music is or is not to be a part of education. Of the three things mentioned in our discussion, which does it produce?—education or amusement or intellectual enjoyment, for it may be reckoned under all three, and seems to share in the nature of all of them. Amusement is for the sake of relaxation, and relaxation is of necessity sweet, for it is the remedy of pain caused by toil; and intellectual enjoyment is universally acknowledged to contain an element not only of the noble but of the pleasant, for happiness is made up of both. All men agree that music is one of the pleasantest things, whether with or without songs; as Musaeus says:

'Song to mortals of all things the sweetest'.

Hence and with good reason it is introduced into social gatherings and entertainments, because it makes the hearts of men glad: so that on this ground alone we may assume that the young ought to be trained in it. For innocent pleasures are not only in harmony with the perfect end of life, but they also provide relaxation. And whereas men rarely attain the end, but often rest by the way and amuse themselves, not only with a view to a further end, but also for the pleasure's sake, it may be well at times to let them find a refreshment in music. It sometimes happens that men make amusement the end, for the end probably contains some element of pleasure, though not any ordinary or lower pleasure; but they mistake the lower for the higher, and in seeking for the one find the other, since every pleasure has a likeness to the end of action.[17] For the end is not eligible for the sake of any future good, nor do the pleasures which we have described exist for the sake of any future good but of the past, that is to say, they are the alleviation of past toils and pains. And we may infer this to be the reason why men seek happiness from these pleasures.

But music is pursued, not only as an alleviation of past toil, but also as providing recreation. And who can say whether, having this use, it may not also have a nobler one? In addition to this common pleasure, felt and shared in by all (for the pleasure given by music is natural, and therefore adapted to all ages and charac-

[16] Cp. VI.
[17] Cp. *Nic. Eth.* vii. 1153b 33.

ters), may it not have also some influence over the character and the soul? It must have such an influence if characters are affected by it. And that they are so affected is proved in many ways, and not least by the power which the songs of Olympus exercise; for beyond question they inspire enthusiasm, and enthusiasm is an emotion of the ethical part of the soul. Besides, when men hear imitations, even apart from the rhythms and tunes themselves, their feelings move in sympathy. Since then music is a pleasure, and virtue consists in rejoicing and loving and hating aright, there is clearly nothing which we are so much concerned to acquire and to cultivate as the power of forming right judgements, and of taking delight in good dispositions and noble actions.[18] Rhythm and melody supply imitations of anger and gentleness, and also of courage and temperance, and of all the qualities contrary to these, and of the other qualities of character, which hardly fall short of the actual affections, as we know from our own experience, for in listening to such strains our souls undergo a change. The habit of feeling pleasure or pain at mere representations is not far removed from the same feeling about realities[19]; for example, if any one delights in the sight of a statue for its beauty only, it necessarily follows that the sight of the original will be pleasant to him. The objects of no other sense, such as taste or touch, have any resemblance to moral qualities; in visible objects there is only a little, for there are figures which are of a moral character, but only to a slight extent, and all do not participate in the feeling about them. Again, figures and colours are not imitations, but signs, of moral habits, indications which the body gives of states of feeling. The connection of them with morals is slight, but in so far as there is any, young men should be taught to look, not at the works of Pauson, but at those of Polygnotus,[20] or any other painter or sculptor who expresses moral ideas. On the other hand, even in mere melodies there is an imitation of character, for the musical modes differ essentially from one another, and those who hear them are differently affected by each. Some of them make men sad and grave, like the so-called Mixolydian, others enfeeble the mind, like the relaxed modes, another, again, produces a moderate and settled temper, which appears to be the peculiar effect of the Dorian; the Phry-

[18] Cp. Plato, *Rep.* iii. 401, 402; *Laws,* ii. 659 C–E.

[19] Cp. Plato, *Rep.* iii. 395.

[20] Cp. *Poet.* 1448^a 5, 1450^a 26.

gian inspires enthusiasm. The whole subject has been well treated by philosophical writers[21] on this branch of education, and they confirm their arguments by facts. The same principles apply to rhythms[22]; some have a character of rest, others of motion, and of these latter again, some have a more vulgar, others a nobler movement. Enough has been said to show that music has a power of forming the character, and should therefore be introduced into the education of the young. The study is suited to the stage of youth, for young persons will not, if they can help, endure anything which is not sweetened by pleasure, and music has a natural sweetness. There seems to be in us a sort of affinity to musical modes and rhythms, which makes some philosophers say that the soul is a tuning, others, that it possesses tuning.

VI And now we have to determine the question which has been already raised,[23] whether children should be themselves taught to sing and play or not. Clearly there is a considerable difference made in the character by the actual practice of the art. It is difficult, if not impossible, for those who do not perform to be good judges of the performance of others.[24] Besides, children should have something to do, and the rattle of Archytas, which people give to their children in order to amuse them and prevent them from breaking anything in the house, was a capital invention, for a young thing cannot be quiet. The rattle is a toy suited to the infant mind, and education is a rattle or toy for children of a larger growth. We conclude then that they should be taught music in such a way as to become not only critics but performers.

The question what is or is not suitable for different ages may be easily answered; nor is there any difficulty in meeting the objection of those who say that the study of music is vulgar.[25] We reply (1) in the first place, that they who are to be judges must also be performers, and that they should begin to practise early, although when they are older they may be spared the execution; they must have learned to appreciate what is good and to delight in it, thanks to the knowledge which they acquired in their youth. As to (2) the vulgarizing effect which music is supposed

[21] Cp. *Rep.* 398 E sqq.
[22] *Rep.* iii. 399 E, 400.
[23] Bk. 8, V.
[24] Cp. Bk. 8, V.
[25] Cp. Bk. 8, V, VI.

to exercise, this is a question which we shall have no difficulty in determining, when we have considered to what extent freemen who are being trained to political virtue should pursue the art, what melodies and what rhythms they should be allowed to use, and what instruments should be employed in teaching them to play; for even the instrument makes a difference. The answer to the objection turns upon these distinctions; for it is quite possible that certain methods of teaching and learning music do really have a degrading effect. It is evident then that the learning of music ought not to impede the business of riper years, or to degrade the body or render it unfit for civil or military training, whether for bodily exercises at the time or for later studies.

The right measure will be attained if students of music stop short of the arts which are practised in professional contests, and do not seek to acquire those fantastic marvels of execution which are now the fashion in such contests, and from these have passed into education. Let the young practise even such music as we have prescribed, only until they are able to feel delight in noble melodies and rhythms, and not merely in that common part of music in which every slave or child and even some animals find pleasure.

From these principles we may also infer what instruments should be used. The flute, or any other instrument which requires great skill, as for example the harp, ought not to be admitted into education, but only such as will make intelligent students of music or of the other parts of education. Besides, the flute is not an instrument which is expressive of moral character; it is too exciting. The proper time for using it is when the performance aims not at instruction, but at the relief of the passions.[26] And there is a further objection; the impediment which the flute presents to the use of the voice detracts from its educational value. The ancients therefore were right in forbidding the flute to youths and freemen, although they had once allowed it. For when their wealth gave them a greater inclination to leisure, and they had loftier notions of excellence, being also elated with their success, both before and after the Persian War, with more zeal than discernment they pursued every kind of knowledge, and so they introduced the flute into education. At Lacedaemon there was a choragus who led the chorus with a flute, and at Athens the in-

[26] Cp. Bk. 8, VI.

strument became so popular that most freemen could play upon it. The popularity is shown by the tablet which Thrasippus dedicated when he furnished the chorus to Ecphantides. Later experience enabled men to judge what was or was not really conducive to virtue, and they rejected both the flute and several other old-fashioned instruments, such as the Lydian harp, the many-stringed lyre, the 'heptagon', 'triangle', 'sambuca', and the like—which are intended only to give pleasure to the hearer, and require extraordinary skill of hand.[27] There is a meaning also in the myth of the ancients, which tells how Athene invented the flute and then threw it away. It was not a bad idea of theirs, that the Goddess disliked the instrument because it made the face ugly; but with still more reason may we say that she rejected it because the acquirement of flute-playing contributes nothing to the mind, since to Athene we ascribe both knowledge and art.

Thus then we reject the professional instruments and also the professional mode of education in music (and by professional we mean that which is adopted in contests), for in this the performer practises the art, not for the sake of his own improvement, but in order to give pleasure, and that of a vulgar sort, to his hearers. For this reason the execution of such music is not the part of a freeman but of a paid performer, and the result is that the performers are vulgarized, for the end at which they aim is bad.[28] The vulgarity of the spectator tends to lower the character of the music and therefore of the performers; they look to him—he makes them what they are, and fashions even their bodies by the movements which he expects them to exhibit.

VII We have also to consider rhythms and modes, and their use in education. Shall we use them all or make a distinction? and shall the same distinction be made for those who practise music with a view to education, or shall it be some other? Now we see that music is produced by melody and rhythm, and we ought to know what influence these have respectively on education, and whether we should prefer excellence in melody or excellence in rhythm. But as the subject has been very well treated by many musicians of the present day, and also by philosophers[29] who

[27] Cp. Plato, *Rep.* iii. 399 C, D. [28] Cp. Plato, *Laws,* iii. 700.
[29] Cp. *Rep.* iii. 398 D sqq.

have had considerable experience of musical education, to these we would refer the more exact student of the subject; we shall only speak of it now after the manner of the legislator, stating the general principles.

We accept the division of melodies proposed by certain philosophers into ethical melodies, melodies of action, and passionate or inspiring melodies, each having, as they say, a mode corresponding to it. But we maintain further that music should be studied, not for the sake of one, but of many benefits, that is to say, with a view to (1) education, (2) purgation (the word 'purgation' we use at present without explanation, but when hereafter we speak of poetry,[30] we will treat the subject with more precision); music may also serve (3) for intellectual enjoyment, for relaxation and for recreation after exertion. It is clear, therefore, that all the modes must be employed by us, but not all of them in the same manner. In education the most ethical modes are to be preferred, but in listening to the performances of others we may admit the modes of action and passion also. For feelings such as pity and fear, or, again, enthusiasm, exist very strongly in some souls, and have more or less influence over all. Some persons fall into a religious frenzy, whom we see as a result of the sacred melodies—when they have used the melodies that excite the soul to mystic frenzy—restored as though they had found healing and purgation. Those who are influenced by pity or fear, and every emotional nature, must have a like experience, and others in so far as each is susceptible to such emotions, and all are in a manner purged and their souls lightened and delighted. The purgative melodies likewise give an innocent pleasure to mankind. Such are the modes and the melodies in which those who perform music at the theatre should be invited to compete. But since the spectators are of two kinds—the one free and educated, and the other a vulgar crowd composed of mechanics, labourers, and the like—there ought to be contests and exhibitions instituted for the relaxation of the second class also. And the music will correspond to their minds; for as their minds are perverted from the natural state, so there are perverted modes and highly strung and unnaturally coloured melodies. A man receives pleasure from

[30] Cp. *Poet.* 1449^{b} 27, though the promise is really unfulfilled. The reference is probably to a lost part of the *Poetics*.

what is natural to him, and therefore professional musicians may be allowed to practise this lower sort of music before an audience of a lower type. But, for the purposes of education, as I have already said,[31] those modes and melodies should be employed which are ethical, such as the Dorian, as we said before[32]; though we may include any others which are approved by philosophers who have had a musical education. The Socrates of the *Republic*[33] is wrong in retaining only the Phrygian mode along with the Dorian, and the more so because he rejects the flute; for the Phrygian is to the modes what the flute is to musical instruments —both of them are exciting and emotional. Poetry proves this, for Bacchic frenzy and all similar emotions are most suitably expressed by the flute, and are better set to the Phrygian than to any other mode. The dithyramb, for example, is acknowledged to be Phrygian, a fact of which the connoisseurs of music offer many proofs, saying, among other things, that Philoxenus, having attempted to compose his *Mysians* as a dithyramb in the Dorian mode, found it impossible, and fell back by the very nature of things into the more appropriate Phrygian. All men agree that the Dorian music is the gravest and manliest. And whereas we say that the extremes should be avoided and the mean followed, and whereas the Dorian is a mean between the other modes,[34] it is evident that our youth should be taught the Dorian music.

Two principles have to be kept in view, what is possible, what is becoming: at these every man ought to aim. But even these are relative to age; the old, who have lost their powers, cannot very well sing the high-strung modes, and nature herself seems to suggest that their songs should be of the more relaxed kind. Wherefore the musicians likewise blame Socrates,[35] and with justice, for rejecting the relaxed modes in education under the idea that they are intoxicating, not in the ordinary sense of intoxication (for wine rather tends to excite men), but because they have no strength in them. And so, with a view also to the time of life when men begin to grow old, they ought to practise the gentler modes and melodies as well as the others, and, further, any mode, such as the Lydian above all others appears to be, which is suited to

[31] Bk. 7, VII.
[32] Bk. 8, V.
[33] Plato, *Rep.* iii. 399 A.
[34] Cp. Bk. 8, V.
[35] *Rep.* iii. 398 E sqq.

children of tender age, and possesses the elements both of order and of education. Thus it is clear that education should be based upon three principles—the mean, the possible, the becoming, these three.

POETICS

Translated by

THOMAS TWINING

BOOK FIRST

GENERAL AND COMPARATIVE VIEW OF POETRY AND ITS PRINCIPAL SPECIES

INTRODUCTION MY design is to treat of POETRY in general, and of its several species; to inquire what is the proper effect of each—what construction of a fable, or plan, is essential to a good poem—of what, and how many, parts each species consists; with whatever else belongs to the same subject: which I shall consider in the order that most naturally presents itself.

I Epic poetry, tragedy, comedy, dithyrambics, as also, for the most part, the music of the flute and of the lyre—all these are, in the most general view of them, *imitations;* differing, however, from each other in three respects, according to the different means, the different objects, or the different manner of their imitation.

II For as men, some through art and some through habit, imitate various objects by means of colour and figure, and others, again, by voice; so, with respect to the arts above-mentioned, rhythm, words, and melody are the different means by which, either singly or variously combined, they all produce their imitation.

For example: in the imitations of the flute and the lyre, and of any other instruments capable of producing a similar effect—as the syrinx, or pipe—melody and rhythm only are employed. In those of dance, rhythm alone, without melody; for there are dancers who, by rhythm applied to gesture, express manners, passions, and actions.

The *epopoeia* imitates by words alone, or by verse; and that verse may either be composed of various metres, or confined, according to the practice hitherto established, to a single species. For we should otherwise have no general name which would comprehend the mimes of Sophron and Xenarchus, and the Socratic dialogues; or poems in iambic, elegiac, or other metres, in which the epic species of imitation may be conveyed. Custom, indeed, connecting the poetry or making with the metre, has denominated some elegiac poets, i. e. makers of elegiac verse; others epic poets, i. e. makers of hexameter verse; thus distinguishing poets, not according to the nature of their imitation, but according to that of their metre only. For even they who compose treatises of medicine or natural philosophy in verse are denominated poets: yet Homer and Empedocles have nothing in common except their metre; the former, therefore, justly merits the name of poet; while the other should rather be called a physiologist than a poet.

So, also, though any one should choose to convey his imitation in every kind of metre promiscuously, as Chaeremon has done in his *Centaur,* which is a medley of all sorts of verse, it would not immediately follow that, on that account merely, he was entitled to the name of poet. But of this enough.

There are, again, other species of poetry which made use of all the means of imitation: rhythm, melody, and verse. Such are the dithyrambic, that of nomes, tragedy, and comedy; with this difference, however, that in some of these they are employed all together, in others, separately. And such are the differences of these arts with respect to the means by which they imitate.

III But as the objects of imitation are the actions of men, and these men must of necessity be either good or bad (for on this does character principally depend; the manners being, in all men, most strongly marked by virtue and vice), it follows that we can only represent men either as better than they actually are, or worse, or exactly as they are: just as, in painting, the pictures of Polygnotus were above the common level of nature; those of Pauson below it; those of Dionysius faithful likenesses.

Now it is evident that each of the imitations above-mentioned will admit of these differences, and become a different kind of imitation, as it imitates objects that differ in this respect. This may be the case with dancing; with the music of the flute and of the lyre; and also with the poetry which employs words or verse only, without melody or rhythm: thus, Homer has drawn men superior to what they are; Cleophon, as they are; Hegemon the

Thasian, the inventor of parodies, and Nicochares, the author of the *Deliad*, worse than they are.

So again, with respect to dithyrambics and nomes: in these, too, the imitation may be as different as that of the *Persians* by Timotheus, and the *Cyclops* by Philoxenus.

Tragedy, also, and comedy, are distinguished in the same manner; the aim of comedy being to exhibit men worse than we find them, that of tragedy, better.

IV There remains the third difference—that of the manner in which each of these objects may be imitated. For the poet, imitating the same object, and by the same means, may do it either in narration—and that, again, either personating other characters, as Homer does, or in his own person throughout, without change —or he may imitate by representing all his characters as real, and employed in the very action itself.

These, then, are the three differences by which, as I said in the beginning, all imitation is distinguished: those of the means, the object, and the manner; so that Sophocles is, in one respect, an imitator of the same kind with Homer, as elevated characters are the objects of both; in another respect, of the same kind with Aristophanes, as both imitate in the way of action; whence, according to some, the application of the term drama (i.e. action) to such poems. Upon this it is that the Dorians ground their claim to the invention both of tragedy and comedy. For comedy is claimed by the Megarians; both by those of Greece, who contend that it took its rise in their popular government, and by those of Sicily, among whom the poet Epicharmus flourished long before Chionides and Magnes: and tragedy, also, is claimed by some of the Dorians of Peloponnesus. In support of these claims they argue from the words themselves. They allege that the Doric word for a village is *come,* the Attic, *demos;* and that comedians were so called, not from *comazein*—to revel—but from their strolling about the *comai,* or villages, before they were tolerated in the city. They say, further, that to do, or act, they express by the word *dran;* the Athenians by *prattein.*

And thus much as to the differences of imitation—how many, and what, they are.

V Poetry in general seems to have derived its origin from two causes, each of them natural.

To *imitate* is instinctive in man from his infancy. By this he is distinguished from other animals, that he is, of all, the most imitative, and through this instinct receives his earliest education. All men, likewise, naturally receive pleasure from imitation. This is evident from what we experience in viewing the works of imitative art; for in them we contemplate with pleasure, and with the more pleasure the more exactly they are imitated, such objects as, if real, we could not see without pain; as the figures of the meanest and most disgusting animals, dead bodies, and the like. And the reason of this is, that to learn is a natural pleasure, not confined to philosophers, but common to all men; with this difference only, that the multitude partake of it in a more transient and compendious manner. Hence the pleasure they receive from a picture: in viewing it they learn, they infer, they discover what every object is; that this, for instance, is such a particular man, etc. For if we suppose the object represented to be something which the spectator had never seen, his pleasure, in that case, will not arise from the imitation, but from the workmanship, the colours, or some such cause.

Imitation, then, being thus natural to us, and, secondly, melody and rhythm being also natural (for as to metre, it is plainly a species of rhythm), those persons in whom originally these propensities were the strongest, were naturally led to rude and extemporaneous attempts, which, gradually improved, gave birth to Poetry.

VI But this Poetry, following the different characters of its authors, naturally divided itself into two different kinds. They who were of a grave and lofty spirit chose for their imitation the actions and the adventures of elevated characters; while poets of a lighter turn represented those of the vicious and contemptible. And these composed originally satires, as the former did hymns and encomia.

Of the lighter kind, we have no poem anterior to the time of Homer, though many such in all probability there were; but from his time we have; as his *Margites*, and others of the same species, in which the iambic was introduced as the most proper measure; and hence, indeed, the name of iambic, because it was the measure in which they used to *iambize* (i.e. to satirize) each other.

And thus these old poets were divided into two classes: those who used the heroic, and those who used the iambic verse.

And as, in the serious kind, Homer alone may be said to deserve the name of poet, not only on account of his other excellences, but also of the dramatic spirit of his imitations; so was he likewise the first who suggested the idea of comedy, by substituting ridicule for invective, and giving that ridicule a dramatic cast; for his *Margites* bears the same analogy to comedy, as his Iliad and Odyssey to tragedy. But when tragedy and comedy had once made their appearance, succeeding poets, according to the turn of their genius, attached themselves to the one or the other of these new species: the lighter sort, instead of iambic, became comic poets; the graver, tragic, instead of heroic: and that on account of the superior dignity and higher estimation of these latter forms of poetry.

Whether tragedy has now, with respect to its constituent parts, received the utmost improvement of which it is capable, considered both in itself and relatively to the theatre, is a question that belongs not to this place.

VII Both tragedy, then, and comedy, having originated in a rude and unpremeditated manner—the first from the dithyrambic hymns, the other from those phallic songs which in many cities remain still in use—each advanced gradually towards perfection by such successive improvements as were most obvious.

TRAGEDY, after various changes, reposed at length in the completion of its proper form. Aeschylus first added a second actor; he also abridged the chorus, and made the dialogue the principal part of tragedy. Sophocles increased the number of actors to three, and added the decoration of painted scenery. It was also late before tragedy threw aside the short and simple fable and ludicrous language of its satyric original, and attained its proper magnitude and dignity. The iambic measure was then first adopted: for originally the trochaic tetrameter was made use of as better suited to the satyric and saltatorial genius of the poem at that time; but when the dialogue was formed, nature itself pointed out the proper metre. For the iambic is, of all metres, the most colloquial; as appears evidently from this fact, that our common conversation frequently falls into iambic verse; seldom into hexameter, and only when we depart from the usual melody of speech. Episodes, also, were multiplied, and every other part of the drama successively improved and polished.

But of this enough: to enter into a minute detail would, perhaps, be a task of some length.

VIII COMEDY, as was said before, is an imitation of bad characters; bad, not with respect to every sort of vice, but to the ridiculous only, as being a species of turpitude or deformity; since it may be defined to be a fault or deformity of such a sort as is neither painful nor destructive. A ridiculous face, for example, is something ugly and distorted, but not so as to cause pain.

The successive improvements of tragedy, and the respective authors of them, have not escaped our knowledge; but those of comedy, from the little attention that was paid to it in its origin, remain in obscurity. For it was not till late that comedy was authorized by the magistrate and carried on at the public expense; it was at first a private and voluntary exhibition. From the time, indeed, when it began to acquire some degree of form, its poets have been recorded; but who first introduced masks, or prologues, or augmented the number of actors—these, and other particulars of the same kind, are unknown.

Epicharmus and Phormis were the first who invented comic fables. This improvement, therefore, is of Sicilian origin. But, of Athenian poets, Crates was the first who abandoned the iambic form of comedy, and made use of invented and general stories or fables.

IX Epic poetry agrees so far with tragic as it is an imitation of great characters and actions by means of words; but in this it differs, that it makes use of only one kind of metre throughout, and that it is narrative. It also differs in length, for tragedy endeavours, as far as possible, to confine its action within the limits of a single revolution of the sun, or nearly so; but the time of epic action is indefinite. This, however, at first was equally the case with tragedy itself.

Of their constituent parts some are common to both, some peculiar to tragedy. He, therefore, who is a judge of the beauties and defects of tragedy is, of course, equally a judge with respect to those of epic poetry; for all the parts of the epic poem are to be found in tragedy; not all those of tragedy in the epic poem.

BOOK SECOND

OF TRAGEDY

I Of the species of poetry which imitates in hexameters, and of comedy, we shall speak hereafter. Let us now consider TRAGEDY; collecting first, from what has been already said, its true and essential definition.

Tragedy, then, is an imitation of some action that is important, entire, and of a proper magnitude—by language, embellished and rendered pleasurable, but by different means in different parts—in the way, not of narration, but of action—effecting through pity and terror the correction and refinement of such passions.

By pleasurable language I mean a language that has the embellishments of rhythm, melody, and metre. And I add, by different means in different parts, because in some parts metre alone is employed, in others, melody.

II Now as tragedy imitates by acting, the decoration, in the first place, must necessarily be one of its parts: then the *melopoeia* (or music) and the diction; for these last include the means of tragic imitation. By diction I mean the metrical composition. The meaning of *melopoeia* is obvious to every one.

Again, tragedy being an imitation of an action, and the persons employed in that action being necessarily characterized by their manners and their sentiments, since it is from these that actions themselves derive their character, it follows that there must also be manners and sentiments as the two causes of actions, and, consequently, of the happiness or unhappiness of all men. The imitation of the action is the fable: for by fable I now mean the contexture of incidents, or the plot. By manners, I mean whatever marks the characters of the persons; by sentiments, whatever they say, whether proving anything, or delivering a general sentiment, etc.

Hence all tragedy must necessarily contain six parts, which together constitute its peculiar character or quality: fable, manners, diction, sentiments, decoration, and music. Of these parts, two relate to the means, one to the manner, and three to the object of imitation. And these are all. These specific parts, if we may so call them, have been employed by most poets, and are all to be found in almost every tragedy.

III But of all these parts the most important is the combination of incidents or the fable. Because tragedy is an imitation, not of men, but of actions—of life, of happiness and unhappiness; for happiness consists in action, and the supreme good itself, the very end of life, is action of a certain kind—not quality. Now the manners of men constitute only their quality or characters; but it is by their actions that they are happy, or the contrary. Tragedy, therefore, does not imitate action for the sake of imitating manners, but in the imitation of action that of manners is of course involved. So that the action and the fable are the end of tragedy; and in everything the end is of principal importance.

Again, tragedy cannot subsist without action; without manners it may. The tragedies of most modern poets have this defect; a defect common, indeed, among poets in general. As among painters also, this is the case with Zeuxis, compared with Polygnotus: the latter excels in the expression of the manners; there is no such expression in the pictures of Zeuxis.

Further, suppose any one to string together a number of speeches in which the manners are strongly marked, the language and the sentiments well turned; this will not be sufficient to produce the proper effect of tragedy: that end will much rather be answered by a piece, defective in each of those particulars, but furnished with a proper fable and contexture of incidents. Just as in painting, the most brilliant colours, spread at random and without design, will give far less pleasure than the simplest outline of a figure.

Add to this, that those parts of tragedy by means of which it becomes most interesting and affecting are parts of the fable; I mean revolutions and discoveries.

As a further proof, adventures in tragic writing are sooner able to arrive at excellence in the language and the manners than in the construction of a plot; as appears from almost all our earlier poets.

The fable, then, is the principal part—the soul, as it were—of tragedy, and the manners are next in rank; tragedy being an imitation of an action, and through that principally of the agents.

In the third place stand the sentiments. To this part it belongs to say such things as are true and proper; which, in the dialogue, depends on the political and rhetorical arts: for the ancients made their characters speak in the style of political and popular eloquence; but now the rhetorical manner prevails.

The manners are whatever manifests the disposition of the speaker. There are speeches, therefore, which are without manners or character, as not containing anything by which the propensities or aversions of the person who delivers them can be known. The sentiments comprehend whatever is said, whether proving anything affirmatively or negatively, or expressing some general reflection, etc.

Fourth in order is the diction; that is, as I have already said, the expression of the sentiments by words; the power and effect of which is the same, whether in verse or prose.

Of the remaining two parts the music stands next; of all the pleasurable accompaniments and embellishments of tragedy the most delightful.

The decoration has also a great effect, but of all the parts is most foreign to the art. For the power of tragedy is felt without representation and actors; and the beauty of the decorations depends more on the art of the mechanic than on that of the poet.

IV These things being thus adjusted, let us go on to examine in what manner the fable should be constructed; since this is the first and most important part of tragedy.

Now we have defined tragedy to be an imitation of an action that is complete and entire; and that has also a certain magnitude; for a thing may be entire and a whole, and yet not be of any magnitude.

(1) By entire I mean that which has a beginning, a middle, and an end. A beginning is that which does not necessarily suppose anything before it, but which requires something to follow it. An end, on the contrary, is that which supposes something to precede it, either necessarily or probably, but which nothing is required to follow. A middle is that which both supposes something to precede and requires something to follow. The poet, therefore, who would construct his fable properly is not at liberty to begin or end where he pleases, but must conform to these definitions.

(2) Again, whatever is beautiful, whether it be an animal, or any other thing composed of different parts, must not only have those parts arranged in a certain manner, but must also be of a certain magnitude; for beauty consists in magnitude and order. Hence it is that no very minute animal can be beautiful; the eye comprehends the whole too instantaneously to distinguish and compare the parts. Neither, on the contrary, can one of a prodigious size be beautiful; because, as all its parts cannot be seen at once, the whole, the unity of object, is lost to the spectator; as it would be, for example, if he were surveying an animal of many miles in length. As, therefore, in animals and other objects, a certain magnitude is requisite, but that magnitude must be such as to present a whole easily comprehended by the eye; so in the fable a certain length is requisite, but that length must be such as to present a whole easily comprehended by the memory.

With respect to the measure of this length—if referred to actual representation in the dramatic contests, it is a matter foreign to the art itself. For if a hundred tragedies were to be exhibited in concurrence, the length of each performance must be regulated by the hourglass; a practice of which, it is said, there have formerly been instances. But if we determine this measure by the nature of the thing itself, the more extensive the fable, consistently with the clear and easy comprehension of the whole, the more beautiful will it be, with respect to magnitude. In general, we may say that an action is sufficiently extended when it is long enough to admit of a change of fortune, from happy to unhappy, or the reverse, brought about by a succession, necessary or probable, of well-connected incidents.

V A fable is not one, as some conceive it to be, merely because the hero of it is one. For numberless events happen to one man, many of which are such as cannot be connected into one event; and so, likewise, there are many actions of one man which cannot be connected into any one action. Hence appears the mistake of all those poets who have composed *Herculeids*, *Theseids*, and other poems of that kind. They conclude that because Hercules was one, so also must be the fable of which he is the subject. But Homer, among his many other excellences, seems also to have been perfectly aware of this mistake, either from art or genius.

For when he composed his Odyssey, he did not introduce all the events of his hero's life—such, for instance, as the wound he received upon Parnassus; his feigned madness when the Grecian army was assembling, etc.—events not connected, either by necessary or probable consequence, with each other; but he comprehended those only which have relation to one action; for such we call that of the Odyssey. And in the same manner he composed his Iliad.

As, therefore, in other mimetic arts, one imitation is an imitation of one thing, so here the fable, being an imitation of an action, should be an imitation of an action that is one and entire, the parts of it being so connected that if any one of them be either transposed or taken away, the whole will be destroyed or changed; for whatever may be either retained or omitted, without making any sensible difference, is not properly a part.

VI It appears, further, from what has been said, that it is not the poet's province to relate such things as have actually happened, but such as might have happened—such as are possible, according either to probable or necessary consequence.

For it is not by writing in verse or prose that the historian and the poet are distinguished: the work of Herodotus might be versified, but it would still be a species of history, no less with metre than without. They are distinguished by this, that the one relates what has been, the other what might be. On this account poetry is a more philosophical and a more excellent thing than history: for poetry is chiefly conversant about general truth, history about particular. In what manner, for example, any person of a certain character would speak or act, probably or necessarily—this is general; and this is the object of poetry, even while it makes use of particular names. But what Alcibiades did, or what happened to him—this is particular truth.

With respect to comedy this is now become obvious; for here the poet, when he has formed his plot of probable incidents, gives to his characters whatever names he pleases; and is not, like the iambic poets, particular and personal.

Tragedy, indeed, retains the use of real names; and the reason is that what we are disposed to believe, we must think possible. Now, what has never actually happened we are not apt to regard as possible; but what has been is unquestionably so, or it could not have been at all. There are, however, some tragedies in which one or two of the names are historical, and the rest feigned: there are even some in which none of the names are historical; such is Agathon's tragedy called *The Flower;* for in that all is invention, both incidents and names; and yet it pleases. It is by no means, therefore, essential that a poet should confine himself to the known and established subjects of tragedy. Such a restraint would, indeed, be ridiculous; since even those subjects that are known are known comparatively but to few, and yet are interesting to all.

From all this it is manifest that a poet should be a poet or maker of fables, rather than of verses; since it is imitation that constitutes the poet, and of this imitation actions are the object: nor is he the less a poet, though the incidents of his fable should chance to be such as have actually happened; for nothing hinders, but that some true events may possess that probability, the invention of which entitles him to the name of poet.

VII Of simple fables or actions, the episodic are the worst. I call that an episodic fable, the episodes of which follow each other without any probable or necessary connection; a fault into which bad poets are betrayed by their want of skill, and good poets by the players: for in order to accommodate their pieces to the purposes of rival performers in the dramatic contests, they spin out the action beyond their powers, and are thus frequently forced to break the connection and continuity of its parts.

But tragedy is an imitation, not only of a complete action, but also of an action exciting terror and pity. Now that purpose is best answered by such events as are not only unexpected, but unexpected consequences of each other: for, by this means, they will have more of the wonderful than if they appeared to be the effects of chance; since we find that, among events merely casual, those are the most wonderful and striking which seem to imply design: as when, for instance, the statue of Mitys at Argos killed the very man who had murdered Mitys, by falling down upon him as he was surveying it; events of this kind not having the appearance of accident. It follows, then, that such fables as are formed on these principles must be the best.

VIII Fables are of two sorts, simple and complicated; for so also are the actions themselves of which they are imitations. An action (having the continuity and unity prescribed) I call simple, when its catastrophe is produced without either revolution or discovery; complicated when with one or both. And these should arise from the structure of the fable itself, so as to be the natural consequences, necessary or probable, of what has preceded in the action. For there is a wide difference between incidents that follow from, and incidents that follow only after, each other.

IX A revolution is a change (such as has already been mentioned) into the reverse of what is expected from the circumstances of the action; and that produced, as we have said, by probable or necessary consequence.

Thus, in the *Oedipus*, the messenger, meaning to make Oedipus happy, and to relieve him from the dread he was under with respect to his mother, by making known to him his real birth, produces an effect directly contrary to his intention. Thus also in the tragedy of *Lynceus*, Lynceus is led to suffer death, Danaus follows to inflict it; but the event, resulting from the course of the incidents, is that Danaus is killed and Lynceus saved.

A discovery—as, indeed, the word implies—is a change from unknown to known, happening between those characters whose happiness or unhappiness forms the catastrophe of the drama, and terminating in friendship or enmity.

The best sort of discovery is that which is accompanied by a revolution as in the *Oedipus*.

There are also other discoveries; for inanimate things of any kind may be recognized in the same manner, and we may discover whether such a particular thing was, or was not, done by such a person. But the discovery most appropriated to the fable and the action is that above defined; because such discoveries and revolutions must excite either pity or terror, and tragedy we have defined to be an imitation of pitiable and terrible actions: and because, also, by them the event, happy or unhappy, is produced.

Now discoveries, being relative things, are sometimes of one of the persons only, the other being already known; and sometimes they are reciprocal: thus, Iphigenia is discovered to Orestes by the letter which she charges him to deliver, and Orestes is obliged, by other means, to make himself known to her.

These, then, are two parts of the fable—revolution and discovery. There is a third, which we denominate disasters. The two former have been explained. Disasters comprehend all painful or destructive actions: the exhibition of death, bodily anguish, wounds, and everything of that kind.

X The parts of tragedy which are necessary to constitute its quality have been already enumerated. Its parts of quantity—the distinct parts into which it is divided—are these: prologue, episode, exode, and chorus; which last is also divided into the parode and the *stasimon*. These are common to all tragedies. The *commoi* are found in some only.

The prologue is all that part of a tragedy which precedes the parode of the chorus; the episode, all that part which is included between entire choral odes; the exode, that part which has no choral ode after it.

Of the choral part, the parode is the first speech of the whole chorus; the *stasimon* includes all those choral odes that are without anapaests and trochees.

The *commos* is a general lamentation of the chorus and the actors together.

Such are the separate parts into which tragedy is divided. Its parts of quality were before explained.

XI The order of the subject leads us to consider, in the next place, what the poet should aim at and what avoid in the construction of his fable; and by what means the purpose of tragedy may be best effected.

Now since it is requisite to the perfection of a tragedy that its plot should be of the complicated, not of the simple kind, and that it should imitate such actions as excite terror and pity (this being the peculiar property of the tragic imitation), it follows evidently, in the first place, that the change from prosperity to adversity should not be represented as happening to a virtuous character; for this raises disgust rather than terror or compassion. Neither should the contrary change, from adversity to prosperity, be exhibited in a vicious character: this, of all plans, is the most opposite to the genius of tragedy, having no one property that it ought to have; for it is neither gratifying in a moral view, nor affecting, nor terrible. Nor, again, should the fall of a very bad man from prosperous to adverse fortune be represented: because, though such a subject may be pleasing from its moral tendency, it will produce neither pity nor terror. For our pity is excited by misfortunes undeservedly suffered, and our terror by some resemblance between the sufferer and ourselves. Neither of these effects will, therefore, be produced by such an event.

There remains, then, for our choice, the character between these extremes: that of a person neither eminently virtuous or just, nor yet involved in misfortune by deliberate vice or villainy, but by some error of human frailty; and this person should also be someone of high fame and flourishing prosperity. For example, Oedipus, Thyestes, or other illustrious men of such families.

XII Hence it appears that, to be well constructed, a fable, contrary to the opinion of some, should be single rather than double; that the change of fortune should not be from adverse to prosperous, but the reverse; and that it should be the consequence, not of vice, but of some great frailty, in a character such as has been described, or better rather than worse.

These principles are confirmed by experience; for poets formerly admitted almost any story into the number of tragic subjects; but now, the subjects of the best tragedies are confined to a few families—to Alcmaeon, Oedipus, Orestes, Meleager, Thyestes, Telephus, and others, the sufferers or the authors of some terrible calamity.

The most perfect tragedy, then, according to the principles of the art, is of this construction. Whence appears the mistake of those critics who censure Euripides for this practice in his tragedies, many of which terminate unhappily; for this, as we have shown, is right. And as the strongest proof of it we find that upon the stage, and in the dramatic contests, such tragedies, if they succeed, have always the most tragic effect; and Euripides, though in other respects faulty in the conduct of his subjects, seems clearly to be the most tragic of all poets.

I place in the second rank that kind of fable to which some

assign the first: that which is of a double construction like the Odyssey, and also ends in two opposite events, to the good and to the bad characters. That this passes for the best is owing to the weakness of the spectators, to whose wishes the poets accommodate their productions. This kind of pleasure, however, is not the proper pleasure of tragedy, but belongs rather to comedy; for there, if even the bitterest enemies, like Orestes and Aegisthus, are introduced, they quit the scene at last in perfect friendship, and no blood is shed on either side.

XIII Terror and pity may be raised by the decoration—the mere spectacle; but they may also arise from the circumstances of the action itself; which is far preferable and shows a superior poet. For the fable should be so constructed that, without the assistance of the sight, its incidents may excite horror and commiseration in those who hear them only: an effect which every one who hears the fable of the *Oedipus* must experience. But to produce this effect by means of the decoration discovers want of art in the poet; who must also be supplied by the public with an expensive apparatus.

As to those poets who make use of the decoration in order to produce, not the terrible, but the marvellous only, their purpose has nothing in common with that of tragedy. For we are not to seek for every sort of pleasure from tragedy, but for that only which is proper to the species.

Since, therefore, it is the business of the tragic poet to give that pleasure which arises from pity and terror, through imitation, it is evident that he ought to produce that effect by the circumstances of the action itself.

XIV Let us, then, see of what kind those incidents are which appear most terrible or piteous.

Now such actions must, of necessity, happen between persons who are either friends, or enemies, or indifferent to each other. If an enemy kills, or purposes to kill, an enemy, in neither case is any commiseration raised in us, beyond what necessarily arises from the nature of the action itself.

The case is the same when the persons are neither friends nor enemies. But when such disasters happen between friends—when, for instance, the brother kills, or is going to kill, his brother, the son his father, the mother her son, or the reverse—these, and others of a similar kind, are the proper incidents for the poet's choice. The received tragic subjects, therefore, he is not at liberty essentially to alter; Clytaemnestra must die by the hand of Orestes, and Eriphyle by that of Alcmaeon; but it is his province to invent other subjects, and to make a skilful use of those which he finds already established. What I mean by a skilful use I proceed to explain.

The atrocious action may be perpetrated knowingly and intentionally, as was usual with the earlier poets, and as Euripides, also, has represented Medea destroying her children.

It may, likewise, be perpetrated by those who are ignorant at the time of the connection between them and the injured person, which they afterwards discover; like Oedipus, in Sophocles. There, indeed, the action itself does not make a part of the drama: the *Alcmaeon* of Astydamas, and Telegonus in the *Ulysses Wounded,* furnish instances within the tragedy.

There is yet a third way, where a person upon the point of perpetrating, through ignorance, some dreadful deed, is prevented by a sudden discovery.

Beside these, there is no other proper way. For the action must of necessity be either done or not done, and that either with knowledge or without: but of all these ways, that of being ready to execute knowingly, and yet not executing, is the worst; for this is, at the same time, shocking and yet not tragic, because it exhibits no disastrous event. It is, therefore, never, or very rarely, made use of. The attempt of Haemon to kill Creon in the *Antigone* is an example.

Next to this is the actual execution of the purpose.

To execute through ignorance, and afterwards to discover, is better: for thus the shocking atrociousness is avoided, and, at the same time, the discovery is striking.

But the best of all these ways is the last. Thus, in the tragedy of *Cresphontes,* Merope, in the very act of putting her son to death, discovers him, and is prevented. In the *Iphigenia,* the sister in the same manner discovers her brother; and in the *Helle,* the son discovers his mother at the instant when he was going to betray her.

On this account it is that the subjects of tragedy, as before remarked, are confined to a small number of families. For it was not to art, but to fortune, that poets applied themselves to find incidents of this nature. Hence the necessity of having recourse to those families in which such calamities have happened.

Of the plot or fable and its requisites enough has now been said.

XV With respect to the manners, four things are to be attended to by the poet.

First, and principally, they should be good. Now manners, or character, belong, as we have said before, to any speech or action that manifests a certain disposition; and they are bad or good as the disposition manifested is bad or good. This goodness of manners may be found in persons of every description: the manners of a woman or of a slave may be good; though, in general, women are, perhaps, rather bad than good, and slaves altogether bad.

The second requisite of the manners is propriety. There is a manly character of bravery and fierceness which cannot, with propriety, be given to a woman.

The third requisite is resemblance; for this is a different thing from their being good and proper, as above described.

The fourth is uniformity; for even though the model of the poet's imitation be some person of ununiform manners, still that person must be represented as uniformly ununiform.

We have an example of manners unnecessarily bad in the character of Menelaus in the tragedy of *Orestes:* of improper and unbecoming manners in the lamentation of Ulysses in *Scylla,* and in the speech of Menalippe: of ununiform manners in the *Iphigenia at Aulis;* for there the Iphigenia who supplicates for life has no resemblance to the Iphigenia of the conclusion.

In the manners, as in the fable, the poet should always aim either at what is necessary or what is probable; so that such a character shall appear to speak or act, necessarily or probably, in such a manner, and this event to be the necessary or probable consequence of that. Hence it is evident that the development also of a fable should arise out of the fable itself, and not depend upon machinery as in the *Medea,* or in the incidents relative to the return of the Greeks in the Iliad. The proper application of machinery is to such circumstances as are extraneous to the drama; such as either happened before the time of the action, and could not by human means be known; or are to happen after, and require to be foretold: for to the Gods we attribute the knowledge of all things. But nothing improbable should be admitted in the incidents of the fable; or, if it cannot be avoided, it should, at least, be confined to such as are without the tragedy itself; as in the *Oedipus* of Sophocles.

Since tragedy is an imitation of what is best, we should follow the example of skilful portrait-painters; who, while they express the peculiar lineaments, and produce a likeness, at the same time improve upon the original. And thus, too, the poet, when he imitates the manners of passionate men (or of indolent, or any other similar kind), should draw an example approaching rather to a good than to a hard and ferocious character: as Achilles is drawn by Agathon and by Homer. These things the poet should keep in view; and besides these, whatever relates to those senses which have a necessary connection with poetry: for here, also, he may often err. But of this enough has been said in the treatises already published.

XVI What is meant by a discovery has already been explained. Its kinds are the following:

First, the most inartificial of all, and to which, from poverty of invention, the generality of poets have recourse—the discovery by visible signs. Of these signs, some are natural; as the lance with which the family of earth-born Thebans were marked, or the stars which Carcinus has made use of in his *Thyestes:* others are adventitious; and of these some are corporal, as scars; some external, as necklaces, bracelets, etc., or the little boat by which the discovery is made in the tragedy of *Tyro*. Even these, however, may be employed with more or less skill. The discovery of Ulysses, for example, to his nurse by means of his scar, is very different from his discovery by the same means to the herdsmen. For all those discoveries, in which the sign is produced by way of proof, are inartificial. Those which, like that in the 'Washing of Ulysses', happen suddenly and casually are better.

Secondly, discoveries invented at pleasure by the poet, and on that account still inartificial. For example, in the *Iphigenia,* Orestes, after having discovered his sister, discovers himself to her. She, indeed, is discovered by the letter; but Orestes by verbal proofs, and these are such as the poet chooses to make him produce, not such as arise from the circumstances of the fable. This kind of discovery, therefore, borders upon the fault of that first mentioned; for some of the things from which those proofs are drawn are even such as might have been actually produced as visible signs.

Another instance is the discovery by the sound of the shuttle in the *Tereus* of Sophocles.

Thirdly, the discovery occasioned by memory; as when some recollection is excited by the view of a particular object. Thus, in the *Cyprians* of Dicaeogenes, a discovery is produced by tears shed at the sight of a picture: and thus, in the 'Tale of Alcinous', Ulysses, listening to the bard, recollects, weeps, and is discovered.

Fourthly, the discovery occasioned by reasoning or inference; such as that in the *Choephorae:* 'The person who is arrived resembles me—no one resembles me but Orestes—it must be he!' And that of Polyides the Sophist, in his *Iphigenia;* for the conclusion of Orestes was natural: 'It had been his sister's lot to be sacrificed, and it was now his own!' That also, in the *Tydeus* of Theodectes: 'He came to find his son and he himself must perish!' And thus, the daughters of Phineus, in the tragedy denominated from them, viewing the place to which they were led, infer their fate: 'there they were to die, for there they were exposed!' There is also a compound sort of discovery arising from false inference in the audience; as in *Ulysses the False Messenger:* he asserts that he shall know the bow which he had not seen; the audience falsely infer that a discovery by that means will follow.

But of all discoveries the best is that which arises from the action itself, and in which a striking effect is produced by probable incidents. Such is that in the *Oedipus* of Sophocles: and that in the *Iphigenia;* for nothing more natural than her desire of conveying the letter. Such discoveries are the best, because they alone are effected without the help of invented proofs or bracelets, etc.

Next to these are the discoveries by inference.

XVII The poet, both when he plans and when he writes his tragedy, should put himself as much as possible in the place of a spectator; for by this means, seeing everything distinctly as if present at the action, he will discern what is proper, and no inconsistencies will escape him. The fault objected to Carcinus is a proof of this. Amphiaraus had left the temple: this the poet, for want of conceiving the action to pass before his eyes, overlooked; but in the representation the audience were disgusted, and the piece condemned.

In composing, the poet should even, as much as possible, be an actor: for, by natural sympathy, they are most persuasive and affecting who are under the influence of actual passion. We share the agitation of those who appear to be truly agitated—the anger of those who appear to be truly angry.

Hence it is that poetry demands either great natural quickness of parts, or an enthusiasm allied to madness. By the first of these we mould ourselves with facility to the imitation of every form; by the other, transported out of ourselves, we become what we imagine.

When the poet invents a subject, he should first draw a general sketch of it, and afterwards give it the detail of its episodes and extend it. The general argument, for instance, of the *Iphigenia* should be considered in this way: 'A virgin on the point of being sacrificed is imperceptibly conveyed away from the altar, and transported to another country where it was the custom to sacrifice all strangers to Diana. Of these rites she is appointed priestess. It happens, some time after, that her brother arrives there'. But why?—because an oracle had commanded him, for some reason exterior to the general plan. For what purpose? This also is exterior to the plan. 'He arrives, is seized, and at the instant that he is going to be sacrificed the discovery is made'. And this may be, either in the way of Euripides or, like that of Polyides, by the natural reflection of Orestes that 'it was his fate also as it had been his sister's to be sacrificed'; by which exclamation he is saved.

After this, the poet, when he has given names to his characters, should proceed to the episodes of his action; and he must take care that these belong properly to the subject; like that of the madness of Orestes, which occasions his being taken, and his escape by means of the ablution. In dramatic poetry the episodes are short; but in the epic they are the means of drawing out the poem to its proper length. The general story of the Odyssey, for example, lies in a small compass: 'A certain man is supposed to be absent from his own country for many years; he is persecuted by

Neptune, deprived of all his companions, and left alone. At home his affairs are in disorder—the suitors of his wife dissipating his wealth and plotting the destruction of his son. Tossed by many tempests, he at length arrives, and making himself known to some of his family attacks his enemies, destroys them, and remains himself in safety'. This is essential; the rest is episode.

XVIII Every tragedy consists of two parts—the complication and the development. The complication is often formed by incidents supposed prior to the action, and by a part, also, of those that are within the action; the rest form the development. I call complication all that is between the beginning of the piece and the last part, where the change of fortune commences; development all between the beginning of that change and the conclusion. Thus, in the *Lynceus* of Theodectes, the events antecedent to the action and the seizure of the child constitute the complication; the development is from the accusation of murder to the end.

XIX There are four kinds of tragedy, deducible from so many parts, which have been mentioned. One kind is the complicated, where all depends on revolution and discovery; another is the disastrous, such as those on the subject of Ajax or Ixion; another, the moral, as the *Phthiotides* and the *Peleus;* and fourthly, the simple, such as the *Phorcides,* the *Prometheus,* and all those tragedies the scene of which is laid in the infernal regions.

It should be the poet's aim to make himself master of all these manners; or as many of them, at least, as possible, and those the best: especially considering the captious criticism to which in these days he is exposed. For the public, having now seen different poets excel in each of these different kinds, expect every single poet to unite in himself, and to surpass, the peculiar excellences of them all.

One tragedy may justly be considered as the same with another or different, not according as the subjects, but rather according as the complication and development are the same or different. Many poets, when they have complicated well, develop badly. They should endeavour to deserve equal applause in both.

XX We must also be attentive to what has been often mentioned, and not construct a tragedy upon an epic plan. By an epic plan I mean a fable composed of many fables; as if any one, for instance, should take the entire fable of the Iliad for the subject of a tragedy. In the epic poem, the length of the whole admits of a proper magnitude in the parts; but in the drama the effect of such a plan is far different from what is expected. As a proof of this, those poets who have formed the whole of the destruction of Troy into a tragedy, instead of confining themselves (as Euripides, but not Aeschylus, has done in the story of Niobe) to a part, have either been condemned in the representation or have contended without success. Even Agathon has failed on this account and on this only; for in revolutions, and in actions also of the simple kind, these poets succeed wonderfully in what they aim at; and that is the union of tragic effect with moral tendency; as when, for example, a character of great wisdom, but without integrity, is deceived, like Sisyphus; or a brave but unjust man conquered. Such events, as Agathon says, are probable, 'as it is probable, in general, that many things should happen contrary to probability'.

XXI The chorus should be considered as one of the persons in the drama; should be a part of the whole, and a sharer in the action: not as in Euripides, but as in Sophocles. As for other poets, their choral songs have no more connection with their subject than with that of any other tragedy; and hence they are now become detached pieces inserted at leisure—a practice first introduced by Agathon. Yet where is the difference between this arbitrary insertion of an ode and the transposition of a speech, or even of a whole episode, from one tragedy to another?

XXII Of the other parts of tragedy enough has now been said. We are next to consider the diction and the sentiments.

For what concerns the sentiments we refer to the principles laid down in the books on rhetoric; for to that subject they more properly belong. The sentiments include whatever is the object of speech; as, for instance, to prove, to confute, to move the passions—pity, terror, anger, and the like; to amplify or to diminish.

But it is evident that, with respect to the things themselves also, when the poet would make them appear pitiable, or terrible, or great, or probable, he must draw from the same sources; with this difference only, that in the drama these things must appear to be such, without being shown to be such; whereas in oratory they must be made to appear so by the speaker, and in consquence of what he says: otherwise what need of an orator if they already appear so in themselves, and not through his eloquence?

XXIII With respect to diction, one part of its theory is that which treats of the figures of speech, such as commanding, entreating, relating, menacing, interrogating, answering, and the like. But this belongs, properly, to the art of acting, and to the professed masters of that kind. The poet's knowledge, or ignorance, of these things cannot any way materially affect the credit of his art. For who will suppose there is any justice in the cavil of Protagoras—that in the words, 'The wrath, O goddess, sing', the poet, where he intended a prayer, had expressed a command? For he insists that to say 'Do this' or 'Do it not' is to command. This subject, therefore, we pass over as belonging to an art distinct from that of poetry.

XXIV To all diction belong the following parts: the letter, the syllable, the conjunction, the noun, the verb, the article, the case, the discourse or speech.

(1) A letter is an indivisible sound; yet not all such sounds are letters, but those only that are capable of forming an intelligible sound. For there are indivisible sounds of brute creatures; but no such sounds are called letters. Letters are of three kinds: vowels, semi-vowels, and mutes. The vowel is that which has a distinct sound without articulation, as *a* or *o*. The semi-vowel, that which has a distinct sound with articulation, as *s* and *r*. The mute, that which, with articulation, has yet no sound by itself; but joined with one of those letters that have some sound, becomes audible, as *g* and *d*. These all differ from each other, as they are produced by different configurations, and in different parts, of the mouth; as they are aspirated or smooth, long or short; as their tone is

acute, grave, or intermediate; the detail of all which is the business of the metrical treatises.

(2) A syllable is a sound without signification, composed of a mute and a vowel. For *gr* without *a* is not a syllable; with *a*, as *gra*, it is. But these differences, also, are the subject of the metrical art.

(3) A conjunction is a sound without signification, . . . of such a nature as, out of several sounds, each of them significant, to form one significant sound.

(4) An article is a sound without signification which marks the beginning or the end of a sentence; or distinguishes, as when we say *the* [word] φημί, *the* [word] περί, etc.

(5) A noun is a sound composed of other sounds; significant without expression of time, and of which no part is by itself significant. For even in double words the parts are not taken in the sense that separately belongs to them. Thus, in the word 'Theodorus', 'dorus' is not significant.

(6) A verb is a sound composed of other sounds; significant, with expression of time, and of which, as of the noun, no part is by itself significant. Thus, in the words 'man', 'white', indication of time is not included. In the words 'he walks', 'he walked', etc., it is included; the one expressing the present time, the other the past.

(7) Cases belong to nouns and verbs. Some cases express relation; as 'of', 'to', and the like. Others number; as 'man' or 'men', etc. Others relate to action or pronunciation, as those of interrogation, of command, etc. For ἐβάδισε; [did he go?] and βάδιζε [go] are verbal cases of that kind.

(8) Discourse or speech is a sound significant, composed of other sounds, some of which are significant by themselves: for all discourse is not composed of verbs and nouns; the definition of 'man', for instance. Discourse or speech may subsist without a verb: some significant part, however, it must contain; significant, as the word 'Cleon' is in 'Cleon walks'.

A discourse or speech is one, in two senses: either as it signifies one thing or several things made one by conjunction. Thus, the Iliad is one by conjunction: the definition of man by signifying one thing.

XXV Of words, some are single, by which I mean composed of parts not significant; and some double: of which last some have one part significant and the other not significant, and some both parts significant. A word may also be triple, quadruple, etc., like many used by those who love hard words, as *Hermocaïcoxanthus*. Every word is either common, or foreign, or metaphorical, or ornamental, or invented, or extended, or contracted, or altered.

By common words I mean such as are in general and established use; by foreign, such as belong to a different language, so that the same word may evidently be both common and foreign, though not to the same people. The word *σίγυνον* to the Cyprians is common; to us, foreign.

A metaphorical word is a word transferred from its proper sense; either from genus to species, or from species to genus, or from one species to another, or in the way of analogy.

(1) From genus to species, as:

'Secure in yonder port my vessel stands'.

For to be at anchor is one species of standing or being fixed.

(2) From species to genus, as:

'to Ulysses,
A thousand generous deeds we owe'.

For a thousand is a certain definite many, which is here used for many in general.

(3) From one species to another, as: Χαλκῷ ἀπὸ ψυχὴν ἀρύσας. And *ταμὼν ἀτειρέϊ χαλκῷ*. For here the poet uses *ταμεῖν*, to cut off, instead of *ἀρύσαι*, to draw forth, and *ἀρύσαι* instead of *ταμεῖν*; each being a species of taking away.

(4) In the way of analogy–when, of four terms, the second bears the same relation to the first as the fourth to the third; in which case the fourth may be substituted for the second, and the second for the fourth. And sometimes the proper term is also introduced besides its relative term.

Thus, a cup bears the same relation to Bacchus as a shield to Mars. A shield, therefore, may be called the 'cup of Mars', and a cup the 'shield of Bacchus'. Again, evening being to day what old age is to life, the evening may be called the old age of the day, and old age the evening of life; or as Empedocles has expressed it: 'Life's setting sun'. It sometimes happens that there is no proper analogous term answering to the term borrowed; which yet may be used in the same manner as if there were. For instance, to sow is the term appropriated to the action of dispersing seed upon the earth; but the dispersion of rays from the sun is expressed by no appropriated term; it is, however, with respect to the sun's light, what sowing is with respect to seed. Hence the poet's expression of the sun:

'sowing abroad
His heaven-created flame'.

There is also another way of using this kind of metaphor, by adding to the borrowed word a negation of some of those qualities which belong to it in its proper sense; as if instead of calling a shield the 'cup of Mars', we should call it the 'wineless cup'.

An invented word is a word never before used by any one but coined by the poet himself; for such it appears there are, as ἔρνυγες for κέρατα, horns, or ἀρητήρ for ἱερεύς, a priest.

A word is extended when, for the proper vowel, a longer is substituted, or a syllable is inserted. A word is contracted when some part of it is retrenched. Thus, πόληος for πόλεως, and Πηληϊαδέω for Πηλείδου, are extended words; contracted, such as κρῖ and δῶ, and ὄψ, e. g.: μία γίνεται ἀμφοτέρων ὄψ.

An altered word is a word of which part remains in its usual state, and part is of the poet's making, as in δεξιτερὸν κατὰ μαζόν, δεξιτερός is for δεξιός.

Further, *nouns* are divided into masculine, feminine, and neuter. The masculine are those which end in ν, ρ, σ, or in some letter compounded of σ and a mute; these are two, ψ and ξ. The feminine are those which end in the vowels always long, as η, or ω; or in α of the doubtful vowels; so that the masculine and the feminine terminations are equal in number, for as to ψ and ξ, they are the same with terminations in σ. No noun ends in a mute or a short vowel. There are but three ending in ι: μέλι, κόμμι, πέπερι; five ending in υ: πῶϋ, νᾶπυ, γόνυ, δόρυ, ἄστυ.

The neuter terminate in these two last-mentioned vowels and in ν and σ.

XXVI The excellence of diction consists in being perspicuous without being mean. The most perspicuous is that which is composed of common words, but at the same time it is mean. Such is the poetry of Cleophon and that of Sthenelus. That language, on the contrary, is elevated and remote from the vulgar idiom which employs unusual words. By unusual I mean foreign, metaphorical, extended—all, in short, that are not common words. Yet should a poet compose his diction entirely of such words, the result would be either an enigma or a barbarous jargon; an enigma, if composed of metaphors; a barbarous jargon, if composed of foreign words. For the essence of an enigma consists in putting together things apparently inconsistent and impossible, and at the same time saying nothing but what is true. Now this cannot be effected by the mere arrangement of the words; by the metaphorical use of them it may, as in this enigma:

> *'A man I once beheld,* [*and wondering viewed,*]
> *Who, on another, brass with fire had glued'.*

With respect to barbarism, it arises from the use of foreign words. A judicious intermixture is, therefore, requisite.

Thus, the foreign word, the metaphorical, the ornamental, and the other species before mentioned, will raise the language above the vulgar idiom, and common words will give it perspicuity. But nothing contributes more considerably to produce clearness, without vulgarity of diction, than extensions, contractions, and alterations of words; for here the variation from the proper form, being unusual, will give elevation to the expression, and at the same time, what is retained of usual speech will give it clearness. It is without reason, therefore, that some critics have censured these modes of speech, and ridiculed the poet for the use of them, as old Euclid did, objecting that 'versification would be an easy business if it were permitted to lengthen words at pleasure'—and then giving a burlesque example of that sort of diction.

Undoubtedly, when these licences appear to be thus purposely used, the thing becomes ridiculous. In the employment of all the species of unusual words moderation is necessary; for metaphors, foreign words, or any of the others, improperly used, and with a design to be ridiculous, would produce the same effect. But how great a difference is made by a proper and temperate use of such words, may be seen in heroic verse. Let any one only substitute common words in the place of the metaphorical, the foreign, and others of the same kind, and he will be convinced of the truth of what I say. For example, the same iambic verse occurs in Aeschylus and in Euripides, but, by means of a single alteration—the substitution of a foreign for a common and usual word—one of these verses appears beautiful, the other ordinary. For Aeschylus, in his *Philoctetes,* says:

Φαγέδαινα, ἥ μου σάρκας ἐσθίει ποδός.

'The cankerous wound that eats my flesh'.

But Euripides, instead of ἐσθίει [eats] uses θοινᾶται [feasts on].

The same difference will appear, if in this verse,

Νῦν δέ μ' ἐὼν ὀλίγος τε καὶ οὐτιδανὸς καὶ ἄκικυς,

we substitute common words, and say:

Νῦν δέ μ' ἐὼν μικρός τε καὶ ἀσθενικὸς καὶ ἀειδής.

So again, should we for the following,

Δίφρον ἀεικέλιον καταθεὶς, ὀλίγην τε τράπεζαν,

substitute this:

Δίφρον μοχθηρὸν καταθεὶς, μικράν τε τράπεζαν.

Or change ἠϊόνες βοόωσιν ('the cliffs *rebellow*') to ἠϊόνες κράζουσιν ('the cliffs *resound*').

Ariphrades also endeavoured to throw ridicule upon the tragic poets, for making use of such expressions as no one would think of using in common speech: as δωμάτων ἄπο, instead of ἀπὸ δωμάτων; and σέθεν, and ἐγὼ δέ νιν, and Ἀχιλλέως πέρι, instead of περὶ Ἀχιλλέως, etc. Now it is precisely owing to their being *not* in common use that such expressions have the effect of giving elevation to the diction. But this he did not know.

To employ with propriety any of these modes of speech—the double words, the foreign, etc.—is a great excellence; but the greatest of all is to be happy in the use of metaphor; for it is this alone which cannot be acquired, and which, consisting in a quick discernment of resemblances, is a certain mark of genius.

Of the different kinds of words, the double are best suited to dithyrambic poetry, the foreign to heroic, the metaphorical to iambic. In heroic poetry, indeed, they have all their place; but to iambic verse, which is, as much as may be, an imitation of common speech, those words which are used in common speech are best adapted, and such are the common, the metaphorical, and the ornamental.

Concerning tragedy, and the imitation by action, enough has now been said.

BOOK THIRD

OF THE EPIC POEM

I With respect to that species of poetry which imitates by narration, and in hexameter verse, it is obvious that the fable ought to be dramatically constructed like that of tragedy; and that it should have for its subject one entire and perfect action, having a beginning, a middle, and an end; so that, forming like an animal a complete whole, it may afford its proper pleasure, widely differing in its construction from history, which necessarily treats, not of one action, but of one time, and of all the events that happened to one person or to many during that time; events the relation of which to each other is merely casual. For, as the naval action at Salamis, and the battle with the Carthaginians in Sicily, were events of the same time, unconnected by any relation to a common end or purpose; so also in successive events, we sometimes see one thing follow another without being connected to it by such relation. And this is the practice of the generality of poets. Even in this, therefore, as we have observed, the superiority of Homer's genius is apparent, that he did not attempt to bring the whole war, though an entire action with beginning and end, into his poem. It would have been too vast an object, and not easily comprehended in one view; or had he forced it into a moderate compass it would have been perplexed by its variety. Instead of this, selecting one part only of the war, he has from the rest introduced many episodes—such as the catalogue of the ships and others—by which he has diversified his poem. Other poets take for their subject the actions of one person, or of one period of time, or an action which, though one, is composed of too many parts. Thus, the author of the *Cypriacs* and of the Little Iliad. Hence it is that the Iliad and the Odyssey, each of them furnish matter for one tragedy, or two at most; but from the *Cypriacs* many may be taken, and from the Little Iliad more than eight, as: *The Contest for the Armour, Philoctetes, Neoptolemus, Eurypylus, The Vagrant, The Spartan Women, The Fall of Troy, The Return of the Fleet, Sinon,* and *The Trojan Women.*

Again, the epic poem must also agree with the tragic as to its two kinds: it must be simple or complicated, moral or disastrous. Its parts also, setting aside music and decoration, are the same, for it requires revolutions, discoveries, and disasters, and it must be furnished with proper sentiments and diction; of all which Homer gave both the first and the most perfect example. Thus, of his two poems the Iliad is of the simple and disastrous kind, the Odyssey complicated (for it abounds throughout with discoveries) and moral. Add to this, that in language and sentiments he has surpassed all poets.

II The epic poem differs from tragedy in the length of its plan and in its metre.

With respect to length a sufficient measure has already been assigned. It should be such as to admit of our comprehending at one view the beginning and the end, and this would be the case if the epic poem were reduced from its ancient length, so as not to exceed that of such a number of tragedies as are performed successively at one hearing. But there is a circumstance in the nature of epic poetry which affords it peculiar latitude in the extension of its plan. It is not in the power of tragedy to imitate several different actions performed at the same time; it can imitate only that one which occupies the stage, and in which the actors are employed. But the epic imitation, being narrative, admits of many such simultaneous incidents, properly related to the subject, which swell the poem to a considerable size.

And this gives it a great advantage, both in point of magnificence, and also as it enables the poet to relieve his hearer and diversify his work by a variety of dissimilar episodes; for it is to the satiety naturally arising from similarity that tragedies frequently owe their ill success.

With respect to metre, the heroic is established by experience as the most proper, so that, should any one compose a narrative poem in any other, or in a variety of metres, he would be thought guilty of a great impropriety. For the heroic is the gravest and most majestic of all measures; and hence it is that it peculiarly admits the use of foreign and metaphorical expressions; for in this respect also, the narrative imitation is abundant and various beyond the rest. But the iambic and trochaic have more motion; the latter being adapted to dance, the other to action and business. To mix these different metres, as Chaeremon has done, would be still more absurd. No one, therefore, has ever attempted to compose a poem of an extended plan in any other than heroic verse;

nature itself, as we before observed, pointing out the proper choice.

III Among the many just claims of Homer to our praise, this is one—that he is the only poet who seems to have understood what part in his poem it was proper for him to take himself. The poet, in his own person, should speak as little as possible; for he is not then the imitator. But other poets, ambitious to figure throughout themselves, imitate but little and seldom. Homer, after a few preparatory lines, immediately introduces a man, a woman, or some other character; for all have their character—nowhere are the manners neglected.

IV The surprising is necessary in tragedy; but the epic poem goes further and admits even the improbable and incredible, from which the highest degree of the surprising results, because there the action is not seen. The circumstances, for example, of the pursuit of Hector by Achilles, are such as, upon the stage, would appear ridiculous—the Grecian army standing still and taking no part in the pursuit, and Achilles making signs to them by the motion of his head not to interfere. But in the epic poem this escapes our notice. Now the wonderful always pleases, as is evident from the additions which men always make in relating anything in order to gratify the hearers.

V It is from Homer principally that other poets have learned the art of feigning well. It consists in a sort of sophism. When one thing is observed to be constantly accompanied or followed by another, men are apt to conclude that if the latter is, or has happened, the former must also be, or must have happened. But this is an error. For knowing the latter to be true, the mind is betrayed into the false inference that the first is true also.

VI The poet should prefer impossibilities which appear probable to such things as, though possible, appear improbable. Far from producing a plan made up of improbable incidents, he should, if possible, admit no one circumstance of that kind; or, if he does, it should be exterior to the action itself, like the ignorance of Oedipus concerning the manner in which Laius died; not within the drama, like the narrative of what happened at the Pythian games in the *Electra;* or in the *Mysians,* the man who travels from Tegea to Mysia without speaking. To say that without these circumstances the fable would have been destroyed is a ridiculous excuse: the poet should take care, from the first, not to construct his fable in that manner. If, however, anything of this kind has been admitted, and yet is made to pass under some colour of probability, it may be allowed, though even in itself absurd. Thus in the Odyssey, the improbable account of the manner in which Ulysses was landed upon the shore of Ithaca is such as in the hands of an ordinary poet would evidently have been intolerable; but here the absurdity is concealed under the various beauties of other kinds with which the poet has embellished it.

The diction should be most laboured in the idle parts of the poem—those in which neither manners nor sentiments prevail; for the manners and the sentiments are only obscured by too splendid a diction.

BOOK FOURTH

OF CRITICAL OBJECTIONS AND THE PRINCIPLES ON WHICH THEY ARE TO BE ANSWERED

I With respect to critical objections and the answers to them, the number and nature of the different sources from which they may be drawn will be clearly understood, if we consider them in the following manner.

(1) The poet, being an imitator, like the painter or any other artist of that kind, must necessarily, when he imitates, have in view one of these three objects: he must represent things such as they were or are; or such as they are said to be and believed to be; or such as they should be.

(2) Again, all this he is to express in words, either common, or foreign and metaphorical, or varied by some of those many modifications and peculiarities of language which are the privilege of poets.

(3) To this we must add that what is right in the poetic art is a distinct consideration from what is right in the political or any other art. The faults of poetry are of two kinds, essential and accidental. If the poet has undertaken to imitate without talents for imitation, his poetry will be essentially faulty. But if he is right in applying himself to poetic imitation, yet in imitating is occasionally wrong; as if a horse, for example, were represented moving both his right legs at once; or if he has committed mistakes, or described things impossible, with respect to other arts, that of physic, for instance, or any other—all such faults, whatever they may be, are not essential, but accidental, faults in the poetry.

II To the foregoing considerations, then, we must have recourse in order to obviate the doubts and objections of the critics.

For, in the first place, suppose the poet to have represented things impossible with respect to some other art. This is certainly a fault. Yet it may be an excusable fault, provided the end of the poet's art be more effectually obtained by it; that is, according to what has already been said of that end, if by this means that, or any other part, of the poem is made to produce a more striking effect. The pursuit of Hector is an instance. If, indeed, this end might as well, or nearly as well, have been attained without departing from the principles of the particular art in question, the fault, in that case, could not be justified, since faults of every kind should, if possible, be avoided.

Still, we are to consider further whether a fault be in things essential to the poetic art, or foreign and incidental to it; for it is a far more pardonable fault to be ignorant, for instance, that a hind has no horns, than to paint one badly.

III Further, if it be objected to the poet that he has not represented things conformably to truth, he may answer that he has represented them as they should be. This was the answer of Sophocles, that 'he drew mankind such as they should be; Euripides, such as they are'. And this is the proper answer.

But if the poet has represented things in neither of these ways, he may answer that he has represented them as they are said and believed to be. Of this kind are the poetical descriptions of the Gods. It cannot, perhaps, be said that they are either what is best or what is true; but, as Xenophanes says, opinions 'taken up at random'; these are things, however, not 'clearly known'.

Again, what the poet has exhibited is, perhaps, not what is best, but it is the fact; as in the passage about the arms of the sleeping soldiers:

> '. . . *fixed upright in the earth*
> *Their spears stood by.*'

For such was the custom at that time, as it is now among the Illyrians.

IV In order to judge whether what is said or done by any character be well or ill, we are not to consider that speech or action alone, whether in itself it be good or bad, but also by whom it is spoken or done, to whom, at what time, in what manner, or for what end—whether, for instance, in order to obtain some greater good or to avoid some greater evil.

V For the solution of some objections we must have recourse to the diction. For example:

οὐρῆας μὲν πρῶτον . . .

'On mules and dogs the infection first began'.

This may be defended by saying that the poet has, perhaps, used the word οὐρῆας in its foreign acceptation of sentinels, not in its proper sense, of mules.

So also in the passage where it is said of Dolon:

εἶδος μὲν ἔην κακός.

'of form unhappy'.

The meaning is, not that his person was deformed, but that his face was ugly; for the Cretans use the word εὐειδές—'well-formed'—to express a beautiful face.

Again:

ζωρότερον δὲ κέραιε.

Here the meaning is not 'mix it strong', as for intemperate drinkers, but 'mix it quickly'.

(2) The following passages may be defended by metaphor.

'Now pleasing sleep had seal'd each mortal eye;
Stretch'd in the tents the Grecian leaders lie;
The immortals slumber'd on their thrones above'.

Again:

'When on the Trojan plain his anxious eye
Watchful he fix'd'. . . .

And,

αὐλῶν συρίγγων θ' ὁμαδόν.

For 'all' is put metaphorically instead of 'many'; all being a species of many.

Here also:

'The bear alone,
Still shines exalted in th' aetherial plain,
Nor bathes his flaming forehead in the main'.

Alone is metaphorical: the most remarkable thing in any kind, we speak of as the *only* one.

We may have recourse also:

(3) To accent, as the following passage:

δίδομεν δέ οἱ εὖχος ἀρέσθαι,

and this: τὸ μὲν οὐ καταπύθεται ὄμβρῳ—were solved by Hippias of Thasos.

(4) To punctuation, as in this passage of Empedocles:

αἶψα δὲ θνήτ' ἐφύοντο τὰ πρὶν μάθον ἀθάνατ' εἶναι,
ζωρά τε πρὶν κέκρητο . . .

i. e.

'Things, before immortal,
Mortal became, and mix'd before unmix'd,
[Their courses changed.]'

(5) To ambiguity, as in παρῴχηκεν δὲ πλέων νύξ, where the word πλέων is ambiguous.

(6) To customary speech: thus, wine mixed with water is called οἶνος, wine; hence, Ganymede is said Διὶ οἰνοχοεύειν, to 'pour the wine to Jove'; though wine is not the liquor of the gods. This, however, may also be defended by metaphor.

Thus, again, artificers in iron are called χαλκεῖς, literally, braziers. Of this kind is the expression of the poet, κνημὶς νεοτεύκτου κασσιτέροιο, 'Greaves of new-wrought tin'.

(7) When a word in any passage appears to express a contradiction, we must consider, in how many different senses it may there be taken. Here, for instance:

τῇ ῥ' ἔσχετο χάλκεον ἔγχος

'There stuck the lance'.

the meaning is, was 'stopped' only, or 'repelled'.

Of how many different senses a word is capable may best be

discovered by considering the different senses that are opposed to it.

We may also say, with Glaucon, that some critics first take things for granted without foundation, and then argue from these previous decisions of their own; and, having once pronounced their judgement, condemn, as an inconsistency, whatever is contrary to their preconceived opinion. Of this kind is the cavil of the critics concerning Icarius. Taking it for granted that he was a Lacedaemonian, they thence infer the absurdity of supposing Telemachus not to have seen him when he went to Lacedaemon. But perhaps what the Cephalenians say may be the truth. They assert that the wife of Ulysses was of their country, and that the name of her father was not Icarius, but Icadius. The objection itself, therefore, is probably founded on a mistake.

VI The impossible, in general, is to be justified by referring either to the end of poetry itself, or to what is best, or to opinion.

For with respect to poetry, impossibilities, rendered probable, are preferable to things improbable, though possible.

With respect also to what is best, the imitations of poetry should resemble the paintings of Zeuxis; the example should be more perfect than nature.

To opinion, or what is commonly said to be, may be referred even such things as are improbable and absurd; and it may also be said that events of that kind are, sometimes, not really improbable; since 'it is probable that many things should happen contrary to probability'.

VII When things are said which appear to be contradictory, we must examine them as we do in logical confutation: whether the same thing be spoken of; whether in the same respect, and in the same sense. . . .

VIII Improbability and vicious manners, when excused by no necessity, are just objects of critical censure. Such is the improbability in the *Aegeus* of Euripides, and the vicious character of Menelaus in his *Orestes*.

Thus, the sources from which the critics draw their objections are five: they object to things as impossible, or improbable, or of immoral tendency, or contradictory, or contrary to technical accuracy. The answers, which are twelve in number, may be deduced from what has been said.

BOOK FIFTH

OF THE SUPERIORITY OF TRAGIC TO EPIC POETRY

I It may be inquired, further, which of the two imitations, the epic or the tragic, deserves the preference.

If that which is the least vulgar or popular of the two be the best, and that be such which is calculated for the better sort of spectators—the imitation which extends to every circumstance must evidently be the most vulgar or popular; for there the imitators have recourse to every kind of motion and gesticulation, as if the audience, without the aid of action, were incapable of understanding them: like bad flute-players, who whirl themselves round when they would imitate the motion of the discus, and pull the coryphaeus when Scylla is the subject. Such is tragedy. It may also be compared to what the modern actors are in the estimation of their predecessors; for Myniscus used to call Callipides, on account of his intemperate action, the ape, and Tyndarus was censured on the same account. What these performers are with respect to their predecessors, the tragic imitation, when entire, is to the epic. The latter, then, it is urged, addresses itself to hearers of the better sort, to whom the addition of gesture is superfluous, but tragedy is for the people; and being, therefore, the most vulgar kind of imitation, is evidently the inferior.

II But now, in the first place, this censure falls, not upon the poet's art, but upon that of the actor; for the gesticulation may be equally laboured in the recitation of an epic poem, as it was by Sosistratus; and in singing, as by Mnasitheus, the Opuntian.

Again, all gesticulation is not to be condemned, since even all dancing is not; but such only as is unbecoming—such as was objected to Callipides, and is now objected to others whose gestures resemble those of immodest women.

Further, tragedy, as well as the epic, is capable of producing its effect even without action; we can judge of it perfectly by reading. If, then, in other respects, tragedy be superior, it is sufficient that the fault here objected is not essential to it.

III Tragedy has the advantage in the following respects: It possesses all that is possessed by the epic; it might even adopt its metre: and to this it makes no inconsiderable addition, in the music and the decoration; by the latter of which the illusion is heightened, and the pleasure arising from the action is rendered more sensible and striking.

It has the advantage of greater clearness and distinctness of impression, as well in reading as in representation.

It has also that of attaining the end of its imitation in a shorter compass: for the effect is more pleasurable when produced by a short and close series of impressions, than when weakened by diffusion through a long extent of time; as the *Oedipus* of Sophocles, for example, would be if it were drawn out to the length of the Iliad.

Further: there is less unity in all epic imitation, as appears from this—that any epic poem will furnish matter for several tragedies. For, supposing the poet to choose a fable strictly one, the consequence must be either that his poem, if proportionably contracted, will appear curtailed and defective, or, if extended to the usual length, will become weak and, as it were, diluted. If, on the other hand, we suppose him to employ several fables—that is, a fable composed of several actions—his imitation is no longer strictly one. The Iliad, for example, and the Odyssey contain many such subordinate parts, each of which has a certain magnitude and unity of its own; yet is the construction of those poems as perfect, and as nearly approaching to the imitation of a single action, as possible.

IV If, then, tragedy be superior to the epic in all these respects, and also in the peculiar end at which it aims (for each species ought to afford, not any sort of pleasure indiscriminately, but such only as has been pointed out), it evidently follows that tragedy, as it attains more effectually the end of the art itself, must deserve the preference.

And thus much concerning tragic and epic poetry in general and their several species, the number and the differences of their parts, the causes of their beauties and their defects, the censures of critics, and the principles on which they are to be answered